THE
SOMERSET & DORSET
FROM THE
FOOTPLATE

by

Peter Smith

MENDIPS ENGINEMAN
Copyright © 1972 by Peter Smith and Ivo Peters
FOOTPLATE OVER THE MENDIPS
Copyright © 1978 by Oxford Publishing Co.
This edition copyright © 1987 Oxford Publishing Co.

ISBN 0-86093-403-9

All photographs by Ivo Peters unless otherwise credited.

Typeset by:
Central Lancashire Printers Ltd., Wigan

Printed in Great Britain by:
Biddles Ltd, Guildford & Kings Lynn

Published by:
Oxford Publishing Co.
Link House,
West Street,
Poole, Dorset.

CONTENTS

To Donald Beale. My very good friend.
Also to Hazel my wife and to Lindsey and Sally my daughters, for their
patience and encouragement.

ACKNOWLEDGEMENTS

The period of time that I spent working on the railway would not have been as smooth as it was, had it not been for the unstinted help that I received from various people. This analogy is undoubtedly true of the writing and illustration of this book. My thanks are due to Mr. R. C. Riley and Mr. Ivo Peters, who kindly read through my typescript, and whose advice taught me that there was more to writing a book than I imagined. These good friends also afforded me every possible help and facility in order that I could adequately illustrate it, thus to them, and all the photographers who have allowed me to use their photographs I am greatly indebted.

I own an immense debt of gratitude to my ex footplate mentor, engine driver and ever good friend Donald Beal, who was a tower of strength during the preparation of this book, particularly with regard to the pre 1940 detail and the chapter about Tablet Working. Now, as when on the footplate, he was always most ready to answer the many questions that I put to him and in certain instances kindly undertook himself to check on points requiring amplification when he knew better than I just where to obtain the required information, this usually being straight from the horse's mouth — as it were. For this additional collaboration I am most grateful.

Finally, to Mrs. Gloria Graham and my wife, who succeeded in typing the manuscript from my somewhat illegible hand-writing, my many thanks.

PREFACE TO THE COMBINED EDITION

This compendium is an exposition of steam locomotive footplate work as experienced on the ex Somerset and Dorset Joint Railway between Bournemouth and Bath which remained steam operated right up until closure in March 1966.

'Mendips Engineman', first published in 1972, is the personal account of my career from engine cleaner to driver whilst working on the line during BR days between 1953 and 1963. During this period I naturally became aware of many more facts and anecdotes concerning earlier years on the line extending back to the early 1920s. Much of this material was gleaned from mess room conversations between Donald Beale — my regular driver for five years — and his contemporaries. This suggested another book and following additional research, including many pleasant hours spent in Donald's company following his retirement, I gathered together a sufficient fund of stories and information to produce in 1978, 'Footplate Over The Mendips'.

The long friendship that I have been able to enjoy with Donald extending from my schoolboy train spotter days up to the present time, is something I greatly treasure; but with the steam locomotive and S&D line swept from the BR scene before the 1960s were out, the chances of ever again sharing a steam locomotive footplate with Donald appeared remote. However, the preservationists have seen to it that the steam engine lives on, and that the premier train of the S&D line, the Bournemouth-Manchester 'Pines Express', still runs occasionally at various preservation centres up and down the country — albeit over very confined lengths of permanent way and under the constraints of the light railway order limiting speed to 25 mph. Nevertheless, with appropriate motive power, rolling stock and perhaps complete with headboard adorning the smokebox, the memory of the S&D and the 'Pines Express' lives on in tangible form. In addition, several preserved railways have, on a number of occasions, invited, Donald and me to a re-run of the 'Pines' resulting in the Driver Beale/Fireman Smith footplate partnership becoming fact once more. An update of this particular aspect of S&D remembrance might be appropriate here.

Probably the most notable occasions where this has occured was in connection with two BBC television programmes. The first of these entitled, *'Return to Evercreech Junction'*, was filmed in appalling weather during March 1984 and featured a then and now survey of the northern half of the main line. This film was also a tribute to my good friend Ivo Peters, whose collection of superb photographs and 16 mm cine films which he shot up and down the S&D over the years are now so well known. Some of this material was used in both BBC productions. The footplate scenes for the first programme were filmed on the East Somerset Railway at Cranmore using the BR Class 9F 2-10-0, No. 92203, belonging to David Shepherd, the well known artist, and Donald and I were contracted to appear in the film.

This footplate reunion involving Donald and myself with a 9F was most appropriate, as No. 92203 had been allocated to Bath shed for S&D line work during the summer service of 1960 and during this time we had the pleasure of her company on the 'Pines Express' — not to mention other services — on a good many occasions. A further and most pleasant result of taking part in this film was meeting up once more with two more footplate colleagues who were also taking part — Ray Stokes, who spent his S&D days based at Templecombe shed and David Massey, who was based at Bath Green Park.

Following its screening, the programme was considered sufficiently successful to encourage the BBC to produce a follow up programme. This was filmed during March 1986 and entitled, *'All change at Evercreech Junction'*. Using the same 'then and now' format as before, the southern half of the line was covered interwoven with which was a re-run of the 'Pines Express' and a brief glimpse into the closed world of what was involved in footplate work in the days of steam. For this film the Driver Beale/Fireman Smith footplate team was resurrected once more and a résumé of our respective careers recounted in the narrative; this in effect, was designed to encompass and pay tribute to all S&D enginemen past and present.

Prior to the filming there was some discussion amongst interested parties about which preserved operational locomotive would be most appropriate for a film which was to feature prominently 'The Pines Express'. My suggestion was BR Class 5 4-6-0 No. 73050, now on the Nene Valley Railway, but which during its BR days was a long serving member at Bath Green Park shed and undoubtedly amassed a greater mileage hauling the 'Pines Express' over the S&D than any other preserved locomotive. Unfortunately, various constraints, including the unsuitability of rolling stock and the scenery at this location, rather ruled out the use of this locomotive and thoughts turned to another class of locomotive which had over the years, seen considerable service on the S&D and had graced the 'Pines' on numerous occasions. The Bulleid Light Pacifics.

Of those preserved, No. 34105 *Swanage*, an unrebuilt 'West Country' class Pacific now kept at Ropley on the Mid Hants line, would have been an obvious choice being a one time Bournemouth Central locomotive and often loaned to the S&D for summer service weekend work. Though well advanced in restoration the engine was not ready for steaming and so another Mid Hants Bulleid Pacific was used to haul the BBC version of the 'Pines Express', No. 34016 *Bodmin*. While *Bodmin* was one 'West Country' that, in fact, never worked over the S&D line, rebuilt engines of this type — of which *'Bodmin'* was one — were frequent visitors to the line and often headed the 'Pines Express' following their introduction to this route in June 1959. The magnificently restored No 34016 was therefore a worthy locomotive to represent the many Bulleid Pacifics that had hauled the 'Pines Express' over the S&D and surely after its involvement in this BBC production can now be looked on as having gained some S&D status — if only by proxy.

Finally, may I invite the reader to view Mac Hawkins atmospheric pictures on the dust jacket, taken in fact at Alresford on the preserved Mid Hants line during the filming of *'All Change at Evercreech Junction'* — but evocative of many a location which saw Bulleid Pacifics during the days of steam. Imagine, therefore, the scene as being Bournemouth West in the early 1960s and then, through the medium of this combined volume, join me on 34016 as we head the northbound 'Pines Express' to Bath and experience, hopefully, something of the unique atmosphere of the footplate, and the flavour of the Somerset and Dorset and the life and times of its enginemen.

Peter Smith,
Upton, Poole,
1986

MENDIPS
ENGINEMAN

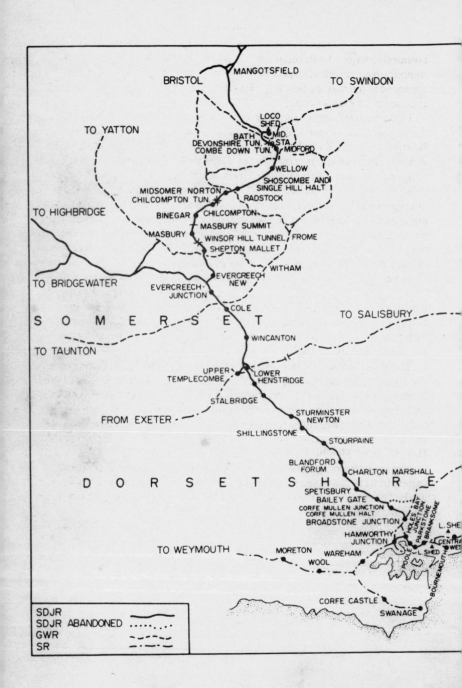

Map of the Somerset and Dorset Joint Railway

PREFACE

I wanted to write a book about the "Somerset and Dorset" railway line of comparatively recent years, for this was the "S&D" that I knew, and it appeared to me that the best way to do this would be to use my own personal experience of it as an engineman

I have enjoyed writing the book immensely, for in doing so I have relived the 10 years that I spent on the footplate, working over the line between Bournemouth and Bath. I have never kept a diary of day to day events whilst at work; consequently precise dates or the arrival and departure times of some of the many summer Saturday extra trains which ran over the "S&D" have taxed my memory on occasions, and I apologise should there be the odd discrepancy in this respect. I have had no difficulty, however, in recalling the many incidents and the people with whom I was connected during my 10 years' working association with the line, for they are still vivid memories of a very happy part of my life. This fascinationg stretch of line is no more, but a railway of such character could hardly be forgotten easily.

In keeping with the character of the line were the men who worked over it. I have heard it said many times that the steam locomotive produced a race of men apart, and I had not been associated with footplatemen for very long before I realised exactly what this meant. I feel very proud to have worked with these men; they have enriched my life more than they will ever know. I am deeply grateful to them.

The steam locomotive is a magnificent machine, with each of them, from the biggest to the smallest types, exuding its own personality. The sight of one at speed or working hard up a gradient has always stirred the deepest emotions within me — this is true as far back in my life as I can remember. I am thankful that I was born in time to have savoured the thrill of firing, and later driving, steam locomotives — not only doing so, but of doing it on the "Somerset and Dorset" as a "Mendip Engineman" in my own right.

The magnificent scenery through which the line passed; the ever changing variety of its motive power; the friendly and loyal railwaymen of all grades who worked on it — these things were the "S&D" railway. I fear we shall never see their like again.

Poole,   P. W. Smith.
Dorset.   1972.

Chapter One

SETTING THE SCENE

As a boy, the steam engine had a tremendous fascination for me. This interest was heightened by the fact that I lived beside the Southern Railway's Waterloo-Weymouth main line at Parkstone, and so was always within sight and sound of trains. I can vividly remember the famous Schools class locomotives going past our back garden on Waterloo-Weymouth trains. *'Radley'*, *'Stowe'*, *'Malvern'*, were three names belonging to this breed of engine which stand out most clearly in my mind. Later on the Lord Nelson and King Arthur classes were the mainstay on this line until ousted by the army of Bulleid Pacifics towards the end of the 1940s.

However, despite this close contact with Southern engines that was accorded me, my interest gradually centred on the LMS engines which worked over the Somerset and Dorset line between Bath Green Park and Bournemouth West, and which shared the metals with the Southern engines between Broadstone Junction and Bournemouth West. The '2P' 4-4-0s, '4F' 0-6-0s, and especially the Stanier Black '5' 4-6-0s, impressed me immensely. The latter class of locomotives were, as far as I was concerned, the absolute cream of engines that passed by the bottom of our garden, and I can still recall the feeling of emptiness, when, during the coal crisis of 1947, the 'Pines Express' which these locomotives used to haul, was withdrawn temporarily; the staccato bark of the 'Staniers' as they lifted twelve coaches up the 1 in 60 gradient of Parkstone Bank, was sorely missed by me. However, it was not long before this train was reinstated, and all was well again. I doubt whether the railway authorities knew how happy they made one small boy when they put this train back on the timetable again.

Why the S&D line and its locomotives should have fascinated me so much at this time I am not quite sure, for I had not then even travelled over it. Perhaps it was my year-round anticipation of its summer service, which brought trains over this line from many distant Midland and Northern Cities — trains which, by the time they had passed my home, had travelled much further in terms of mileage than the Southern long-distance trains. Roofboards proclaiming destinations such as 'Waterloo to Weymouth' seemed to my mind most dull compared with 'Bournemouth to Manchester', 'Liverpool Lime Street' or 'Leeds'.

Then there were the pigeon specials, which often produced one of the S&D '7F' 2-8-0 locomotives, hauling immensely long trains — perhaps fifteen or sixteen vans — which they would pull up Parkstone Bank in seemingly effortless style, without any banking assistance.

Overall, my impression was of splendid locomotives driven forcefully by their drivers as strident exhaust notes bore eloquent testimony. That I was not alone in thinking this, was born out by local station staff, signalmen and many of the general public who said they could always recognise the sound of an S&D train, compared with a Southern train, and took it for granted that if it was class '5' or '7F' hauled, it would not require the service of a banker from Poole up to Branksome, irrepective of the load being hauled.

Leaving school at the age of fifteen, I applied twice for employment as an engine cleaner at Branksome Motive Power Depot — which was the S&D depot in the Bournemouth area — for I had now resolved to become an engine driver. There were no vacancies at Branksome, but I was offered a similar post at Bournemouth Central Depot. As soon as I had passed the routine medical examination my footplate career could begin. I started work at Bournemouth Central at 8 o'clock on September 29th 1953, although not for long, as I had made it known to the Chief Clerk that should a vacancy arise at Branksome, I would like to transfer there. I was fortunate in that this transpired less than two months after my application, and I was successful in obtaining the post. At last I was working on S&D territory. So started what were the ten happiest years of my working life

Branksome Motive Power Depot was quite small, with two roads under cover, and of sufficient length to house four locomotives of the '2P' and '4F' variety, but if its occupants were 'West Country' or Class '5' locomotives, the rear half of their tenders would protrude through the shed entrance, exposed to the elements.

Outside the shed there were two more roads, known as the back road and the pit road, the latter being where incoming locomotives carried out their disposal duties. This road was equipped with a water cock in the pit for direction into the ashpan of engines during raking-out operations. An obvious piece of apparatus to have, one would have thought, but something which Bournemouth Central Depot was not provided with, until quite some time after I started on the railway. If the wind happened to be blowing the wrong way, the consequence of not having a water spray in the disposal pit was, of course, that dust and ash would be blown all over the unfortunate person raking out, plus a liberal deposit under the eyelids; on finally emerging from under the engine one looked more like a miller's lad than a fireman. Both of the outside roads were provided with water columns, and originally there was also a balance type turntable at the approach to the disposal pit, but soon after I started it was removed. The reason for this was that the largest engines that could be turned on it were the '2Ps' and the '4Fs', and by now the majority of engines using Branksome were larger than these, and so had to turn on the Branksome triangle, within which the loco depot was situated on the south side. Consequently, it was considered that all engines could turn by this method, and so save the maintenance cost of the turntable.

Incidentally, what may be described as the base of this triangle, between

Gas Works Junction Signalbox and Bournemouth West Junction Box, was very sharply curved. If a heavy train bound for Bournemouth West Station happened to get stopped at Bournemouth West Junction home signal, (something that its signalman tried to avoid at all costs, but was not always successful in doing), the sharp curve across the high Bourne Valley viaduct, with its check rail, would frustrate any attempt by the unfortunate drivers to restart their trains, however hard they tried. The Bulleid Pacifics especially, could always be relied upon to produce a show of slipping.

These displays brought forth scathing criticism from the S&D men who inevitably gathered to watch the fun, not at the expense of the drivers but of their mounts. "One of our '5s' would walk away with that lot," would be the usual sort of comment heard from the S&D camp, though perhaps expressed in more picturesque language! However, their point was proved over the years. Several times I have seen BR Standard Class '5s' start eleven and twelve coach trains from this spot, without too much difficulty.

The ultimate demonstration in starting heavy trains from this spot, that I personally witnessed, was that of three Great Western 'Hall' Class locomotives working consecutive excursion trains from their home region to Bournemouth, each hauling twelve coaches a piece.

I was shovelling coal forward on the tender of a Class '4F' in the adjacent Branksome loco yard at the time and was convinced, when the first train was stopped, that we would have to go out and bank it away with our engine. It was not so, however; when the starting signal came off, the Western driver, who was accompanied by a Southern pilotman, opened the regulator, but nothing happened. The engine was now wound cautiously into back gear, until the engine just backed the train gently. Winding her quickly into forward gear, the driver whipped the regulator open. The 'Hall' obeyed instantly, moving off without further trouble, and never a hint of a slip, to the accompaniment of that lovely explosive Great Western bark, never quite equalled by engines of any other British railway. The following two 'Halls' did not even have to suffer the indignity of having to 'set back'. When signalled away, they just strode purposefully off, as though it was nothing at all.

I was pleased to note that there were a number of Southern men (who, as a body, had not one good word to say about a 'Western engine') hanging over the cabside of their engines in adjacent carriage sidings watching this spectacle, and I could tell that they were impressed by this demonstation of surefooted strength. To top it off, these ambassadors of a foreign region were beautifully clean with gleaming green paintwork, and their copper-capped chimneys sparkled brightly in the sunlight.

Returning to Branksome 'Loco' proper — the staffing allocation included five sets of enginemen. Their duties consisted of three passenger turns to Templecombe and back, one to Bailey Gate and then back to Poole Yard with a freight train, and the crack duty at the depot, the 'Pines Express', which was worked over the 71½ miles to Bath Green Park and back. Besides the enginemen, there were also four cleaners and three steamraisers, the latter each working consecutive eight hour shifts.

The administration of Branksome came from Templecombe, of which it was a sub-depot, a state of affairs which existed until 1958, when Bournemouth Central Depot took over the task. Branksome shed had no locomotives allocated to it, its duties being performed by engines from either Bath Green Park or Templecombe sheds. Coaling facilities were absent, so engines had to be coaled up sufficiently at their home depots to complete the round trip.

No engine cleaning was perfomed by the cleaners when in shed, their duties being to throw the coal forward on tenders for the return trips of engines off the S&D line, though Bournemouth Central Depot sent over a man of their own for the 'coaling down' of Southern engines, which visited the shed. Other tasks allotted to the cleaners were the loading of ashes and clinker into a wagon, and to keeping the shed 'spick and span', which it usually was despite there being no on the spot supervision.

As a rule Branksome shed had no more than four or five engines on view at any one time, but on a summer Saturday the scene was transformed, with the tiny shed boasting perhaps twenty or so engines in its environs at certain times of the day. The early morning from 5 am until 9 am was a particularly busy period, when engines off overnight trains from the Midlands and North came on shed, prior to working the day expresses back. Engines from a wide range of depots could be seen at such times, with representatives from places such as Nine Elms and Brighton in the South, to Sheffield Millhouses, Leeds Holbeck, or Carlisle, in the Midlands and North. Most of these locomotives were, of course, to supplement the Bath and Templecombe engines, which were overwhelmed by the tremendous increase in traffic over the S&D line on these summer Saturdays.

A locomotive inspector was usually provided for summer Saturdays to sort out the duties of the engines and crews, and to improvise if, due to late running, one or other was not available for their prescribed duties. By far the busiest time for the inspector was the period from 6 am until midday when Branksome shed dispatched, during peak Saturdays, engines for the 6.58 am, 7.40 am, 8.00 am, 8.16 am, 8.40 am, 8.55 am, 9.25 am, 9.45 am, (The 'Pines' Express) 9.55 am, 10.05 am, 10.35 am, 11.12 am, 11.40 am, 12.00 noon, and 12.20 pm, trains over the S&D line, plus a fair number of Southern engines, which used our shed for their 'engine requirements' before working back to Waterloo.

Usually three out of Branksome's five sets of men were removed from their rostered local duties on busy days such as those described, in order to work some of the extra trains. The crew on the 6.58 am and the 'Pines' were normally the only ones left untouched by the intrepid 'list clerk' and that was not always true either. Branksome's passed firemen and passed cleaners worked the vacated times of duty, but if they were not available Bournemouth Central or Templecombe crews filled the gaps. Branksome's passed firemen and passed cleaners also deputised for drivers and firemen away on holiday or those who might be off on sick leave, and they were well used to working the heaviest and fastest trains that the S&D line had to offer, sometimes with pretty ramshackle locomotives, when those responsible for providing the motive power were scraping the bottom of the barrel for engines. Trains regularly worked by Branksome men on summer Saturdays were the 9.45 am, (Pines) 10.05 am, 11.12 am, and 12.20 pm, through to Bath, returning respectively with the 12.24 pm, 2.52 pm, 3.30 pm, (Pines) and 4.25 pm, to Bournemouth. All these were heavy trains, destined for, or coming from the Midlands and North of England. The passed firemen usually had the 'rough end of the stick' on these critical occasions — relatively inexperienced themselves at the regulator, their mates were normally the youngest and least experienced firemen that the depot had to offer. This factor, plus the occasional added burden of inadequate motive power with which to work their trains, placed a heavy responsibility on the shoulders of these young men. They were very capable, however, and feared nothing. I always remember the comment one day of Bournemouth Central locomotive inspector Jack Hookey, (one of the best inspectors that it was my good fortune to meet, and a man much respected by everybody at Branksome Shed.) I was standing by him when he informed passed fireman Bert Short which engine he had to to take out to work the 11.12 am express out of Bournemouth West — a filthy travel stained ex Midland '4F' 0-6-0, saddled with a train of twelve bogies. Upon receiving this information from Jack, Bert's only comment was "O.K. dad, that'll be all right," then he and his young mate cheerfully boarded the footplate, and confidently left the shed. "Bless me" said Jack, "I was worried about having to tell him that, but I believe if I had told him he had Stephenson's Rocket he would have merely replied, 'O.K. Dad,' and off he would have gone."

With all this coming and going, the atmosphere was always charged with excitement as far as I was concerned. I enjoyed every moment of it, as indeed did many more of our men, as they always seemed to get to work earlier on these occasions than their signing on times demanded.

At busy times such as these, Branksome shed's tiny Mess Room was crammed to capacity, with crews from Bath, Templecombe and of course our own men, whose West Country brogues contrasted sharply with the cockney accents of the Nine Elms men. The shed's catering facilites were decidely poor, being restricted to one gas ring (with a large and much blackened iron kettle) and a cold water tap. With all these thirsty engine crews to provide hot water for the inevitable 'tea can' this kettle used to steam at a rate which would have done a class '4F' credit.

Such scenes will never be seen again as Branksome Depot was officially closed in January 1963. It was still used, however, for servicing locomotives between trips until it was demolished two years later.

Finally, mention must be made of the footplate crews stationed at Branksome, whose knowledge, keenness and enthusiasm for their job was of a very high order. That this was recognised was made evident on many occasions, and may be summarised by the following extract from a letter I received from Mr. S. C. Townroe, the Motive Power Superintendent, Eastleigh, dated 24th September 1962, which shows the regard that the Motive Power Dept. had for this splendid group of men:—

"I much appreciate your remarks concerning the running of the 'Pines', for it has been one of those trains on which the locomotive performance has been beyond any criticism."

Inevitably over a period of some nine years, there were new faces amongst the drivers at Branksome, all well remembered by me, but it was the five members of that elite band of men who were there in 1953 to whom I am indebted for teaching me the first principles of footplate work. They taught me to organise and plan my work for the job in hand on the depot, for preparation and forethought were the secret of impeccable performance on the road. It is therefore, with particular pleasure that I remember the names of Arthur Clist, Bert Freakly, Alec Bollwell, Bert Brewer, and Donald Beale who was the youngest hand of that group of men. Their skill and knowledge was available to any young cleaner or fireman who was interested enough to seek it, and many young men who passed through Branksome Depot at one time or another must have given thanks to these men for the excellence of their training. Arthur Clist, Bert Freakly and Alec Bollwell all retired during the middle and late 1950's, but their successors were good as well, for the standard of footplate work at Branksome was maintained right up to the end of its days.

This then was Branksome Depot, and the scene is now set for wandering farther afield on the S&D proper.

Chapter Two

MY FIRING CAREER BEGINS

After nine months in the shed I longed for the day when I would be able to go out firing on the road. Then came the 20th August 1954, when I was sent for by the Area Locomotive Inspector at Bournemouth Central for examination to see whether I was fit to act as a fireman. I was asked a number of questions from the official rule book, emphasis being on the safety aspect of a fireman's duties, but I answered these satisfactorily and he soon pronounced me a passed cleaner. Back at my home shed that afternoon I eagerly scanned the roster, and was delighted to find, for the first time, my name booked up in the fireman's column. I was to have my first firing turn the following day, which was my 16th birthday.

The long awaited day started at the very early hour of 3.30 am, since it was one of the peak summer Saturdays. As well as our own engine we had to prepare two others which were to work trains later that morning. My mate, incidentally, was the imperturbable passed fireman Bert Short, and having prepared a West Country Pacific and two Midland Class '2P's, we went off shed to couple to the 6.50 am stopping train to Bath, which we worked to Templecombe Upper. Our return duty from there was with the 9.10 am from Templecombe (6.55 am ex. Bath Green Park). Going up, we had engine 40698 hauling the modest load of three coaches, but, as far as I was concerned, it was like working the 'Royal Scot'. I shall never forget my pride as we steamed past Branksome shed, and I leaned nonchalantly over the cab side, so that everyone could see me! In actual fact, I was a little concerned in case I could not get 40698 to steam properly. However, I need not have worried for she was a grand engine and steamed very freely, pressure being easily maintained at 180lbs despite the inexpert over-firing that she received by a young passed cleaner anxious to please his driver. When the 6.55 am from Bath pulled in at Templecombe, I was surprised to see that our new mount was to be one of the famous S&D '7F' 2-8-0s, No. 53801, with a load of six coaches. At this time I had never even been on the footplate of one of these engines, let alone fired one, but again I had no cause to be anxious for 53801 hardly noticed the six coaches tacked on behind her, and as she clanked her way characteristically through the beautiful Dorset countryside she left me with plenty of time with which to be able to view it at my leisure. The only slight diversion on this trip occurred between Blandford and Bailey Gate Station, when the big 2-8-0 started to emit painful-sounding groans from the vicinity of her front end. Examination at Bailey Gate soon revealed the cause, a bone dry piston rod on the right hand side of the engine, which had turned black through lack of lubrication. This was a common complaint with these engines when working passenger trains, according to Bert Short, so he applied the stock remedy to deal with the situation temporarily, which was to soak a cloth in cylinder oil and secure it so that it hung down on the affected part in much the same way as a tail trimming. This saw us back to shed without too many more groans from that source.

Thereafter, I did not spend much time in the shed, as rest days, leave days, and occasional sickness among the crews (not to mention extra trains to be covered by Branksome crews), ensured of plenty of firing turns for our four passed cleaners.

One duty that seemed to come the way of the passed cleaners more than the others was the 6.40 pm to Templecombe, the reason being that firemen who had holidays owing usually took them on the late turns in preference to the early ones. Late turns are universally hated by railwaymen, but my personal feelings were the reverse, as I always preferred to work an afternoon or evening job, having never been terribly keen on rising at 4.00 am on a cold and frosty morning, or indeed a wet and warm one! The railway atmosphere was more romantic to me in the late evening or night, and a trip on the 6.40 pm to Templecombe with a Black '5' on a cold crisp moonlight night was something I could really appreciate. Of course, the countryside traversed by the S&D was very beautiful by day, but on nights such as these, places that looked quite ordinary in the daytime took on a new and more fascinating hue. I liked to see the hills around Shillingstone silhouetted against the moonlit sky or the chill, fast-flowing river shining like a molten silver strip as it passed underneath our bridge and wound on into the shadow of the trees at Fiddleford Mill near Sturminster Newton. Then there was the distant light shining from the farmstead set deep in the Dorset fastness near Stalbridge, and many similar sights that more than compensated for having to work a late turn.

The engine normally employed on the 6.40 pm up was a Standard or Stanier class '5', except during the first six months of my firing career when West Country Pacifics used to power it. At that time three were shedded at Bath Green Park, but they were removed in favour of the class '5's. The return working of this duty was with the 9.03 pm from Templecombe (7.00 pm ex Bath Green Park), normally the duty of a class '2P'.

Being a passed cleaner I did not have a regular driver, but fired to all of them as circumstances dictated, mostly on the Templecombe stopping trains. later on, in 1955, two shunting turns were allotted to our depot in exchange for two of our passenger trains which were re-allocated to Bournemouth Central. Bournemouth Central men had never previously had any working over the S&D line, and this development was viewed with displeasure by the Branksome men. The Southern Authorities defended their action, their argument being that it was necessary to have men who knew the road at that depot to enable them to work over it in an emergency.

The two shunting turns we inherited were the Bournemouth West carriage

Shunter and the Poole Goods Shunter. This brought Branksome men into contact for the first time, with Dugald Drummonds 'M7' 0-4-4 tanks. Our crews soon came to scorn these engines and it became a standing joke to enquire of the Bournemouth drivers when changing over, "Where did you get this from, out of the Ark?" Even allowing for the fact that these engines were pretty old and not designed for such duties, they seemed rather poor tools. Shunting Poole Yard was an exasperating affair. The 'M7' supplied for the duty was never one in the best condition and often seemed incapable of pulling out a whole road of wagons, so causing us to have to shunt it out in two rakes. Then there were the brakes; at least I think they had brakes, for there were occasions when they seemed to be practically non-existent. When the shunter in charge of knocking-up operations gave the driver the stop signal, he would dutifully apply his vacuum brake, but it didn't have much effect, and the weight of any reasonable train would nearly pull one back into the siding again, necessitating another go at knocking the wagons into some other road. All this made shunting a most laborious task. Sometimes we had to bank passenger trains with them up to Branksome, another nerve-wracking ordeal. You needed second valve on these engines when banking, otherwise you might as well have stayed in the siding for all the good you were doing. To get second valve on these engines fitted with a big reversing lever (some of them were fitted with steam reversers) one had to shut off steam (it was necessary to nick up the reverser to the required position), and then struggle like mad to get the regulator wide open as soon as possible. While this effort took place, as we would be banking loose-coupled, the main train might well have left us behind, with the result that we sometimes chased it as far as Parkstone, instead of pushing it! In any case, if you opened the second valve with more than half a glass of water the engine primed, so it really didn't matter. What made these engines seem worse was the fact that they were compared with the more modern tank engines that we had on the S&D, the Ivatt Class '2' 2-6-2s, which were very snappy performers in or out of the shunting yard.

By way of illustration of what these competent engines could do, there was an occasion when driver Bert Jones of Templecombe shed on 41248 had a load of no less than ten coaches, when working the 12.23 pm from Templecombe to Bournemouth West. The train weighed 335 tons, but the little tank made light of it, and hauled this heavy load up the 1 in 80 of Corfe Mullen bank and the 1 in 60 of Parkstone bank unassisted, including stopping and starting at Parkstone Station. This was an outstanding feat, even allowing for the fact that these were comparatively modern engines.

I had to wait some time before I was booked up for the 'Pines Express', but eventually the day arrived when they were scraping the bottom of the barrel for men and I was the only one available. The engine was Black '5' 45440, which was probably the longest reigning Class '5' at Bath shed, and certainly the darling of the depot at the time. My driver was Albert Brewer, and the load was one of eleven coaches. I thought I knew all there was to know about firing by now, but by the time we reached Broadstone Bank I began to wonder. Full regulator working combined with cut offs in the region of 50-55% was altogether much sterner stuff than I had experienced hitherto, and 180lbs of steam and half a glass of water at this early stage of the run was not at all healthy. However, with some kindly advice from Bert Brewer, plus a demonstration of firing, which showed that the passing years had not robbed him of any of his skill with the shovel, we made out quite well after all. By the time I was making my first ascent of the Mendip Hills, 45440 was thoroughly behaving herself and we passed over the top at Masbury Summit, 811ft. above sea level, in great style. From there I was able to sit down practically all the way into Bath, and enjoy my first sight of the enchanting scenery which surrounds the line to the outskirts of that ancient and beautiful City. I also learned of the beauties or otherwise of those two obnoxious single line tunnels situated between Midford and Bath, Combe Down Tunnel and Devonshire Tunnel. A trip up through Devonshire Tunnel on a heavy Southbound train, with its 1 in 50 gradient, a pilot engine in front of you working flat out, plus your own on 50% and the regulator hard over was not exactly a joyous experience, and definitely not something for anybody with a nervous disposition. The din inside was tremendous, the heat inside tremendous, and the relief to get outside was tremendous: yes, taking it all round, the S&D was certainly a rugged railway, and had no use for weaklings amongst its men or its engines.

Two days later I was again drafted on the 'Pines' with the same engine and driver, but this time I performed my task without any prompting at all, and with Driver Brewer expressing himself well pleased with my performance upon arrival back at Branksome that night. Those words of praise meant a good deal to me!

However, at this stage of my career, such important duties seldom fell to the responsibility of a relatively inexperienced fireman and Templecombe duty No. 72 was the sort of turn which was more appropriate to my skill and knowledge, and indeed an excellent job for young passed cleaners to cut their teeth on.

Part of this diagram was worked by Branksome men, and a very pleasant and easy job it was as well. At no time was any sense of real urgency required and the general tenor of this turn of duty matched many people's conception of the S&D.

The first part of this duty consisted of preparing two class '2P' locomotives. One of these was our own engine, while the other worked the 11.40 am Bristol Temple Meads later in the morning.

Ringing off shed at 8.10 am we would amble down to the West Station, and back on to our train, usually to be found in platform 2. After coupling up operations had been completed there was just time to watch the departure of 'The Royal Wessex' for Waterloo from platform 3 at 8.20 am, and to appraise its occupants, some of whom would be already tucking into their breakfasts. We still had ample time to exchange pleasantries with our Guard and to put the country's affairs in order before departure. Then at 8.50 am we would get the right away, a tug at the regulator from the driver, and the '2P', with its three coach train, would be set in motion.

There was no particular hurry, and we would saunter easily along, stopping at all stations to Bailey Gate, which was as far as Branksome men went on this duty. Here footplates would be exchanged with the Templecombe crew of the 6.35 am Evercreech Junction-Poole freight, the 8.50 am ex Bournemouth West completing its sedate journey to Templecombe under their care.

We would now spend the rest of our working day completing the duties of the 6.35 am Poole freight, probably hauled by '4F' 0-6-0 No. 44102, for this engine had the virtual monopoly of this turn of duty. Except for the occasions when she was stopped for 'washouts', periodical examinations, or away for general overhaul, this engine was the first choice for this freight train. Certainly this was true from 1953 when I started work on the S&D until the year 1960, when the advent of the Standard '4' M.T. 4-6-0s at Templecombe depot (44102's home shed) ousted her from this job.

Bailey Gate Station was situated some twelve miles from Bournemouth, and was a typical wayside station, set amongst the peaceful green fields of Dorset's farmland. On the down side of the line, trailing points off the main line gave access to a United Dairies cheese factory, and it was this, rather than its passenger traffic, that made Bailey Gate one of the more prosperous stations on the S&D system; and provided us, on the 6.35 freight, with anything up to two hours shunting if business was brisk in the factory.

However, after the initial change-over, shunting was necessarily brief, as both the up and down lines had to be cleared by 10.00 am for the passage of trains.

First of all on the down line, the 6.55 am from Bath Green Park to Bournemouth West would put in an appearance, stopping for two minutes or so at the station before continuing its journey. We would now be listening for the sound that heralded the approach of the up 'Pines Express'. With the distant, home, starting and advanced starting signals nodding their approval, the sound of an engine being worked vigorously at speed would soon be heard on the lilting breeze. Seconds later, with the roar of a Class '5' exhaust swelling to a crescendo, the train would come into view, hurtling around the gentle curve towards the station, making nearly 70 mph with the engine's exhaust rising well clear of the chimney, before being borne behind it on its own artificially produced gale. Then, with the characteristic change in sound, the engine would sweep by — our shedmates on the footplate exchanging 'waves' with us — followed urgently by its twelve maroon coaches, beating out their message on the Bailey Gate pointwork.

In a moment, she was by, the train rapidly disappearing under the road-bridge at the north end of the station. Only the sound of her lingered on, and that too soon melted into the Dorset countryside. The morning show was over; the cows in the adjacent field, who had temporarily suspended their habitual chewing to gaze at the train resumed chewing, and with the ground signal guarding the exit of our siding, now in the off position, we were able to resume our shunting activities.

Shunting would now be carried on in much the same fashion as it is on railways the world over, but there was one move often employed by the resident shunter which intrigued me. This was carried out if it was necessary to transfer any vans for the watercress traffic at Bailey Gate, which was quite substantial, from the down to the up siding, and it was effected without our engine having to leave the down line.

We would vigorously propel the unattached vans for some 50 yards before stopping abruptly, leaving the vans to carry on across the connection to the up line and as far up the rising grade beyond as impetus would carry them, and that was quite a considerable distance. Thereafter, we could forget them, the shunt being completed by gravity and our guard. A few minutes later the vans would come trundling into sight again down the 1 in 100 gradient, under the roadbridge and through the station platform to the signalbox. Here our guard, who in all probability had spent the interim period enjoying a cup of tea with the signalman, would appear, and 'walk' them into the up siding, bringing them to a stand by means of a hand brake a few inches from the buffer stop.

By 11.15 am shunting would be completed and our train for Poole Yard assembled. Soon the guard would appear (usually from the direction of the signalbox once more, as guards and signalmen always seem to have plenty to talk about), to tell us our load for the climb of Corfe Mullen bank, up which the maximum load allowed for a '4F' 0-6-0 was = 37 wagons. He also told us whether we had to shunt 'Carters Sidings' or not.

'Carters Sidings' were located some 1½ miles up the old original S&D line, which ran to Wimborne in the early days of this railway, but was now terminated at this point. This section of line was retained solely to afford access to these sidings, which were visited on an average about twice a week until the clay pit which produced the traffic for the line was shut down, about 1959. Thereafter, the line was used as a refuge sidings for goods or perhaps pigeon trains, when it was necessary to let passenger trains get ahead of them.

If our guard had made the cryptic remark 'Carters' before leaving Bailey Gate, we could expect the left hand signal to be off on the gantry at Corfe Mullen Junction, and our engine, instead of nosing to the right at Corfe Mullen Box, would carry on curving to the left, and soon to the right, finally straightening out for the remainder of the run up to the sidings.

Actually, the whole train was not taken the full length of the spur. When the entire train was in clear of the ground signal protecting the exit, the train was halted. The guard would screw his handbrake on tightly, and then proceed to walk the length of the train to where it was necessary to detach the empty ingoing wagons. He then joined us on the footplate for a truly rural ride up the rather rickety track to the sidings.

The countryside hereabouts is very pleasant, and running as we were on an embankment, a good view was to be had of the flat water-meadows around the old market town of Wimbourne, which was now close at hand.

On the right hand side the single track main line to Bournemouth, opened on December 14th, 1885, was climbing away above us, soon to disappear in a wooded cutting. We would, of course, be rejoining this line when our business was completed at the clay sidings.

Twenty minutes usually sufficed to see us back and coupled on to the main train once more, and with the ground signal 'pulled off' we would propel the now complete train onto the main line.

Now, with the Corfe Mullen starting signal displaying the 'right away' for the Bournemouth line, and with the single line tablet picked up by means of the Whittaker mechanical tablet-catching apparatus, the battle royal would begin. This was especially so if we had a full load behind the tender, for the 1 in 80 grade of Corfe Mullen bank began within a few yards of passing the starting signal and lasted for about two miles, the summit being marked by a very high three-arched overbridge.

The regulator of our class '4' would be yanked over on the stop, and with the reverser not far from full forward gear, Midland Railway enthusiasts may well imagine the lusty roar that old 44102 would be emitting as, racked to the frames, she fought her way up the summit at some 10-12 mph with safety valves sizzling, and rolling from side to side under the pressure of her own piston thrusts, rather like the action of someone climbing up a rope ladder.

The effort on the part of the engine was transitional, with the water level in the boiler dropping steadily all the way, and the injectors being left off to maintain full boiler pressure. But as the climb was relatively short, a boiler full of water and a full firebox at the commencement would allow me to lean over the side of the cab and enjoy the sound and the scenery, which in Autumn and winter, when the trees were stripped of their foliage, included a most appealing view of Wimbourne Minster from the left hand side of the cab.

After breasting the top of the bank there was a short plateau before the line dipped downhill on a gradient of 1 to 97, bisecting the golf course laid out amidst the heathlands around Broadstone. The '4Fs' tender brake would now be screwed firmly on, and both of her injectors would be set, working on full bore, in order to raise the water level in the boiler to something more than the inch showing in the gauge glass, when the engine dipped her nose down the hill.

Continuing coasting down the bank we next joined up with the Ringwood and Salisbury line at Broadstone Junction, giving up the single line tablet in the process and leaving the S&D at this point.

Still with steam shut off we would carry on drifting down from Broadstone, mostly on 1 in 75 grades, through Creekmoor Halt until sea level was reached, with the backwaters of Holes Bay lapping up nearly to our tender axlebox journals.

Joining up with the Weymouth — London main line at Holes Bay Junction, our engine would almost immediately lurch to the left to enter one of the two reception sidings in Poole Goods Yard.

Leaving our train here, all that remained for us to do was to run light engine to Branksome Depot, via Gas Works junction, in order that our loco would be facing the right way for her return working, which was the 3.05 pm goods from Poole Yard to Templecombe Upper Yard manned by a Templecombe crew.

This was the only main line goods working that Branksome shed had regularly diagrammed to it, and was retained right up to the closure of the depot. Inevitably, over a period of ten years, parts of the diagram were altered in the mid fifties, with Branksome losing the 8.50 am up to Templecombe Depot. Branksome crews then took over the goods at Blandford Station, after working the 6.50 am Bournemouth West-Bath train as far as Templecombe, and the 6.55 am Bath Green Park-Bournemouth, from that point to Blandford.

This turn of duty was often used for 'breaking-in' young passed cleaners, and introducing them gently to the rigours of firing on the main line. It provided them with an excellent chance to put a little theory into practice, without jeopardising too much if the theory did not stand up. But most important of all, it was far more likely to catch the interest of the younger men than the boring shunting turns normally doled out to them by most depots' list clerks.

Chapter Three

A NEW TEAM IS BORN

I first came into contact with Donald Beale when I was still a young train spotter, viewing engines from the extreme ends of station platforms. We used to exchange regular pleasantries in those days, and I always found him most friendly and jovial to talk to. So what with this attribute, plus our mutual admiration of the steam locomotive, it was only natural that we very soon became firm friends.

To the uninitiated, Donald Beale was an engine driver at Branksome Loco Depot, who had spent the majority of his railway career working over the S&D line. His native town was Bath in Somerset, and this was where he had started on the railway, as an engine cleaner, in the year 1919. Over the lengthy period from this time until we came into contact with one another, Donald had amassed a wealth of knowledge and experience concerning the S&D, and of the locomotives that had worked over it.

Right from those early platform meeting days, I have always respected his judgement on anything to do with his work, and later on, when I was a young passed cleaner, I would wish fervently that by some miracle I would some day be his regular fireman. It did not seem reasonable to suppose that this would every happen, promotion being by means of strict seniority only, and vacancies advertised in all loco depots within the particular region one was in. But in 1958, the hoped-for miracle came to pass. Donald's regular fireman most unexpectedly resigned from the railway, and I, who was by now the senior passed cleaner at the depot, duly applied for the vacancy when it was advertised.

A month of suspense now had to be endured, and I, always the pessimist, was convinced that out of all the loco depots on the Southern Region somebody with longer service than I had would surely apply for the post. However, upon returning to the depot one Saturday evening after working the down 'Pines' with Donald, the steamraiser on duty greeted us with the news that I had in fact got the job that I wanted so much. I was now a registered fireman, and had for my driver the man that I would have chosen had the choice been in my own hands.

Donald's artistry in the realm of locomotive handling was legendary on the S&D line, and his many feats of top grade performance on the road are well known to large numbers of railway observers.

Donald had many good friends amongst the older drivers at Bath, some of whom he had spent much time on shed with, cleaning S&D locos in the 'good old days' when they were painted blue and kept in immaculate condition.

I never failed to become absorbed with interest when listening to these senior drivers reminiscing in the mess room about bygone days on the S&D. Days when the drivers wore long white beards and, judging by the remarks passed about these old boys, I should imagine that some of them were most eccentric to say the least. Bath men used to work lodging turns to Wimborne, the then terminus of the S&D line, and also to Birmingham and Derby on the Midland main line. The motive power provided for them was usually either a class '2P', or a '4F' if on goods work. These engines were, of course, new at that time. The class '2P's, I gather, were very well liked except one, which was equipped with a Dabeg feed water heater and which, for some reason, earned a bad reputation for itself.

In addition to these duties at Bath, the men were also sent on loan to Highbridge, which was the S&D headquarters and was then a thriving railway community. This section of the S&D known locally as 'the branch' was the one stretch that I never worked over, much to my regret. Dear old Chummy Andrews of Highbridge shed frequently asked me to take a trip down the branch with him, but I never got around to it.

It was always interesting to question these drivers about some of the engines that had run over the 'Dorset' comparatively recently, but before I started work on the line. These included such engines as the Horwich Crabs, Midland Compounds, and the Midland '3P', No. 40741, which was at Templecombe for a short time in 1950. One driver surprised me considerably by claiming to have piloted an LNER locomotive to Blandford on an ambulance train during the last war. This was a rebuilt Great Eastern 'B12' 4-6-0 locomotive, a type chosen for its high route availability for working these mercy trains over much of Southern England during that unhappy period. A similar train was noted by my good friend Ivo Peters, who saw it passing over a road bridge near Bitton just after dawn one morning on its way into Bath. He was told later that the 'B12' had been turned at Bath and then continued on over the S&D line to Blandford.

The engines that Donald disliked most of all in recent years were the rather ugly looking class '4' 2-6-0s, nicknamed 'Doodlebugs' by the S&D men, three of which were shedded at Bath in 1950. One of them was given two test runs on the 'Pines' but was found wanting; nevertheless they were often rostered to heavy passenger trains on summer weekends. I gather they gave their handlers some of the most anxious moments experienced for many a long day on these jobs.

The engines concerned were 43013/17/36: all of them as originally built with double blastpipe and chimney, which was mainly the cause of the trouble with them. The blast pipe dimensions were out of proportion to the size of the boiler and firebox, resulting in inferior steaming. This was proved when an engine of this type was thoroughly tested on the Rugby testing plant, which resulted in the entire class being fitted with single blastpipes and draughting arrangements more suited to the dimensions of the locomotives.

Donald told me that working such a train as the 'Pines' with one of these engines in original state could indeed be a trial: if you had a reasonable head of steam, you had no water in the boiler, (relatively speaking that is), and if you had ample water — then there was no steam! But he did speak appreciatively of their very free running qualities when coasting, and which helped considerably in times of stress, which were many.

Part of the skill of handling steam engines is the ability of the driver to interpret correctly how far he can push an engine when mortgaging the boiler to procure a high draw bar horsepower for some particular reason — but which is beyond the capacity of the boiler to sustain. This may be when lost time is being regained on an uphill section, or again, it may be necessary to use this technique when coaxing a badly steaming engine along the road. Where some drivers would play safe and ease a bad steamer in an attempt to recoup the boiler, and lose time in the process, the absolute expert might well extend the engine further, losing both boiler pressure and water level in so doing but confident of his assessment that these two commodities would last out until an easier stretch of track was reached. Both steam and water could then be recovered and with little or perhaps no lost time into the bargain. This sort of thing could not always be accomplished of course circumstances being the overriding factor, but if it was possible then Donald, with his skill and knowledge of the road, was the person to demonstrate it to the full, for he had complete confidence in his ability on the footplate.

To give an example of this ability, I will describe a trip that we shared on the up 'Pines', when our engine, Standard class '5' No. 73116, had a very dirty tubeplate and, as we discovered later on Bath shed, the smokebox door was drawing air nearly all the way round its circumference. This last factor alone was a pretty good guarantee of a rough trip, let alone anything else.

Despite the fact that she had a glorious hand built fire made up in her, No. 73116 refused to steam freely right from the start and by the time we were passing Branksome Station, some 1¼ miles out from our point of departure, boiler pressure was already back to 180lbs, and the injector was still off. Normally, it would have been started as we passed Bournemouth West Carriage sidings, with safety valves ready to lift. But this was only giving us notice of real troubles still to come.

73116, with her eleven coach load, made the going extremely gruelling for me. I was constantly at work on the fire, shutting the firehole door after every shovelfull of coal, which was being fed onto a blinding, white hot fire over the hinged flap fitted on these engines for the purpose of restricting the intake of cold air into the firebox. Liberal use was also made of the pricker to break up any fuel which showed any tendency to cake in the firebox. But as we progressed up through Dorset things went from bad to worse, until we reached what I considered 'rock bottom', when we came to a cautious halt at the Stalbridge stop with the water just visible in the gauge glass, 120lbs of steam on the clock, and the perspiration pouring off me from my efforts with shovel and fireirons.

Donald, throughout, had been seated on the other side of the cab, looking as relaxed as though we had a 'full pot' and were blowing off. However, when we expired in Stalbridge Station, I decided it was a foregone conclusion that we would stop for a while and have a 'blow up'. But Donald thought otherwise, and when given the 'tip' to start by the guard, opened 73116 up again. We had not recovered to more than 140lbs of steam, and about an inch of water showing in the glass.

"We'll never make it to Templecombe No. 2!" I exclaimed, being very surprised that we were in fact going on so soon in view of the adverse grades — moderate though they were by S&D standards — still to be surmounted before Templecombe No. 2 Junction box was passed. Donald grinned. "She will be all right son", he answered, at the same time opening up the regulator to the full position. "Things will be tight when I shut off for the Templecombe slack, but after that we should be able to recover a bit". His judgement was 'right on the nail', and with Templecombe safely behind us, good use was made of the falling gradients between there and Wincanton to test the coasting ability of our mount, which proved to be excellent. Perhaps I should point out that by now we were no longer attempting to keep time on this train, but were just concerned in keeping it rolling. I have no idea of how overdue we were at any particular point on this journey, being far too pre-occupied with steam production. I do remember, however, that from Stalbridge onwards up to Masbury Summit our speeds were little better than those of a smartly worked freight train, but at least we remained a 'going concern.'

With steam reapplied, we staggered on past Wincanton and managed to get speed up towards the 50 mph mark before shutting off once more at the high arched bridge at Shepton Montague. Now there was the chance for some real recovery of our resources, as we coasted down the winding valley leading to the picturesque little station at Cole beyond which the GWR West of England main line was bridged. The short rise encountered after traversing Cole curve was breasted without steam and then it was downhill almost all the way to Evercreech Junction — and things were looking up on 73116. We ran in to the Evercreech stop with 190lbs on the clock, and half a glass of water.

A Templecombe class '2P' was coupled to the front of us here for the climb over the Mendips and on to Bath, and a few words with her driver, Ray Stokes of Templecombe shed, advising him of our situation brought forth doughty assistance from that quarter. Masbury was cleared without further loss of time, even though we were losing steam and water levels all the way up. The struggle was over. It was coasting and light steaming now, right into Bath except, of course, for the short but sharp climb from Midford up through Combe Down Tunnel.

I am unaware of our exact time of arrival at Bath, but know that it was round about 12.15 pm, roughly 20 minutes late. Not a satisfactory conclusion to a run on a crack express to be sure, but had it not been for some excellent enginemanship on Donald's part it could have have been a whole lot worse. Many lesser men would have given up the engine en route or stopped for a 'blow up' somewhere, procedures which would have caused more loss of time and dislocation to other trains than Donald's method.

The foregoing gives an insight into the skill, judgement and accurate road knowledge necessary if the driver of a steam locomotive was to emerge the victor of such a situation. This sort of effort in fact was more demanding of an engine crew's skill than many of the spetacular performances which grace the pages of the locomotive-running articles in the Railway Magazine.

Modern diesel and electric traction ended trips like this for engine crews, no doubt with considerable relief on the part of the travelling public, but not necessarily to engine crews at large. Though we sweated and cussed at the time of these contretemps, it brought us perhaps even greater satisfaction to get a train through such difficult circumstances than to put up a brilliant performance on the road under more favourable conditions. Steam locomotives only responded to skill and physical effort, unlike today's motive power which, by comparison, require little skill and, of course, no physical effort. This has removed a good deal of the interest and pride in the job which locomen used to experience; the job now is too clinical. Put the controller over on a diesel and it will develop 2,000 hp, no more no less, irrespective of who is the driver. Steam power, on the other hand, reflected in its performance the skill and amount of physical effort available on the footplate. This is why some drivers such as Ted Hailstone, Bill Hoole, and Sam Gingell emerged head and shoulders above many of their colleagues. Donald ranked with this elite band of men.

In 1962, at the age of 24, I was successful in passing the examination allowing me to act as driver. I was elated. My ambition was fulfilled. But could ever a candidate for this examination have been better prepared than I? Besides my attending 'Mutual Improvement Classes' at Branksome shed and swotting diligently at home, Donald took advantage of every spare moment to school me in all aspects of footplate work. In addition, I was allowed to handle locomotives on all types of trains, ranging from shunting work to express passenger trains, while Donald acted as fireman. During the summer of 1960, it was 'booked working', as it were, that I would be the driver on the 12.24 pm Bath-Bournemouth West (7.25 am ex-Nottingham). This gave me my first opportunity to drive the B.R. Standard class '9' 2-10-0s which had just been allocated to Bath shed. I recall that on every occasion except one, that we worked it No. 92203 was the engine rostered on the job. The 3.40 pm Bournemouth West to Bristol (TM) was another train which I invariably drove as far as Templecombe, returning with the 6.05 pm train to Bournemouth West (4.25 pm ex Bath Green Park). This went on for at least three years before my examination, so that when the practical part of this test was undertaken, which was to work the 'Pines' to Bath and back, I was more than at home on the driver's seat.

I received a 100% pass, for which Donald must claim a large share of the credit. It is true to say that many drivers on British Railways took a similar interest in their 'Mates' progress towards the 'regulator', but equally, there were, unfortunately, some who took no interest at all. These men had my sympathy, because if they sustained their interest long enough to learn the theoretical side of the examination, they were ill prepared for the practical side — some of them having never been allowed to touch the regulator by their drivers. Fortunately men of this mentality were comparatively rare, but they highlighted the part that drivers played in the preparation of firemen to assume their responsibility, by the number of examination failures involving firemen teamed with such drivers.

Donald retired on July 8th, 1966, not long after the closure of the S&D line, a great loss to railway enthusiasts and to lovers of the S&D in particular.

Earlier I mentioned the practical part of my 'drivers' examination, something that every candidate for this post hopes will pass off without incident, and so avoid stretching already taut nerves to breaking point.

The engine that has always remained my personal favourite was on the job that day, 73052, a BR Class '5', and in Ron Hyde I had an excellent fireman. The load was one of eleven bogies for 385 tons, and the set-up looked good.

Due to 73052s late arrival on the first part of her diagram that day — the 2.40 am Bath to Bournemouth West mail train — the preparation crew were unable to give much attention to the fire. Normally this would not matter much, but on this occasion, the coal on the tender was very inferior stuff, mostly slack in fact, first class for forming a layer of clinker over the firebars but not so hot for steam production.

As far as Blandford we did quite well, pressure being maintained by dint of shutting off the exhaust steam injector for brief periods, this having the effect of rallying the boiler pressure, but lowering the water level in the boiler. Round about Shillingstone, however, we reached the point where the injector had to stay on, and pressure gradually dropped back.

Adapting techniques and using all the experience that Donald had passed on to me, plus some first rate backing up from Ron Hyde on the shovel, no time was lost. Things were tight at Masbury Summit, just scraping over the top with 150lbs of steam in the boiler and half an inch of water showing on the gauge. On the 1 in 63 descent to Binegar I had to keep the regulator cracked open to keep the water level up in the boiler. But the use of two injectors soon brought the level up to a comfortable position, and that particular worry, at least, was over. On arrival at Bath Green Park Station Jack Evans, the examining inspector, who until now had said nothing since leaving Bournemouth, congratulated me on my handling of 'a tricky situation', adding "I'll bet you won't forget this trip in a hurry".

Bath Green Park was a veritable mecca for train spotters, especially on summer Saturdays, when locomotives representing the four pre-nationalized companies could often be seen on the depot. To Donald and myself, with insatiable appetites for steam engines, this was like food and drink. Should one of us spot an unusual engine on shed as we ran into Green Park Station, it was certain that as soon as our immediate work was completed we would be standing on the visitors footplate, eagerly noting and pointing out the detail differences between it and the engines we regularly handled. Unusual engines that we have noted at Bath include ER Bls, WR Halls and Granges, LMR Royal Scots, Patriots and Jubilees, and ex LNWR Super D 0-8-0s. Add to this list the odd Britannia Pacific and of course the SR West Countrys, T9s, etc. etc., and one wonders where else in the country such a diverse collection of locomotive classes could be seen in each other's company at one time. Possibly Oxford was Bath's biggest rival for this distinction.

Donald and I have shared many exciting times together, although few frightening ones I am glad to say. But an incident in which we were involved with a West Country Pacific in Devonshire Tunnel can be categorised under the heading of terrifying.

It occurred on a very hot and sultry summer Saturday in 1960, when we were working the Southbound Pines with 34105 'Swanage' and a '2P' as pilot to Evercreech Junction. We got away from Bath Station, but immediately we were on the move it was apparent that the brakes were rubbing on the train, possibly as a result of the engine which had brought it into Bath running with a train pipe vacuum in excess of the 'Standard 21'. Be that as it may, Donald and our assisting engine's driver signalled agreement to each other to make for Midford Station, and to stop there and pull the strings on the brake cylinders throughout the train. This action allowed atmospheric pressure access to the top of the brake pistons — thus creating an equilibrium between top and bottom of the brake cylinders, which caused the pistons to fall by gravity to the bottom of the cylinders and released the brakes. But first we had to get to Midford and the way that the train pulled on the first taste of 1 in 50 from Bath Junction up to the Co-op coal sidings, it was going to need considerable effort on the part of our two locomotives to make it.

At the immediate approach to Devonshire Tunnel our engine was working in full forward gear with full regulator, and I imagine the '2P' on the front of us was being similarly worked. A pensive glance passed between Donald and myself and with our speed down to 10-12 mph we knew neither of us was going to relish the passage of this single line bore, a ¼ mile long and on a rising grade of 1 in 50. The clearance between a 'West Country's' chimney top and the roof of the tunnel was less than 12″ which resulted in the exhaust striking the tunnel roof and rebounding down around the locomotive.

As we entered the tunnel, I took a deep breath of fresh air, covered my mouth with a damp cloth and sat down on the footboards. Poor Donald however, stuck to his post, apprehensive lest 34105 should lose her feet, but soon the heat and fumes became so intense, that he too was forced to the footboards. I sat there in the fumes and heat laden atmosphere with my lungs nearly bursting, listening to the Pacific's rasping exhaust, as she fought her way up through the stygian darkness of this 'hell hole'. Then she slipped, and it wasn't in a half hearted fashion either. The engine shuddered and vibrated like a trapped lion in a snare, and all I could see through the thick sulphurous atmosphere was a cascade of burning coals, showering all around our cab. Add to this scene the din that the engine was making in this confined space, and it all added up to a terrifying situation. Donald forced himself off the floorboards and tried to slam the regulator shut, but to add to the problem the engine was now priming badly, making the regulator very stiff. I quickly jumped up to help him and together we managed to close it. By now we had both been forced to suck into our lungs the obnoxious semi-superheated gases that we had to substitute for oxygen. Each gasp taken was like swallowing a red hot poker, and my chest was tightening up instantaneously as the foul smoke-laden air reached my lungs. Donald was heroically pumping the regulator of 34105 in an effort to keep her going, and save us from asphyxiation. We couldn't tell how much farther there was to go before we would break daylight, or even if we would, for it was difficult to judge just how fast we were moving. In fact we made it, and were some yards out of the tunnel before we realised it such was the density of the smoke and fumes on our footplate and surrounding the engine. We quietly gave thanks to that '2P' on the front of us, which had never slipped once, and undoubtedly had saved all of us from an extremely nasty situation, if not a tragedy. For if we had come to a stand in that tunnel I don't think any of us on the two engines would have been in a fit state to do much to save himself or the train. As it was, speaking personally, I was unable to get my breath properly for some time afterwards, and my chest felt as though it was constricted with steel bands. What sort of temperatures we had endured in that tunnel I have no idea, but both Donald and myself were soaked to the skin in perspiration when we emerged into the daylight. Having survived, we made it safely through Combe Down Tunnel to Midford where we stopped to release the brake cords on the train as planned.

The back corners of the Pacific's firebox were virtually empty of fire. I was shocked at the amount of live coal which must have been thrown out of the engine's chimney during that terrifying slip back in the tunnel. Whilst our guard pulled the strings I set about rebuilding the fire, but I was still wheezing badly, and had to stop frequently for breath. Bournemouth West at this juncture looked a mighty long way away. But the true value of a good Mate on the footplate was now displayed by Donald's insistence on taking turns with me to fire the engine on to Evercreech Junction, and by this time I was feeling rather better. Even though he was in as much physical distress as myself this was great courage, I feel, from a 60 year old man under these conditions. The pilot crew incidentally did not get the full effect of the two engines' exhausts as we did, but it was no picnic for them either, in that Dantes Inferno that passed under the name of Devonshire Tunnel.

Exchanging the tablet at speed via the Whittaker tablet exchange apparatus could be a difficult undertaking at times, especially if the engine's equipment was not maintained properly, as was often the case with engines loaned from Bournemouth Central. The square end of the catcher's arm which slotted into a bracket on the engine's tender was the usual trouble, it being too slack a fit, thus allowing the catcher to vibrate at speed and slop about in the bracket. I have walked several miles during my time on the S&D retrieving dropped tablets on this account.

Sometimes trouble was encountered in giving up the tablet due to the fireman's inability to insert the pouch in between the spring-loaded lugs at the back of the catcher, where outgoing tablets were positioned for collection. If this occurred most drivers would slow down approaching the collecting signalbox and hand it to the signalman at a train speed of about 10 mph, thus losing time. Donald, on the other hand, kept the train going at speed if the exchange point was adjacent to the station platform such as Shillingstone, Sturminster Newton or Stalbridge, giving a series of pop whistles to alert the signalman and station staff during our approach. When this happened they knew what to do — stand well away from the platform edge and watch the tablet all the way, for Donald was going to launch if from the footplate, and attempt to land it flat surface down on the platform. On contact the pouch would slide along as if on ice before striking some part of the station building finally bouncing off to a halt, to be picked up by the station staff. Donald was a dab hand at this, and the procedure never let him down, although someone did lose all the spokes out of the front wheel of his bicycle at Sturminster one day, and British Rail got the bill for their replacement.

In pursuit of punctual running Donald would use his initiative to the full, but there were times when his optimism was way above my own. This was very much the case when we were running towards Blandford Station one Saturday with the 11.12 am Bournemouth-Manchester (SO) express. This train was booked non-stop from Poole to Evercreech Junction, and we were approaching the station at about 40 mph when I noticed that the signalman had not got his tablet apparatus set up for us to collect the token for the Blandford-Shillingstone section. I shouted a warning to Donald and crossed quickly to the right hand side of the cab where I saw an astonished signalman walking along the down platform towards the apparatus with the tablet in his hand, (we had evidently arrived there sooner than he anticipated). I expected Donald to slap the brakes on, stop the train, and I would have to run back for the tablet. But he never touched the brake, instead he joined me on the side of the footplate, leaned over the cab side and motioned the signalman to throw him the tablet. Without time to think about it, he obliged launching it into space instantly. Now a tablet and pouch together weighed about 4lbs, and the metal loop on it could cause considerable personal injury if it should strike one under such conditions, (that is if it did not go through the side cab window first). I took evasive action, but Donald caught the pouch as sweet as a nut, and hung it nonchalantly on the gauge glass lamp bracket as he recrossed the cab to the regulator, which in turn was yanked wide open once more, and we stormed the 1 in 80 bank to Milldown at speed.

I recall yet another demonstration of Donald's astonishing ability to improvise at a moment's notice. Driver Bert Freakly and myself, (still a passed cleaner then), were travelling up to Bath 'on the cushions' of the 'Pines' in order to work an extra Sheffield-Bournemouth train later in the day, when between Bailey Gate and Spetisbury the speed of the train dropped off so

Very occasionally an ex-L.S.W.R. "T9" 4-4-0 was turned out by Bournemouth Central shed to cover an S & D diagram, usually as the result of a failure to the rostered loco-motive — as in this case No. 30706 deputising for a Standard class "4" photographed after arrival at Bath with the 3.35pm. from Bournemouth on 2nd February 1956.

Our old friend of Chapter two, "4F" No. 44102, puts in some hard work, as she leaves Chilcompton Tunnel with a stopping passenger train for Templecombe.

Stanier class "5" 4-6-0. No. 44826 shares some hard work with ex-Midland "2P" 4-4-0. No. 40505, about to enter Chilcompton tunnel on the southbound "Pines" in the early 1950s.

Bournemouth West Station

S & D "7F" 2-8-0 No. 53806 was the last of this class to retain the original large diameter boiler with which they were built. She was still so fitted when this photograph was taken of her departure from the West station with the 12.25pm. express to Birmingham.

Yet another combination of double heading. Bert Brewer and Donald Beale are on class "5" No. 44888 and "West Country" class No. 34043 *Combe Martin* respectively, as they speed through Wellow with a down express.

W.D. on test

The 2-8-0 No. 90125 gets its first taste of S & D gradients as she climbs the 1 in 50 Devonshire bank out of Bath. Note the fitted vans immediately behind the engine, which proved so useful during the run photographed on January 22nd 1959. (See Chapter 4.)

The footplate playout of S & D "7F" 2-8-0. No. 53809

Bath shed during one of its less congested moments. In the background right an express is seen starting away from Green Park Station.

S & D "7F" 2-8-0 No. 53808 heads a Bath—Evercreech Junction freight working away from Midford in wintery conditions. The Mendips could be a most unpleasant place for engine crews in conditions like these.

Radstock station — where the contretemps mentioned in Chapter 7 occurred. The busy level crossing referred to is just visible in the background under the footbridge. This location also featured in the Bulleid Pacific fire described in chapter 4. The locomotives in this photograph are Stanier class "5" No. 45440 and pilot engine "2P" No. 40634.

Standard class "5" No. 73054 has just crossed the Western Region Paddington—Plymouth main line, and is about to pass through Cole Station with a Saturday "extra". 73054 appears to be steaming as well as ever.

Class "2P" No. 40563, and Standard class "5" No. 73050, come off the S & D line at Bath Junction, and coast along the Midland line towards Bath Green Park Station.

Bath Green Park station from the buffer stop end. On the left of the picture, S & D "7F" 2-8-0 No. 53806, piloted by a Johnson "3F" 0-6-0, No. 43441, has just worked in on a summer Saturday extra. Whilst on the right, an Ivatt 2-6-2 tank is preparing to leave with a local train for Bristol (Temple Meads).

March 29th 1960. The S & D has its first view of a Class "9F" 2-10-0. No. 92204 on her southbound test run; seen here passing a line of stored locomotives on Templecombe shed. Driver Bill Rawles and Fireman Ron Bean of Bath shed are in charge.

Golfer's crossing: Standard Class "5". No. 73052 finds the crossing is clear, but not Broadstone down distant signal, as she heads southwards with a Saturdays only express from the north of England.

Blandford Forum station looking south. Standing in the up platform on a stopping train to Bath is Bulleid Pacific No. 34041 *Wilton.*

Descending Broadstone bank, "9F" 2-10-0 No. 92233 hauling the down "Pines" is about to pass "U" class 2-6-0 No. 31619 coming up on the 4.57pm. Bournemouth West to Salisbury. The line on the embankment (right) led to Hamworthy Junction and the S.R. Weymouth main line. One S & D freight working used this line, the 6.0am. Evercreech Junction—Hamworthy Junction which ran as required.

The unique pairing referred to in Chapter 7 of a "West Country" class 4-6-2 and class "9" 2-10-0, photographed at Shepton Montague in August 1962.

This is believed to be the occasion to which I refer in Chapter 7 when "4F" 0-6-0 No. 44559 piloted by "2P" No. 40563, hurtles out of the mile and a quarter long Combe Down Tunnel with the northbound "Pines Express".

Fireman Aubrey Punter takes a well earned rest as *Evening Star* makes the echoes ring in Masbury cutting with the last northbound "Pines Express" on September 8th 1962.

. . . and later in the day after arrival on Bath shed, *Evening Star*, Aubrey Punter, and I (left), pose for Ivo Peters.

Midland "2P" No. 40700 about to depart from Bath Green Park with the 3.30pm. Bristol Temple Meads (4.25pm. from Bath) Bournemouth semi-fast.

Few people, I think, realized the danger to which S & D firemen exposed themselves when inserting or retrieving the tablet from the mechanical tablet catcher apparatus. This photograph of a down express approaching Midford shows the fireman on the class "5" carrying out the operation.

Looking every inch a top class express passenger locomotive rather than a freight engine, "9F" No. 92245 wheels the up "Pines Express" around the curves near Midford.

March 1954

"U" class on test. Southern "Mogul" No. 31621 and Midland "2P" No. 40563 climb out of Bath with the 4.25pm. to Bournemouth West. This load was more than No. 31621 could comfortably handle, however, especially when unassisted south of Evercreech. Bert Freakly drove the engine from Templecombe onwards and he was not impressed with its capabilities. The trials took place between March 1st—6th. The trains selected for the trials were the 11.40am. Bournemouth West to Bath, and 4.25pm. return. The engine was set to work 8 bogies unassisted and 12 piloted.

Standard class "4" 2-6-0 No. 76008, pauses at Shepton Mallet with the 1.10pm. Bournemouth West to Bath. S & D "7F" 2-8-0 No. 53802 approaches from the Bath direction with a Bath—Evercreech Junction freight.

The 'doyen' of the class, "7F" No. 53800 approaching Evercreech Junction from the south with an express train.

This view southwards from Midford is an example of the severe track curvature encountered between Bath and Evercreech. Here the down "Pines" hurries by with class "5" No. 73051 piloting Bulleid rebuilt Pacific No. 34028 *Eddystone*. Donald Beale and I are in charge of the latter engine. The class "5" was (unusually) piloting us through to Bournemouth, in order to work an unbalanced return train later that evening.

drastically that obviously something was wrong up front. At Blandford Station we looked out of our carriage window and saw Donald standing on a bucket on the off side of the engine, 73050, examining something underneath her framing. It was the auxiliary steam pipe from the steamchest to the pressure gauge which had become uncoupled and Donald was attempting to recouple it; (incidentally, I was amazed that a ¼″ open ended steam pipe like this could have such a drastic effect on the engine's boiler pressure). Unfortunately the threads on the pipe were burred, and our combined efforts — for we had now joined Donald on the track — failed to join it up. Donald then decided to detach the length of pipe and take it to a garage situated near the station, to see if they could turn a new thread on the pipe end. The pipe was detached whilst orders were sent to Templecombe shed for another engine in case this idea was not successful. But in fact it was; a garage mechanic turned the thread and hurried back with Donald to help him fit the pipe to the engine.

Some 25 minutes after its arrival at Blandford the 'Pines Express' departed, 73050 restored to full health again. Now Donald set about some time recovery. Bert Freakly and I sat in the train and listened in awe to the '5' as Donald got down to recovering as much time as he could. Frank Stickley was Donald's mate then, and he must take a share of the credit for his efforts during this part of the run. Bert was an ex-London North Western man hailing from Stoke, and himself noted for 'tapping them' a little, but even he got worried at times during this run. Several times I heard him muttering to himself aloud, "Careful Don, you'll empty your boiler in a minute." But Donald knew how far you could push these '5's, and he was doing it.

Donald was the envy and despair of most ordinary mortals like me, but his determination that nothing would prevent him from running his trains on time stimulated anyone who was working with him, so that we too, were forced at times to join the ranks of the super-human for a while anyway.

One of the last trains to run over the S&D line was a special, organised by 'The Locomotive Club of Great Britain', which toured the line on March 5th, 1966, and it was fitting that Donald was in charge of one of the two engines taking part in the working — an immaculate West Country Pacific 34006, *Bude*. It took place only four months prior to Donald's retirement, and one is tempted to say that two great characters in their own right were being retired. The Somerset and Dorset Railway and Driver Donald Beale.

Chapter Four

FOOTPLATE OBSERVATIONS

The S&D line tested, perhaps more than most stretches of railway, every aspect of a locomotive's capabilities. Its steaming was tested to the absolute utmost, especially on the northern part of the line, and the general curvature of the road would quite soon reveal any defect in the riding qualities of an engine. If an engine was to be used for freight work, it was imperative that it should have braking capabilities of the highest order. More than one engine has failed on this score between Bath and Evercreech Junction when on test for use as a possible freight locomotive for this line. The only side of locomotive performance that was not taken to its farthest extent, especially with the larger types, was in the realms of speed, since the wandering course of the S&Ds alignment precluded anything in the way of very fast running. However, engines had to be able to run up to 70 mph which was the maximum speed laid down for the S&D line, and this is not exactly hanging about. So it can safely be said that if there were any latent defects in a locomotive's design, the 71½ miles between Bournemouth and Bath could be relied upon to reveal them in double-quick time.

As stated earlier, it was an Old LMS '2P' on which I had performed my first firing turn, and this class will serve to introduce a summary of the engines regularly worked by Branksome men on the S&D, and also a footplate commentary of the sort of performances and the snags one could expect on the trains that we ran with them.

The '2P's 4-4-0s.

One would have thought that the '2P's were not really suitable locomotives for work over the S&D, having regard to the terrain traversed in conjunction with their 6′9″ driving wheels, but in actual fact they did sterling work over the entire length of the line, and indeed before the war, they were the locomotives that powered the 'Pines Express'. In those days the normal load on this train was 6 bogies, which they hauled unassisted over the Mendip Hills, a severe test for such an engine.

In comparatively recent years, the Saturday working of the 9.03 pm down from Templecombe (7 pm ex-Bath) used to provide quite a tough test for one of these locomotives, by reason of the normal four coach load of this train being supplemented at Templecombe by a further four coaches attached at the rear, these being empty stock for Bournemouth West carriage sidings. It was not unknown to have two or three milk tanks added to this total as well, attached at Templecombe and put off at Bailey Gate by the train engine. This involved uncoupling the engine and milk tanks, which would be marshalled immediately behind the tender, and pulling forward some twenty yards or so before backing the milk tanks into the dairy sidings. This procedure often lost us five minutes or so on schedule, and had many passengers' heads thrust out of the carriage windows, looking into the darkness and, upon seeing their locomotive steaming off up the line, wondering what on earth had gone wrong. With now just the eight coaches this train used to weigh in the region of 240 tons, and presented a real test of '2P' haulage capacity, for after slowing to 25 mph at Corfe Mullen Junction in order to negotiate the points leading on to the single line and to pick up the tablet from the mechanical apparatus, the engine was faced immediately with the 1 in 80 bank up to Broadstone. This might be thought a severe test in itself, but in the early 1950s this train had to stop at Corfe Mullen Halt, which consisted of a very small platform set in a deep cutting slap in the middle of the 1 in 80 climb. As one might well imagine, starting away again from this spot demanded a considerable amount of skill, especially so on damp or dewy nights, but having surmounted this obstacle the '2P's main work still wasn't over for the night. After leaving Poole came the even steeper Parkstone bank, and once again a stop had to be made in the middle of a difficult climb, at Parkstone Station. The gradient, after easing to 1 in 300 for the length of the station platform, immediately resumed its former steep incline, climbing away on a curve through a deep wooded cutting — a formidable start for an engine of such moderate power. It was a tribute to the engines, and no less to the Branksome engine crews, that stalling on either of these two banks was unheard of. The first time that I fired on this duty with the full eight coach Saturday complement we had engine No. 40700, which was the last engine of this series to be built. My driver on this occasion was a passed fireman, Gordon Bailey, 'Bill' to his mates, a very keen and enthusiastic railwayman who had previously been a fireman on the Midland main line, stationed at Gloucester. This experience had made him almost fanatical with praise of all things connected with the LMS, and as we both seemed to think alike we immediately became very firm friends. It was on this particular duty with 40700 that we left Templecombe 5 minutes late, but Bill Bailey was determined to finish on time if at all possible. Not withstanding a huge hole in the brick arch, 40700 was worked on full regulator virtually throughout the trip. Acceleration was remarkably good away from the station stops, and the engine performed excellently with this load. Still relatively inexperienced, I maintained steam pressure well up to the 180lbs mark all the way, and the coal consumption could not be called heavy under any circumstances. Although the exhaust beats off these engines when being worked hard could not be truthfully described as a bark, the sound we made climbing Parkstone bank that night was well worth hearing, awakening the echoes far across the dark waters of Poole Harbour.

During the early 1950s I also had several trips on the original rebuilt '2P's of Johnson design. Two were shedded at Templecombe at this time, Nos. 40505 and 40509. No. 40505 was withdrawn in 1954 and 40527 arrived on the S&D as a replacement. Despite their having 7' 0½" driving wheels allied to 160lbs boiler pressure, they were little, if at all, inferior to the late Fowler members of this class. Several times I fired them when working the 6.03 pm Templecombe-Bournemouth West (3.30 pm ex Bristol T.M.), hauling eight coaches, and the steep banks were climbed with equal competence to their later sisters.

To see a class '2P' working hard one could not do better than find a good vantage point in the Mendip Hills, and listen to one acting as assisting engine on the 'Pines Express'. The observer could be sure of the sight and sound of two locomotives being worked practically flat out, the stately beat of the class '2P' trying desperately to outdo the vocal efforts of a Standard or Stanier class '5', being worked on about 55% cut off, with absolutely full regulator if the crews were really going for it — great days!

The Fowler '4F' 0-6-0s.

Not liking these engines, I found it hard to understand how Midland locomotive authorities of the past came to select them as their standard goods engines, and multiplied their numbers to a staggering total of 771 units.

There is nothing I can say in their favour. On the footplate they were most uncomfortable. The driver's seat in particular was stuck in a most awkward position, situated as it was over the top of the reversing screw, and if any speed was necessary the unfortunate crew was subjected to a constant bombardment of dust particles blown up from the ashpan, via conveniently placed slots and holes between the footboards and the boiler front. No amount of hosing down with the slacking pipe would subdue it for long.

To this discomfort must be added atrocious riding qualities, while the banging in the axleboxes was usually tremendous and made station stops sweet relief. These axleboxes were rather prone to overheating also, especially when working passenger trains where a bit of speed was necessary. Another weak feature was the boiler, which was incapable of supplying the cylinders with the necessary amount of steam if any hard work was called for, and there was plenty of that on the S&D.

On summer Saturdays we were often saddled with these engines on 10 and 12 coach trains, and it was only the slow Saturday Schedules and frequent signal checks that enabled us to make a fair job without the guard being able to book much time against the engine.

As an example of the work that the authorities expected us to perform with the '4F's, I can do no better than describe a trip that I had one dark wet Saturday night with a return football excursion to Plymouth, which we worked from Christchurch to Templecombe No. 2 Box. Donald was my driver, the engine was No. 44417 of Templecombe, and the load of ten coaches, including two restaurant cars, weighed 350 tons. Prior to our departure from Christchurch a waiter from one of the restaurant cars approached Don and asked if he could get to Templecombe a little early as he wished to see someone. Donald's reply was to the effect that he would be lucky to see

Templecombe at all, let alone early. Leaving Christchurch we stopped at Boscombe to take up our cargo of excited Plymouth Argyll football fans. There was also the Poole stop, which was obligatory in those days. From Poole we were 'non stop' to Templecombe, and the sectional timings were similar to those of the 'Pines'. I was not bothering too much about the finesse of locomotive firing, and left Poole with a boiler full of water, and both safety valves nearly lifting themselves out of the firebox casing, for the fun was about to commence. As early as Creekmoor Halt, on the ascent of Broadstone bank, the water level was down to three parts of a glass, but the engine — true to form — would not stand the injector for long without the pressure fading. She was being worked on the second valve, and God knows where on the reverser. All I knew was that I had to keep the steam pressure well up to the 180lb mark or else she was not going to get up to Broadstone, so I had to let the water go, in the forlorn hope of recovering it elsewhere. With 44417 shooting sparks defiantly into the damp night air, we breasted the climb with 160lb of steam and the water coming into sight occasionally in little surges, which caused Donald to enquire laconically "What's up, son, tide gone out?" It had indeed. But now we were coasting, with both injectors on, but they were so slow putting water in the boiler that we passed Corfe Mullen Box with only about 1½" showing in the glass and the engine blowing off furiously. If we had had nearly any other class of engine, she could have been allowed to coast for a bit longer, (with just a breath of steam on to stop the blowing off, of course) but the 4's coasting ability was virtually nil. So we got stuck into them again. With the engine now working on the first valve the injector could be left on, but again, as usually happened with these engines, the water regulating valve handle was working too freely and the vibration kept moving it, causing the injector to blow out, so Donald worked the injector on his side, and by dint of resting his right foot on the regulating handle, avoided the same thing occurring. The slacking pipe only worked off the fireman's injector, so we were covered in a coat of dust, and past caring just as long as we could keep going. That was the way it went that dark night, when all the way to Templecombe we never recovered the water level to more than a couple of inches, although I did manage to maintain steam pressure in the 140-160 lb region. First valve was largely the order of the day from Corfe onwards, which was entirely inadequate for time-keeping, and Templecombe was reached somewhat late. This was the way the '4F's treated us; granted, this was a heavy train for a class '4', but even with a fully loaded freight train — which was the sort of work for which they were designed — although one might do a bit better as regards steam, the rest of my criticism still holds good.

In 1960 four B.R. Standard '4's were allocated to Templecombe depot (Nos. 75002, 75007, 75023, 75027) and at long last it could turn out an engine which was master of such a duty as that just described, there were few tears shed by Branksome men when Midland '4F's were swept from the scene.
The S&D '7F' 2-8-0s.

The activities of these outstanding and unique freight locomotives were largely confined to the Bath—Evercreech section. During the summer season, however, when engine crews and locomotives were in short supply, these stalwarts were pressed into service on express trains and 'Pigeon Specials'. Their use was condoned by their ability to haul ten bogies over the Mendips unassisted, and in so doing saving both engines and manpower. These were the only occasions that Branksome men normally came into contact with the '7F's, and a shattering experience it could be if any heroics were attempted in the way of fast running. These engines suffered from a malady known as 'shuttling'. This arose when the engines coasted downhill at speeds of 40 mph and over, when due to the engine's coupled wheels being fitted with solid cast balance weights which made no provision for balancing the reciprocating masses, a shuttling effect took place between engine and tender. Going downhill the weight of the train 'leaning' on the tender would compress the intermediate buffer springs until the intermediate buffing blocks came into contact, but the engine would be oscillating in phase with the coupled wheels and kicked the tender away, only to be pushed back into contact again by the train weight pushing from behind. The effect of this on the footplate made the engineman's position unenviable to say the least. This brutal oscillating between engine and tender at some 80 cycles per minute made standing up without holding on impossible, and left the footplate knee deep in coal, and the fire down the front of the firebox. Proper balancing would have cured this problem. To set the picture straight, I might just mention that these were not the only engines to suffer from 'shuttling'. The Standard class '4' 2-6-0s were addicted to it at certain speeds, and some of the Stanier class '8' 2-8-0s and Standard class '9' 2-10-0s were as well, but not all of them. Presumably some were satisfactorily balanced, because many of them rode very well indeed at all speeds. The only way to minimise the effects on engines not so treated, was to keep steam on, and keep out of the way of the train — not always possible to do of course, and some discomfort on the footplate (and possibly in the first two coaches of the train) was inevitable, when working fast trains with engines which were prone to 'shuttling'.

With their 4' 8½" coupled wheels they were, of course, unsuitable engines for passenger train working, but on freight work the Bath men acknowledged none better. They were immensely strong engines, easily master of the maximum freight train loads laid down for them. Steaming was excellent also, with a very moderate coal consumption, and their braking capabilities were superb; quite the most powerful of any engine that I have ever been on in fact, as well they might be in view of the gradients encountered.

The engines were fitted with Ferodo brake blocks instead of the usual cast-iron variety, and these lasted much longer than the latter type of brake block. One could always detect these blocks, because of the distinctive smell that they gave off when heavy braking was in progress.

Unfortunately, the '7F's were fitted with the same type of axle boxes as the '4F's, and consequently were subject to the usual knocking and banging from that quarter, and hot boxes were not unknown with them either. In every other aspect though, they were excellent locomotives.

When drafted to some of the summer extra passenger workings, ten coaches over the Mendips was no mean task for one of these engines. They had plenty of power for the job, but if absolute timekeeping was attempted it tested their steaming capabilities to the utmost. On the long climbs it was good policy to let them settle down to a speed that the boiler could cope with without trouble, and forget the timebook until later on in the journey. Any attempt to mortgage the boiler could be fraught with disaster on such lengthy climbs.

Despite the fact that passenger work was not their strong point, as freight engines they were never bettered by any of the various types that were tested over the S&D at different times. To sum up, I can only add that the few times that I did have one on freight work (always on 72 duty, deputising for 44102) it was an immense pleasure, and the eleven engines which comprised the class certainly gave the S&D line outstanding service, and contributed in no small way to the general colour of the line.

WD 2-8-0 and GWR 0-6-2T (5600 class)

As mentioned above, various types of locomotives had been tested between Bath and Evercreech Junction, with a view to finding a replacement for the ageing S&D '7F's. It is amusing to relate the happenings during the braking trials of the WD 2-8-0 No. 90125 and the GWR 0-6-2T No. 6641 and the reason why they did not supersede the S&D engines becomes obvious. The trials took place on January 22nd 1959 and December 4th 1959 respectively.

The WD engine was tried on the 11.00 am Bath Yard to Evercreech Junction freight train. Bath men were in charge of her with a locomotive inspector in attendance, and the train was made up to a full load for this class of engine. Someone had the forethought to couple several vacuum fitted vans next to the engine — 'For use in an emergency'. The Western Region Inspector did not know the line, and when they managed — just — to pull up in Shepton Mallet station to take water, he remarked, "Well, that was all right then, wasn't it?", not realising that there was more downhill still to come. Water safely aboard they pulled away from Shepton and set about the second stage of the headlong descent to Evercreech Junction. After Prestleigh Viaduct, the train was in full control, pushing the WD downhill at ever increasing speed. As they shot through Evercreech New Station, flames streaming back from the 2-8-0s tortured brake blocks, the Inspector said, "Will you be able to pull up by Evercreech North, driver?," to which the driver replied, "Evercreech North be b........d, we'll be lucky to stop by Wincanton!" The fitted vans were promptly brought into use!

The Great Western 0-6-2T was tried on an up coal train from Midsomer Norton to Bath. With considerable forethought, the signalman at Midsomer Norton had arranged for the level crossing gates at Radstock to be closed to road traffic before he allowed the 0-6-2T to depart. Having got away it was soon sailing down the 1 in 50 bank in tremendous style at ever quickening speed, and it was said to have 'shot through Radstock as if it was on skates!' They did manage to stop before Writhlington, but the engine was considered to be so poor as regards braking ability that the test was abandoned forthwith.

By these incidents the excellence of the S&D 2-8-0s work on freight trains over the Mendip Hills can be measured. They performed their onerous tasks adequately for 50 years or so, and knew no superiors.

The Standard '4' 4-6-0 and 2-6-0s

The British Railways standard class '4's came into regular service on the S&D line in the mid 1950's — the 2-6-0s in 1955 and the 4-6-0s in 1956 — and took over some of the diagrams previously worked by the Midland '2P' and '4F' classes.

The 4-6-0s were allocated to Bath shed (Nos. 75071, 72, 73) but the 2-6-0s were shedded at either Bournemouth or Eastleigh.

They were immediately liked by the enginemen at large who were quick to appreciate their comfortable cabs, rocking grates and self-cleaning smoke-boxes. The last two features, in particular, greatly eased the hard and unpleasant task of engine disposal duties, and their larger capacity boilers made them eminently more suitable as express engines than their predecessors, when required to assume that role.

I particularly liked the 75,000 breed, and I have occasionally had them on heavy trains which they handled most capably. The 76,000 type I was not so fond of, their steaming characteristics being not unlike the 'Doodlebugs', which design they closely resembled. Their one advantage over the 4-6-0 type was in starting heavy goods trains on adverse gradients such as from Templecombe No. 2 Box up to Templecombe Upper Yard. The 2-6-0s could always start away whereas the 4-6-0s often had to be banked in the rear away from this point. Even the Midland '4F's had this ascendancy over the 4-6-0s here! The reason for this could be found in the smaller diameter wheels fitted to the other two classes, 5' 3" as opposed to the 5' 8" of the 4-6-0s.

Bath's 4-6-0s were fitted with double blast pipes and chimneys during their stay, but Templecombe's engines were of the single chimney variety. The difference in performance on the road between the single and double chimney engines was hardly detectable. As these engines were mostly employed on four or five coach stopping trains when they were handled by Branksome men, the opportunity to extend them and see what they could do, was comparatively rare, and did not provide the scope to make any comparison between the two draughting arrangements.

Both the 4-6-0s and the 2-6-0s did excellent, if largely unspectacular work, during their comparatively short reign on the S&D, and I was very glad to see them come, and to have had the opportunity to work on them. I only wish the power of the engines had been used to speed up the stopping passenger trains on this line, for were easily capable of improving on the existing schedules. On the odd occasion, for instance, when Templecombe was left 20 minutes late with the 3.30 pm ex Bristol T.M., it was a simple matter with a 75,000 class to arrive punctually at Bournemouth West, and it was a great shame, in my opinion, that schedules more in keeping with the power of these engines were not introduced.

The 'West Country' Pacifics.

Three Bulleid light Pacifics were shedded at Bath when I first went to Branksome, Nos. 34040, 41, 42, being the engines concerned, and they worked the best turns over the S&D line. They were not universally liked amongst the footplate crews, Bath men disliking them intensely and the Templecombe and Branksome men tolerating them but having no great love of the design. The reason for this was not prejudice, but due to the fact that their ability, efficiency, and reliability on the road did not match up to the class '5's that they had replaced. It was originally hoped that they would be able to handle heavier loads that the class '5's, but during a series of tests carried out in 1951 (in which, incidentally, Donald was involved) over the S&D, to gauge their suitability for the line, No. 34109 *Sir Trafford Leigh Mallory* was sent over the Mendips with 10 bogies unassisted. The engine kept her feet during the climb, but it was a near thing at Masbury Summit, with speed down to about 10 mph, this load being more than they could comfortably handle. Consequently their loading had to be restricted to the same tonnage as that allowed the class '5's. This, briefly, is the reason why the standard '5's in turn ousted them from Bath depot in 1954. But of course, Bulleid Pacifics worked over the S&D line right up to its closure, especially during the summer season, when at weekends Bournemouth Central depot had to loan Branksome at least four members of the class in order that we could cope with our diagrams, and it is fair to say that our men had more experience of handling them than any other enginemen on the S&D.

Due to the healthy appetites of these engines, coal — or rather the shortage of it — often proved an embarrassment to Branksome men on the 'Pines' job in the up direction, Bath being reached with sometimes only a couple of hundredweight left in the tender. Bearing in mind that engines had to be coaled at Bath sufficiently for the round trip to Bournemouth and back, this meant that the following procedure had to be carried out in order to accomplish this with any certainty. Whilst coaling was in progress under the coal stage, the firemen would have to fill up the firebox to its absolute limit, which was something like one ton of coal. Next, the best part of a tub of coal would be stacked on the footplate, followed by the topping-up of the tender to the maximum capacity it could safely hold. One day I stacked so much on the tender of one of these engines that the shed master ordered it to be gauged, in case it would not clear Devonshire Tunnel roof. I would add that it was quite safely stacked by virtue of wedging large blocks of coal around the edge of the tender and using them as a retaining wall. If these precautions were carried out, the engine stood a good chance of making the round trip satisfactorily. Some drivers would not allow the full firebox technique, or have coal on the footplate, and so visits to Bournemouth Central for coal intermediately were a frequent occurrence.

These engines also had an inordinate thirst, and if paired with tenders of

4,500 gallons water capacity, through-working without replenishing the tank en route could not be confidently recommended. Donald and I have done it several times, with 400 ton trains, but on two occasions the injector blew out when passing Branksome Station on the southbound run, the tender tank being bone dry — too close for comfort. By contrast, the Standard '5's fitted with tenders of 4,250 gallon capacity could work a similarly loaded train from Bath to Bournemouth without intermediate replenishment, and still have ample water left.

The riding qualities of these Pacifics were very good, though they sometimes rolled alarmingly on certain sharp curves, especially on the Radstock—Bath section of the line. But this did not mean that their footplate was always entirely comfortable for its occupants. Being so closed in as they were, and having the manifold in the cab, there were occasions when the heat on the footplate was nearly unbearable, especially during the summer months. This, coupled with the fact that they tended to be rather dirty and dusty engines to ride on, meant that the swirling coal dust stuck readily to one's sweating brow, not to mention overalls, thus making it impossible to keep even reasonably clean. Again, these engines compared unfavourably with the Standard or Stainier '5's, whose cabs were very clean and comfortable to work in.

The steam reverser fitted on the original air smoothed Pacifics was most unreliable, and the position of the cut off indicator on the sector plate quite frequently bore no relation to how the engine was actually being worked. For instance, I have frequently witnessed engines of this type hauling 400 ton trains up adverse grades — say, 1 in 100 — with perhaps 160lbs per square inch showing on the steam chest pressure gauge, and the cut off indicator cheerfully pointing to the 'mid gear' position. Indeed, I have seen drivers experimenting with them, pull them up to a position marked as 15% cut off in *Back Gear!* Still the engine would be rasping away at the chimney top, and generally tearing into the job with tremendous gusto.

It was, of course, obvious that something was wrong somewhere, and when ultimately these engines were rebuilt the method of working them changed completely. With heavy trains, full regulator was now the order of the day, with the cut off rarely brought up inside 25%. No longer any mid gear stuff, but at least the indicator was now telling the truth!

The rebuilt light Pacifics were more efficient, measured in terms of coal and water consumption, than their original counterparts, though still consuming more than a class '5' on a comparable job.

The slipping propensities of these engines are well known, and the S&D line brought out these characteristics in no uncertain manner; I could mention many occasions when this weakness led to a considerable amount of time being lost on the road.

The maximum load allowed one of these engines, unassisted from Bath to Evercreech Junction, was 270 tons, the same as that allowed the class '5's, but if any windy or damp conditions were encountered on the Mendips a load such as this was more than enough for them, and many an engine crew has fought a grim battle with the elements when in charge of a West Country Pacific.

As an illustration of what could occur if over-confidence ruled a driver when handling one of these engines, I recall an occasion when the Sheffield relief to the 'Pines' was running, and arrived in Bath with nine coaches for Donald and myself to haul southward, with No. 34043 *Combe Martin* unassisted. The day was one of sunshine and occasional rain showers.

Our guard gave us the load as 302 tons, and Donald was considering asking for an assisting engine. But the remarks of a Bath crew on a nearby 'Ivatt' tank made his mind up for him. "Better get assistance mate", shouted the driver "even you Branksome men won't make it with one of them", he called, with mild sarcasm, and a broad smile upon his face. "That settles it," said Donald with a grin, "Can't turn down a challenge like that, we go on our own".

No. 34043 was a strong engine for her class, but a rather poor steamer, and I knew it was going to be a gruelling trip for the first eighteen miles out of Bath, even if she kept her feet.

We left at 2.52 pm, just ahead of the main portion of the 'Pines'. The first climb up to Combe Down Tunnel passed off without incident. Steam pressure fell to about 215lbs inside the tunnel, but I had managed to rally it by the time Radstock was passed, and Donald took a real bash at the main climb. *Combe Martin* was really purring, as with 240lbs boiler pressure we approached Midsomer Norton Station, and an air of confidence prevailed upon our footplate.

Then she slipped, furiously and quite unexpectedly, for the first time on the trip. It occurred just as we were passing over the points leading off to Norton Hill Colliery. Speed dropped rapidly, and despite all of Donald's coaxing plus the sanders on, she just slipped and slipped, as we struggled against the 1 in 50 up towards Chilcompton Tunnel.

With the speed down to walking pace, I dropped down on to the side of the track and feverishly picked up fine gravel and earth, placing it under the spinning wheels. Donald and I could both hear the maniacal laughter of our afore-mentioned Bath friend ringing in our ears, and it looked as though our acceptance of this particular challenge was doomed to failure any second.

Our engine slithered into Chilcompton Tunnel at walking pace and then, miraculously, suddenly held her feet. She held it too when we got out in the open, so just saving our bacon. Soon after leaving the tunnel the gradient eased to 1 in 88, followed by a stretch of 1 in 300 through Chilcompton Station, before a further section of 1 in 50 led up to Moorewood sidings. This brief respite in the climb enabled us to get sufficient way on to clamber thankfully up this final half mile stretch of 1 in 50.

From Moorewood up to Masbury the gradients were not quite so severe, which was fortunate since the time spent on the side of the track trying to keep 'Coombe Martin' going had not been exactly helpful to an engine that required constant vigilance in order to maintain boiler pressure. So over this final stretch we were now faced with the additional problem of maintaining sufficient steam and water to get to the top.

We did in fact make it up the final 1 in 60 - 1 in 70 grades, but only just, gasping our way over the summit with speed back to walking pace once more, only 140lbs pressure showing on the gauge and the water just visible in the glass as she dipped her nose gratefully down the 1 in 50 towards Evercreech.

One fact concerning the rebuilt Pacifics which appears to be little known is that when operating over the S&D line a maximum speed limit of 50 mph had to be imposed upon them, due to the heavier axle loading as a result of rebuilding. But this restriction was honoured more in the breach than in the observance. The highest speed that I have personally noted on the speedometer with a rebuilt on the S&D was 85 mph, passing Bailey Gate Station in the down direction. The engine was No. 34042 *Dorchester*. It occurred on September 8th 1962. I was the driver (whisper it gently) on the occasion of my last trip over the S&D line throughout from Bath to Bournemouth. Working the 2.52 pm down from Bath which stopped at Templecombe Upper. Here we had to wait for a late running Southern train on the West of England main line with which we were booked to connect. This duty performed, we set back to Templecombe No. 2 Junction Box ready to resume our run southwards. The signalman here informed me that the down 'Pines' was rapidly catching us up, so "get a move on," he winked. We did! The stretch of line from Spetisbury through Bailey Gate to Corfe Mullen Junction had often won prizes for being the 'best maintained length'. Being reasonably straight it was eminently suitable for high speed, and some of the fastest running seen on the S&D line took place on this section of track — though not normally as fast as on this occasion.

Reference has already been made to the heavy coal consumption of the 'unrebuilts', and this brings to mind an incident that occured involving No. 34102 *Lapford*. It happened in the month of December 1960, during the short period when the 'Pines Express' had to be diverted via West Moors, Salisbury and Westbury to Bath and the North. This was necessary due to a bad slip in the embankment at Midford which literally left the rails suspended in mid air. No. 34102 had worked throughout to Birmingham New Street on 5th December via the emergency route and this story concerns the southbound run with this engine the following day.

A set of Branksome men — Jim Tranter and Alan Northover — plus a Western Region pilotman took over the eleven-coach 'Pines' at Dr. Days Junction, Bristol, and matters continued normally through Bath Spa Station, and on towards Salisbury.

Nearing Westbury, however, the fireman drew the pilot driver's attention to the quantity of coal remaining in *Lapford's* tender, considering it not enough to reach Bournemouth. He further suggested coming off the train at Westbury to replenish stocks at the loco depot.

The pilot driver had a look at it, but considered it enough to reach their destination and overruled the fireman. It was getting dark at the time, and it seems probable that the pilot driver, a Western man and unused to Bulleid

Pacifics, had been deceived in the failing light into not appreciating his critical coal shortage. And the Branksome crew, having their first trip over this — to them — strange route, were not inclined to argue further.

Salisbury was safely past, and the train was running on the Alderbury Junction - West Moors Branch, near Downton, when the fireman stepped out of the tender and ceremoniously put a shovelful of coal on the fire. "That's it then", he said, "I've just swept the tender out." This bit of news caused quite a stir on the footplate. There were still about 30 miles to go, and it included two stiff banks to climb. Fortunately, the engine had a big fire in her, and the only thing to do was to nurse the engine along, and try to eke it out.

As the train progressed southwards, the driver scribbled out a note for the Wimborne signalman, outlining their plight, and requesting substantial banking assistance from Poole up to Branksome. The note was thrown from the footplate, as the train passed through Wimborne Station.

The Poole banker proved to be No. 30548, one of the Maunsell 'Q' class 0-6-0s. And make no mistake. *Lapford* was going to need all the help she could get from that 'Q', for things were looking pretty grim on the footplate by now. 170lbs boiler pressure, and a decidedly 'ashy looking' fire was not the best combination with which to face Parkstone bank.

However, 30548 'gave her all' on the rear during the climb, giving an almost frightening display of pyrotechnics. In fact, she probably got one or two shots into orbit, in the bid to put Britain in the space race, and get the 'Pines' up to Branksome. I know, because I watched this spectacle from my home alongside Parkstone Bank.

Bournemouth West was reached with the fire just alight, and some small coal spillage was shovelled from under the footplate and put onto the fire in order to generate sufficient steam pressure to propel the empty train up to the carriage sidings.

Upon arrival at this point, the fire went out, but it was of no consequence now; there was steam enough to see 'Lapford' safely onto the disposal pit at Bournemouth Central. I would dearly liked to have heard the disposal men's comments, when they climbed onto the footplate, and saw the state she was in, 60lbs of steam and the fire completely out — which was just as well, there being not a drop of water visible in the gauge glass — and the tender completely empty of coal. One could not work it much finer than that.

Needless to say, after this experience reached their ears, the Southern Authorities put a stop to these through engine workings to Birmingham, and from then on, until the S&D line was reopened on December 9th, engines were changed at Bristol, the Pacific from the up 'Pines' making a quick turn around, and working the southbound 'Pines' to Bournemouth. (I believe engines were changed at Westbury on one occasion, the 'Pines' being hauled by a 'U' class 2-6-0 as far as this point.)

This was the sort of controversial situation with which these engines were often connected; driving or firing them was rarely a dull affair, and one often wondered what was going to happen next. Despite being placed in the category of '7P' for power classification, I personally always had the feeling that on a train such as the 'Pines' they never had full control of the job. Certainly, they did not have the mastery of the S&D grades as did the class '5's.

Finally, reference must be made to another weakness of the unrebuilt Pacifics, namely, their susceptibility to catching fire, usually after heavy and prolonged braking had taken place, such as when descending the Mendip Hills. The reason was due to slivers of hot metal from the tortured brake blocks being shot up into the oil-soaked lagging under the airsmoothed casing. The lagging became soaked in oil from the sump which housed the middle big end. It was virtually impossible to maintain this sump 'Oil tight' and oil loss from this quarter was substantial, and contributed to starting these fires.

Donald was involved in one of the many occasions when an outbreak of fire occurred, and I think it well worth describing because of the humorous side to what was really a serious situation. This 1951 incident illustrates Donald's sangfroid on the footplate, already referred to, and was related to me by his fireman on this occasion, 'Bill' Bailey.

Whilst descending the Mendip Hills with the up 'Pines', the fireman noticed smoke and fumes coming from under the casing of Pacific No. 34040 *Crewkerne* and concluded that it was on fire. Since this was a fairly frequent occurrence with these engines, and the fires usually burnt themselves out quite quickly, he was not too perturbed. But after passing Midsomer Norton the smoke and heat was so bad that he called Donald over to his side of the cab to see it. Donald's comment to this was, "That's nothing, you ought to see it on my side." The fireman went to look, and was shocked to see flames pouring out from under the casing.

Donald, knowing he would have to stop to extinguish this blaze, had decided to make for Radstock, so as to get his train under protection of fixed signals.

Upon arrival, Donald and his mate gathered the nearest fire extinguisher from the train, and very soon had the blaze out. Meantime however, someone had called the fire brigade, and they roared up, bell clanging, just as Donald was about to continue on his journey.

"It's all right, thanks, the fire's out," Donald called to the Fire Chief. "Stop where you are, I'm in charge of this fire and the safety of the train," this worthy official said. "That's a debatable point, and anyway, I tell you there is no fire now, it's out," Donald returned, "I'm going on."

"I command you to stop where you are," screamed the by now irate fire-chief. Donald and his mate climbed aboard 34040, sat down comfortably, poured themselves a cup of tea from the tea-can, and put their feet up. "Let me know when you have finished, won't you?" Donald called.

While all this was going on, the gallant firemen themselves had been trying to open a drum of foam with which they were going to spray the engine, and it was only after repeated attacks with hatchets and crowbars that the drum relented. Had the engine been on fire, it would have probably been a burnt out shell by now.

But to cap this Keystone Cops type of demonstration, when foam was eventually turned on, the firemen holding the hosepipe happened to be facing a stone wall , which was soon splattered in the snowy white chemical, which caused Donald to shout impatiently to the unfortunate firemen. "It's the engine that's supposed to be on fire, not the wall." Once the engine had been sprayed with 750 gallons of foam and the fire-chief had satisfied his honour, he allowed the train to continue, which it did, now ½ hour late and with the engine piled high with the white foam, and looking as if it had come straight from the 'Arctic region', instead of the 'Southern Region'.

The guard was not having a smooth trip in the train either. Walking up through the corridor, he was called by a prim old lady, who demanded to know the reason for the long delay, "I am very sorry, Madam, but the engine's got a fire in it," the guard told her.

"Don't talk such nonsense, my man, don't you know an engine's always got a fire in it?" the old lady retorted sharply. The guard could not think of an adequate reply at that moment, and after a brief, but helpless silence he continued sorrowfully along the corridor.

That really concludes this chapter, as, although Branksome men handled many other types of locomotives on the S&D such as the '3F' 0-6-0s, and the occasional Southern 'T9' 4-4-0, not to mention the trials of the 'U' and 'U1' 2-6-0s with which Branksome shed was involved, our acquaintance with these was so brief that I do not consider that I have done enough work on them to give a true picture of their merits or otherwise. But there are two classes of locomotives with which I have had rather more than a nodding acquaintance — the class '5' 4-6-0, and the class '9F' 2-10-0 — superb engines, both of them. Consequently, to do them justice in describing their work over the S&D line, both of these classes have demanded a chapter each in their own right.

Chapter Five

THE FABULOUS 'FIVES'

Ever since Stanier 'Black Five' No. 5440 was allocated to Bath shed in 1938, these were without doubt the most popular engines, amongst engine crews and shed staff alike, ever to run on the S&D.

Much has been written in praise of these locomotives over the years. All of it is well deserved, as memories of the work that they performed on the mountainous grades of the S&D year in and year out bear eloquent testimony. The maximum load these engines were allowed on the Evercreech Junction, Bath section, was 270 tons: this was equivalent to a load of eight coaches, roughly speaking, which these engines easily mastered. In fact they have, on occasions, hauled nine coaches, adding up to some 300 tons, when traffic conditions demanded it. When I first came to 'fire' one hauling such a load, I was very surprised to note that even then, the engine was not too severely taxed.

It was of course on 'Bath Duty No. 1', 'The Pines Express', that these engines performed their most spectacular work, and on which train they remained supreme from their introduction to it in March, 1938, until the 'Pines' was re-routed via Basingstoke and Oxford in September, 1962. They have worked it over this route also on a number of occasions. In stating that they were resident on this job, I am not forgetting the time when the Bulleid light Pacifics worked it, or the annual visits of the Standard Class '9's for the summer service from 1960 onwards: but these periods represent only a mere fraction of the 25 years that the fabulous '5's spent doing this job with impeccable regularity.

These engines are only medium sized in terms of power classification, as all railway enthusiasts doubtless know; but to the majority of non-footplate staff on the railway, and to the bulk of the travellers in the Poole — Bournemouth area, they were thought of as the most powerful engines at work in the district. The reason for this mistaken impression is hard to define. Perhaps the fact that engine crews rarely requested assistance with them, irrespective of the load being hauled, had some bearing on the matter. Or then again, their judgement may have been swayed by the tremendous bark at the chimney top which these engines emitted when working hard. The sound of a Class '5' hauling 400 tons up the 1 in 60 gradient of Parkstone bank could be heard for miles around, and was in marked contrast to the efforts of Southern main line engines, only the 'King Arthurs' offering any comparison, and even they fell some way short of equalling the Great Western-type sounds that the '5's produced. These features, together with several incidents in which they were involved, were the reason for their 'big engine' reputation, and who would say they did not earn it?

One of these incidents to which I was a witness took place in 1949. The engine involved was a Stanier 'Black Five' No. 44826.

A nine-coach London bound train had been halted by Parkstone's up home intermediate signal being at danger, and its engine — a 'West Country' Pacific — upon being given the signal to restart, was unable to haul its load more than a few yards up the 1 in 60 grade which extends from that point. Three or four reversals by its driver in an attempt to get going were of no avail. So complying with rules and regulations, the guard protected the train in the rear and the fireman was sent to telephone for assistance.

Whilst all this activity was going on at Parkstone, the down "Pines", with a twelve coach load, had left Poole and was stopped at Poole's outer home signal. Therefore, when the signalman at Poole received a request for assistance he had little option but to send the heavily loaded 'Pines' up, to bank it away. No. 44826 set off up the 1 in 60 grade, stopping once to pick up the guard of the ailing London train before buffering up behind it. Incidentally, restarting a train of this weight on such a gradient is worthy of mention, but was overshadowed by what was to take place in the next few minutes.

The two trains were rapidly coupled together and ready to go. The driver of the 'West Country' (who I now know well of course), told me that due to his engine blowing off steam noisily at the safety valves, he did not hear the '5's crow whistles signifying readiness to proceed. Next moment, he was astounded to feel his engine start to move and realised immediately that the 'Pines' driver behind him had opened up his engine, and, incredibly, was now pulling twelve coaches and pushing nine, plus an engine. Apart from the short strip at 1 in 300 through Parkstone Station platform, a good deal of the trains were standing on the 1 in 60 and even 1 in 50 gradients. Overcoming his amazement, the 'West Country' driver quickly applied steam on his engine as 44826 continued moving forward, though very slowly; but what a splendid locomotive to be able to shift such a load at all in such onerous conditions! The driver of the London train is still at Bournemouth depot today, and when arguments are raging in the mess room concerning the merits of various steam locomotives, he usually quotes this incident, and reckons it the most prodigious feat of strength with any type of steam engine that he has ever witnessed.

When I went to Branksome shed in 1953, there were two Black Staniers allocated to Bath: the original 45440, and 44917. These engines doubled on the Midland main line and the S&D, on the latter section acting mostly as deputies for failed 'West Countries', which were working S&D main line trains at that time. But 1954 saw the departure of the light Pacifics from Bath depot, and their replacements proved to be an initial allocation of three brand new Standard class '5's, No. 73050/51/52. These were the engines that I came to like above any type that I worked upon anywhere. The same can be said of the

Branksome engine crews generally, who took to these engines immediately, despite being told by crews from other depots (notably Bristol Barrow Road men), that they were inferior to the Stanier variety. No. 73050 came straight to Bath from the International Railway Congress exhibition at Willesden where delegates from many parts of the world were shown the latest rolling stock, equipment, etc., that British Railways had at that time. Needless to say, she arrived in immaculate condition, and since her paintwork was especially prepared for this exhibition, she would always polish up much brighter than the others after being cleaned.

This particular locomotive was, for a long time, generally regarded as what is termed a 'weak' engine, requiring at least 5% longer cut offs, as shown on the reverser drum, than the other two locos to do equivalent work. This notion persisted until one day when Donald and I were booked to work a heavy empty stock train from Bournemouth West Carriage Sidings to Broadstone, tender first. In this direction, the engine tore into her work and climbed the 1 in 75 of Broadstone bank with 390 tons working in 28% cut off. Upon arrival back at Branksome shed, Donald wound the reverser back until the quadrant block was in the centre of the expansion link. When so positioned, the indicator on the footplate was reading 7% in forward gear, instead of in mid gear, as it should have done. So that was it! The incorrect setting of the reversing drum indicator on the footplate had given the engine a reputation that was unwarranted. She was in fact just as good as the other two engines, but just wanted a bit of 'understanding'.

Bath's allocation of Standard '5's was gradually strengthened to eight, numbers 73019/28/47/49/50/51/52/54. These were augmented in the summer season by numbers 73087/116, which were loaned from the Southern Region. All were used indiscriminately on S&D or Midland line work.

The two Staniers were transferred away from Bath in 1958, after which the B.R. engines dominated the scene between Bath and Bournemouth on the best trains. The Mendips, however, had not heard the last of the Staniers, as in the summer time especially, they still made frequent excursions southward.

With the Stanier and Standard engines of this type working side by side, it was inevitable that comparisons would be made between them. The British Railways variety were considerably slightly the better engine by Branksome crews, and, I believe, by the S&D crews in general. If one heard the occasional driver or fireman running them down, further enquiry usually elicited the fact that the men concerned were in a link whose work did not bring them into contact with these engines very much, and consequently were basing their opinions on prejudice.

The Standard '5's appeared to be slightly stronger, and definitely the more free running engines of the two. I must emphasise how slight this difference was; indeed, it would be surprising if there was a vast difference between them, as they were virtually the same design, with only detailed changes made to the Standard design here and there. However, on the very heavy trains that ran on the S&D in the late 1950's and early 1960's, sometimes with gross loads approaching 500 tons the 'Seventy-Threes', as they were called, seemed to time them better and appeared to have more in reserve than the Staniers. Presumably, those 'detailed differences' made all the difference.

The fuel economy of these engines was excellent, both types being moderate on both coal and water in relation to the work performed, (allowances being made for the fact that the 'Black Fives' were fitted with continuous blowdown.) Maintenance was also very moderate, making the engines almost always available for revenue earning traffic. Sometimes, however, the early members of the Staniers had to be taken off the main line work, due to their getting extremely rough riding as the higher mileages between 'shopping' were reached. The trouble was always the wear to the trailing driving axleboxes, but later engines of this class were fitted with manganese steel liners to their axleboxes, which greatly improved matters. It was, however, usually the state of the 'boxes' that dictated the timing of their next visit to the repair shop. As one driver put it to me, "They ride like a glove when they come out of the shop, and like a bag of nails when they are due in again."

One of the 'detailed differences' applied to the 'Standards' was the fitting throughout of 'Timken' roller bearing axleboxes, and these appeared to be in the same condition at 100,000 miles as they were when new. These engines gave their crews a very good ride, though in common with all the 'Standards' I have ridden on, a rather hard one. (The class 'Nines' I exempt from this statement.) Unlike the Staniers, their riding was very much the same when they were proposed for 'shopping', as it was when they came out. To my mind, the rather hard ride of these engines was definitely preferable to the tremendous axlebox thump, and its consequent cab shake and vibration to which the 'Black Fives' subjected their crews at the higher mileages.

With regard to steaming capabilities, both types were beyond praise, but here again, when extremely high rates of steaming were reached, I fancy the Standards had the edge. They could stand a tremendous thrashing without the slightest suspicion of flagging. In fact, what they got on the S&D as regards this had to be seen to be believed. 55% and full regulator was resorted to on many occasions for almost the entire climb of the Mendips, when one of the superannuated class '2P' 4-4-0s, turned out by Templecombe shed supposedly to assist the 'Pines', had an off day for steaming. Notwithstanding the limited help from that quarter, Masbury Summit would be cleared at some 25/30 mph, with the '5' cheerfully blowing off. The glorious deep-throated bark of these fabulous engines, which reverberated around the red rocks in Masbury Cutting before escaping across the open hills, is a sound that will remain forever in my memory.

A very high standard of firing was of course demanded for such all-out efforts as these, but as anyone who was familiar with locomotive performance on the 'Pines' would testify, it was usually forthcoming.

We occasionally had a firing instructor riding on the footplate with us to Bath on the 'Pines'. These gentlemen were based at Eastleigh, and their area for tuition included the whole of the S&D line until 1958, when the Western Region took over the running of the Northern end of the line. They were all lavish with their praise of the enginemanship of Branksome crews, and positively staggered at the performance of the '5's, especially their steaming ability. Initially, of course, the instructors had had no experience of these engines, and were a bit disdainful of them, particularly as they had replaced their sacred Bulleid Pacifics on these trains, but later on they became positively enthusiastic about the '5's.

I sometimes offered the instructors the shovel, "in order to give them some experience of firing this type of locomotive", as I put it to them, but really I only wanted to see what kind of job they would make of it. Except for one solitary occasion, they all declined the offer.

The "sport" who agreed to "have a go" took the shovel over as we were passing Broadstone Station, still attired in his overcoat and trilby hat. When Blandford was reached, however, the voracious demands for steam from 73052, with her 400 tons load, had caused him to shed his overcoat and jacket. Stalbridge saw him down to his shirt, which was previously white, but now looked as though it had been washed in brand X washing powder, and the trilby had been thrown unceremoniously into the fireman's corner. 73052 was not doing too well for steam either, due entirely to his method of firing this type of engine. At Wincanton, and with the Mendip Hills looming ahead, Donald requested that I should take over the firing once more. With pressure dropped to the 160 lb. range, it was not before time.

After the Evercreech Junction stop, which gave me a chance to pull the boiler round and get the fire to my liking, we then gave the Instructor a front seat view of 73052 unleashed, giving him an exposition of the way that the '5's could take it and thrive upon it. We were going 'hammer and tongs' near Winsor Hill Tunnel, when I remarked to him what a good engine we had, as she forged assuredly up the long 1 in 50 with a simply deafening exhaust and the needle on the pressure gauge stuck absolutely on the red line. "My God, she wants to be, to stand this B---- lot", he shouted back as Donald dropped her down a couple of 'nicks', for the final fling up to the Summit.

As I indicated earlier, I had perhaps unkindly baited our Firing Instructor into 'showing his hand'. He did in fact command the respect of both Donald and myself for having the 'guts' to have a go, and we all became firm friends. After a number of trips over the S&D, he was quite candid in his view that never had he seen engines worked so hard for such a prolonged time, and steam with such consistent freedom. He was quite lyrical in his praise, and from someone used to the steaming abilities of the Bulleid Pacifics, this was praise of the very highest order.

It was round about this time that Nine Elms depot was receiving its first allocation of these engines, and it was not long before complaints of 'poor steamers' were voiced by their handlers. But it cut no ice with our Firing instructor, who by now was starting to run across the '5's on some Waterloo-Bournemouth runs. He would just relate the performance that he had witnessed from them in the hands of the 'Midland Men', as we were known at Branksome, most of whom were well known to the top link crews at Nine Elms who used our 'loco' during a number of their duties for servicing and meal breaks between out and home runs. Whether these ovations had any effect or not I could not say, but history shows how the '5's gradually became very well liked indeed. They were also based at Stewarts Lane depot, and performed remarkabe work between Victoria and Dover or Ramsgate, especially on the Chatham line. Many drivers and firemen eventually preferred them to a 'West Country' on express trains over their routes. In this connection, I remember being quite thrilled in the mess room at Bournemouth Central one day, when two Bournemouth crews in the top link took my side in an argument concerning these engines. Once again, many men were expressing opinions about the engines without having the experience of working on them. The top link men had had experience on them by now, and succeeded in silencing the rest by indicating a preference for a '5' on the Bournemouth two hour trains to a 'West Country', explaining that the '5's were easily capable of handling these jobs, which resulted in easier work for the fireman. I have worked these trains, and these sentiments are mine exactly.

The 'Pines' up and down comprised the 'Bath No. 1 duty', and it meant a pretty hard day out for an engine rated no higher than Class 'Five' in category. Perhaps the term 'day out' is slightly inappropriate, since the diagram took nearly 26 hours to complete. The salient details of it are as follows:—

Bath M.P.D. depart 2.15 am for goods yard. Depart goods yard 2.40 am with freight and mail vans for Bournemouth West; arrive 7.20 am. Engine proceeds to Branksome shed for engine requirements; arrive approx. 8.15 am via Triangle. Depart shed 9.15 am for Bournemouth West, arrive 9.25 am. Depart 9.45 am. up 'Pines Express' for Bath; arrive 11.56 am. Arrive at Bath shed 12.10 pm., engine disposed and prepared. Depart shed 2.50 pm. Depart from Bath station 3.06 pm down 'Pines'; arrive Bournemouth 5.32 pm. Shunt stock to carriage sidings, engine returns to Branksome shed via Triangle; arrive 6.15 pm approx. Depart 7.10 pm for Branksome Goods yard. Depart with freight 7.25 pm for Poole Yard; arrive 7.45 pm. Depart with freight for Bath Goods Yard at 8.10 pm; arrive 3.15 am. (next day).

A distance of nearly 300 miles, and difficult miles at that, especially in view of the weight of the trains hauled. While the 2.40 am. down was not usually too heavy a train, the up and down 'Pines' and the 8.10 pm. goods — the latter conveying Dorset Clay destined for the Stoke area — undoubtedly were, and gave the '5's 'a hard day's night'. Bath, Templecombe and Branksome crews took part in this diagram at some stage or another.

The 2.40 am. and the 8.10 pm were always referred to as the 'down' and 'up mails' respectively by S&D staff. The down train did have mail vans attached for Poole and Bournemouth. The 8.10 pm; did not, however, its make-up consisting of freight vehicles only.

Incidentally, the use of the term 'mail' to both of these trains afforded me some amusement one day in the mess room at Branksome. A Templecombe driver, who had worked the 8.10 pm up the previous week, was extolling to me the virtues of No. 73052, saying that she had 'walked' a full load of clay up Broadstone Bank, on no more than 35% cut off, with full regulator when working the 'up mail'. It was this last statement which visibly shocked a Nine Elms fireman who had overheard the conversation. "What was that?" he exclaimed, looking up from his newspaper. "A full load of clay on the mail?" I immediately cottoned on to his amazement, but did not explain the facts. No doubt his conception of a mail train was some twelve coaches speeding through the night with its crested mail vans in the formation, but not under any circumstances could his imagination be stretched so far as to picture a load of loose-coupled clay wagons tacked on the rear. The Templecombe driver did not 'twig' this, however, and thought that the fireman was refuting his claim as to 73052's prowess, and so repeated his statement in his broad Somerset accent, and with great finality. The bemused fireman looked steadily at us both for a moment, as though deciding that, as he had long suspected, the S&D was a queer railway, and its men a little cracked. He then returned to his newspaper, shaking his head sorrowfully.

To conclude this chapter on the '5' locomotives, and to illustrate more fully the sort of work of which they were capable on the S&D, I am now going to describe a run on the up 'Pines' in which Donald Beale and myself were involved. It took place in June, 1961.

We had noticed in the Special Traffic Arrangements book earlier in the week that a load of thirteen coaches was scheduled for us on this particular day. This in itself was not unusual, but the fact that an assisting engine had been laid on for us between Bournemouth West and Broadstone most certainly was. The scheme was no doubt dreamed up by some bright spark in the control office in Southampton, who evidently was not 'with it' practically. It would mean making an unscheduled stop at Broadstone Station to detach the pilot engine and then restarting this big train on reverse curves and immediately resume climbing a 1 in 97 bank, a procedure which would undoubtedly lose time. In any case, Control had never worried themselves about overloading on this train before, being no doubt preoccupied with providing enough bankers at Poole, with which to push their main line engines and men up to Branksome.

When we booked on duty on the morning in question, and duly found an assisting engine in the shape of a Southern 'Mogul' coupled to our engine, Donald blew his top. On his own responsibility, he made the 'Mogul's driver uncouple his engine from ours, and sent him back to Bournemouth shed. Next, an explosive and decidedly one-sided telephone conversation informed Southampton Control of the new arrangement, and told them not to bother in future. They never did!

This then was the prelude to the magnificent performance that No. 73054 was destined to display with a tare load of 450 tons, 490 tons gross. It also helps to explain why this particular run stands out so clearly in my mind.

The maximum load allowed for a locomotive of class '5' capacity was 360 tons from Bournemouth to Corfe Mullen Junction, and 420 tons from that point to Evercreech Junction. This meant that, officially, the 'Pines' was over the load on virtually every occasion on which it was hauled by a Class '5'. I wonder if there was any other express train in the country overloaded to this extent, day in, day out, with assistance not provided or requested. Indeed it was considered a slight on one's capabilities even to dream of having it.

We backed 73054 onto her train at the West Station and, as usual with thirteen bogies, our engine was standing on the track-circuiting, which more or less shut the station up temporarily. Our own starting signal could not be pulled off in consequence, and permission to start against the signal was given verbally by the local signal inspector. With no rear-end assistance, the '5' made a sure-footed start up the initial 1 in 90 bank, accelerating this big train past the carriage sidings — where whistled greetings were exchanged with our shed mates on the station pilot. Our engine was now really getting into them, chopping them off 'four beats to the bar' with a deafening bark, which must have been heard over a large section of the town. No. 73054 was already showing signs of having complete mastery of her train. The front end sounded in excellent fettle, and with the needle of the pressure gauge on the mark, a first class run looked in the offing.

The train was allowed eight minutes from Bournemouth West to Poole, start to stop, and starting 'cold' as it were, it wanted some doing. By dint of keeping our engine at it until we were doing 60 mph near Parkstone, and then briskly reaching 65 mph coasting down the bank to Poole before the severe slowing that proceeded the entrance to the station, time was just kept.

Our exit from Poole was once again very impressive, and our vocal passage through Poole goods yard caused the crew of a Maunsell 'Q' class to watch our passage with undisguised awe. Having regard to his exchange of words with Control earlier, Donald was making sure that all sectional times were maintained, as, no doubt, our progress would be watched and any lost time would be noted and an explanation requested. 73054 was certainly not troubled with overloading, gaining two minutes to Broadstone alone, the 1 in 75 bank being climbed with the cut-off never advanced beyond 45%, with full regulator. The steaming was rock steady, and the final stretch of 1 in 97 of the bank was breasted with the safety valves sizzling, and a full glass of water showing on the gauge.

We must have made a splendid sight as we steamed by Broadstone Golf Course on this gloriously sunny day. Our engine was beautifully turned out, with green paintwork and burnished connecting rods sparkling in the morning sunlight, a sight which caused many golfers to be temporarily distracted from their game.

After coasting down Corfe Bank, Donald opened out to 25% cut off, and full regulator. Bailey Gate Station was passed at a full 70 mph, the maximum permitted on the S&D line, and the undulating gradients on to Blandford were covered at round about 60 mph Donald varied the cut off positions within the limits of 20% to 35% to suit the gradients. The going was most exhilarating all the time, and the steaming was very free — indeed, just a little too free at times, despite the firehole door being wide open practically throughout, and dampers only partially open. I could not prevent 73054 from blowing off occasionally. The coal being fired was of the hard Yorkshire variety, and was onto a moderately thick fire, it being roughly level with the firehole door casting.

Blandford was reached 3½ minutes early, but as our extra coach was attached for a contingent of schoolboys and their attendant luggage from nearby Bryanston School to board, the time won was needed.

Departing on time, the 1 in 80 bank out of the station was attacked vigorously, the cut off not being reduced below 50% until Milldown was reached; thereafter it was gradually reduced to 20% by the time Shillingstone Station came into sight. The speedometer was reaching 65 mph, but there were some sharp up grades from this point in the 1 in 75 — 1 in 80 range, and the engine was opened out whilst speed was at its maximum. Cut off was increased by steps to a maximum of 37%, and the purr at the engine's chimney developed into a full-throated roar. At the top, speed was only a shade under 60 mph, and the easy grades from here onto Sturminster Newton allowed the engine to be pulled up to 20% cut off and the regulator brought back onto the first valve. Notwithstanding, speed had crept up to the 70 mark again as we crossed the River Stour opposite Fiddleford Mill. Considering the severity of the road and a near 500 ton load, I think it is no exaggeration to say that 73054 was very easily master of this load. Extraordinary work for an engine of such moderate dimensions, I feel, and yet typical of what was expected as a matter of course from these engines on the S&D, and on this train in particular.

First valve and 20%, later reduced to 15%, sufficed from Sturminster, and saw us to a stand at Stalbridge Station one minute to the good. From here, the adverse grades onto Templecombe Junction were vigorously attacked—cut off still on 38% with full regulator until steam was shut off for the service slack over the junction. Speed peaked 50 mph on this section, and we passed out of Southampton's control at this point, and into the Western Region, 1½ minutes early.

With brisk running thereafter, including a maximum of 65 mph running down the bank to Cole Station, Evercreech Junction was reached three minutes early. The first part of the run was in the bag. Now for the Mendips.

No water was taken here, or anywhere else, 73054 still having a plentiful supply remaining out of her quota of 4,250 gallons with which we had left Bournemouth. The usual assisting engine was attached for the final run into Bath, which proved to be a Standard '4' 4-6-0 No. 75027, a member of the class which had recently ousted the Midland '2P' 4-4-0s from this duty.

This climb over the Mendips was as exhilarating as the first part of the run had been. The '5' was not worked harder than 45% cut off, with full regulator, and with the substantial assistance of the Class '4', speed was maintained mostly in the 25-30 mph range. The coal was as usual well back in the tender by this time, and frequent trips into it were needed to pull forward fresh supplies which now consisted of 'slack'. Despite this, our engine continued to steam freely, and I was able to set my shovel down now and again, and admire the rolling Mendips scenery surrounding us, something of which I never tired.

The usual brief stop was made at Shepton Mallet, and then we set off over the viaducts high above the town on the last stage of this gruelling climb. It was an exceptionally clear summer's day, and above Winsor Hill Tunnel the distinctive cone of Glastonbury Tor stood out more prominently than usual. Indeed, so clear was it on this grand day, that I could just discern in the far distance to our left a silver strip which denoted the sea in Bridgwater Bay, and I drew Donald's attention to it, because of the rarity of the event.

Masbury Summit was approached some three minutes early. The needle of the pressure gauge was still glued on the red line, with the water level at the top of the glass. The last firing on this journey took place in the vicinity of Masbury up distant signal. It was around here also that the exaust injector was shut off briefly, and this, with the high rate of steaming, dropped the water level in the boiler rapidly. This technique allowed room to apply the second injector if necessary during the long spell of coasting after Masbury, and avoid blowing off at the safety valves.

We coasted down the Northern slopes of the Mendips at speeds between 50 and 60 mph, observing, of course, the severe slack to 15 mph past the slag heaps below Midsomer Norton Station (due to subsidence), and the 40 mph slack through Radstock. Thereafter, light steaming from both engines was all that was necessary to keep the train going at speeds of around about 50 mph, as we wended our way round the unceasing curves on this magnificently maintained stretch of permanent way. Shoscombe and Wellow Stations were quickly passed, and the serenely beautiful Midford Valley was entered.

With the tablet safely on board, the last and very awkward single line stretch from Midford to Bath Junction was tackled. It was a steep climb from Midford Station up to the entrance of Combe Down Tunnel, and here 73054 was worked on 40% cut off and full regulator, at speeds of around about 40 mph. The sound in the single bore tunnel, which was just over a mile long, was as usual simply deafening, but at this speed we were spared the discomfort of smoke and fumes to a large extent.

The summit of this climb coincided with the tunnel exit. Steam was shut off for the last time as we dipped down the steep 1 in 50 bank into Bath in a headlong descent. The blower was turned on full, and faces were shielded behind our arms as we hurtled into Devonshire Tunnel. With speed rising rapidly, it was close on 50 mph, when we emerged again. A brief but appealing view of the City of Bath was enjoyed from the fireman's seat as we swooped down the bank towards Bath Junction, and almost immediately the brakes were hard on as we slowed to negotiate the long bend and join up with the Midland main line.

Giving up the tablet at Bath Junction, our two engines coasted easily over the final half a mile of level track into Bath Green Park Station, easing the 'Pines Express' to a halt under the cavernous roof four minutes early. Another typical run, then, from a standard Class '5', the description of which, in detail, explaining why they were held in such high esteem by the Branksome crews.

I might add to these tributes of class '5' prowess, by remarking on the occasions when the 'Pines Express' has arrived at Bath from the North in the order of 30 minutes behind schedule, and put in an appearance at Bournemouth West Station 'on time'.

Donald and I have achieved this on many occasions, and during the course of one of these runs, the bank from Radstock to Masbury Summit was cleared in 10 minutes dead, pass to pass. The pilot engine to Evercreech Junction was '2P' 40569 and our own train engine was 73052, my old favourite. The total time for the entire run to Bournemouth was 1 hour 58 minutes, a gain on schedule of 28 minutes. Once again the climbs up to Masbury, Broadstone and Branksome were to the accompaniment of a tremendous 'obligato' from the engine's chimney. Passengers waiting on Parkstone Station's down platform for the 5.30 pm train to Templecombe recoiled instinctively as we approached the station, and some unashamedly took cover in the waiting room during our thunderous passage through. But most important of all as far as we were concerned, the needle on the boiler pressure gauge never once strayed from the 'red line', no matter what demands were made upon the boiler.

The '5's were regarded by us with the same pride as Haymarket crews looked upon their 'A4' Pacifics. They were generally maintained in excellent mechanical condition by Bath shed, and such things as hot boxes, hot big ends, bad steaming, injector troubles, or indeed anything that could adversley effect their performance on the road, were rare, and consequently their availability was something that any class of steam engine in the country might well have envied.

There were no frills to these engines, they were honest to goodness, hard working utility locomotives, which could, if required, turn out a performance on the road which would make far larger engines look to their laurels. Indeed, in the heyday of steam locomotive operation, I would have willingly taken one of them, whether driving or firing, on any train in the country, for these were the Rolls Royce of locomotives as far as I am concerned, and that is the esteem in which I shall always remember them.

Chapter Six

THE CLASS NINE 2-10-0s ON EXPRESS PASSENGER TRAINS

March 29th 1960 was the date that the Mendip Hills first echoed to the sonorous exhaust of a BR Class '9' 2-10-0, when a test run was arranged to gauge the suitability of these engines for S&D work. The task set to the locomotive No. 92204 was the haulage of an eleven coach train, weighing 350 tons, from Bath to Bournemouth West and back, and incredibly, she was to be unassisted throughout. Driver Bill Rawles, and fireman Ron ('Runner') Bean were selected to handle her, both excellent men from Bath Green Park shed. When first received, this piece of news caused much speculation amongst the S&D's footplate fraternity, concerning the feasibility of the operation. No. 92204 very soon answered this query, however, by completing both the down and up test runs with comparative ease, and this, despite encountering foul weather, with high winds and heavy rain, not to mention a little snow in the vicinity of Masbury.

A resounding success, then, for the class '9' on this initial introduction to the S&D, and it encouraged the authorities to allocate four engines of the double chimney variety to Bath shed for S&D work, the first of which arrived in time for the commencement of the summer service in June 1960. The load limit for them unassisted was initially set at 385 tons.

The reason for the allocation of the 'Nines' to the S&D was to reduce the necessity for double-heading and so alleviate the footplate staff shortage. There were unconfirmed, but persistent, rumours that the Western Region was considering closing its part of the S&D by reason of it not proving profitable; much of which was due to the neccessity of having to bank or double-head trains if any reasonable load was being hauled.

If this were true it seemed to Donald and myself, at least, that these engines might be the saviour of the line, and we were determined to do well with them.

Our first personal acquaintance with a 'Nine' was on the first day of the summer service that year on the 'Pines Express'. This was my first day back at work after a fortnight's holiday, and as I walked up through the shed with Donald that morning, I was slapped heartily on the back by our steamraiser, Norman Whale, who enquired of me as to whether I was "fit and ready for anything after your holiday", I replied that "Indeed I was". "That's just as well then", said Norman, "because we have got a nice little 'Nine' for you today, and Donald's going to try her out, aren't you Donald?," he said darkly. He received a smile, but no comment in reply. But I knew, come what may, this was going to be a most interesting day.

The 'Nine' was already on her train, so we had to walk the half mile or so to Bournemouth West. As we walked towards the station, we were having our first sight of a 'Nine' in the flesh, so to speak, and she looked huge. By the time we were passing the Bournemouth West Station Box, the number on her huge smokebox was plainly discernible, 92205.

Before climbing on the footplate, Donald and I stood a little way away from 92205 and just looked at her, sizing her up, studying her proportions, and, working on the age-old axiom that if a thing looks right it is right, we both agreed that this 'Nine' did indeed look absolutely right. "Look at her, she's all muscle", breathed Donald to me. This comment suited the engine well, I thought, and it was obvious that this meeting with a 'Nine' was for Donald and myself a case of love at first sight.

We relieved the preparation crew on the footplate and then took stock of our surroundings.

That feeling of hugeness was still with us, the size of the cab, the length and height of the boiler when viewed from the driver or fireman's seat, the 40 sq. ft. of the firebox, all gave an impression of enormity that is frankly difficult to explain.

We have both been on 'West Country' Pacifics many times before, and they are big engines, but somehow they never gave us the same feelings of size and power that we were now experiencing on the footplate of this 'Nine'.

9.45 am, and we were right away. I knew that nothing more than strict timekeeping would be attempted on this trip, giving all three of us time to get to know each other.

On the return journey later in the day, Donald put a few questions to her at various locations and she answered them all with obvious enjoyment.

"What's she like then mate?" "How did she steam?" "Burn much coal?" These were a random sample of the questions that we were inundated with on our arrival back at the depot that evening.

Well, we had not found out exactly what she was made of yet, but enough to inform the lads that true to her appearance, this engine was immensely strong. She had steamed well throughout the day on a not excessive coal consumption, but perhaps most remarkable of all in view of those 5ft. driving wheels was the smoothness of the ride, just like silk, and so quiet was she at speed that the sound of the wheels passing over the railjoints could be heard as clearly as if one was sitting in a carriage.

We were vastly impressed with this, as indeed were we with every aspect of this incredible locomotive. Two days later, however, she was destined to be really extended, and her powers were fully displayed.

Things had gone normally as far as Evercreech Junction, but on arrival there it transpired that the usual assisting engine had not been laid on for us, (we found out later that the operating authorities — tongues in cheek — had cancelled it just to see what we would make of the job alone), and so we had to work the 405 ton train on to Bath single-handed. I must admit that now the chips were down I was rather apprehensive about the ability of the 'Nine' to make it up to Masbury. A reasonable fear I think, after all, the S&D class '7' 2-8-0s, themselves very powerful engines, had their work cut out with 300 tons of this climb, and here we were about to attempt it with over 100 tons more coupled on to the drawbar. But then, just as we were about to depart, my thoughts were scattered by the discovery that at least half of the 'Nine's' brick arch had collapsed. The huge fire bricks were now neatly deposited on top of the fire.

The station staff were slamming carriage doors, the guard was blowing his whistle. We moved fast. Deciding that those bricks must come out now, I got the long pricker down and pulled the white hot bricks across the fire and hooked them out onto the footplate, where Donald, with the aid of the firing shovel, threw them out on to the end of the platform. About two minutes saw the task completed and us heading out towards the Mendips. The weather had been misty when we left Bournemouth, but it had now turned into a real scorcher of a day, with an absolutely clear sky from which the sun beat relentlessly down on the beautiful rolling Mendip countryside. The temperature on the footplate had risen gradually as we progressed up from Bournemouth, and the brick arch incident had raised my personal temperature more than somewhat. I was now dripping with perspiration, and really feeling rather tired; no time for rest though — 92205 was 'into them', and Donald, not being inclined to mince matters with this load, was giving her some 'stick'. The 'Nine' roared lustily, and certainly had an appetite for coal, but my word, was she developing some drawbar horse power!

As we climbed up through the cutting at 'Cannards Grave', I paused from shovelling for a moment, and leaned out to listen to the glorious sound that the engine was making. Every beat from the chimney was sharp and clear, and with the boiler pressure right on the line at 250lbs the feeling of exhilaration was tremendous.

This was the heaviest unassisted load that had ever been taken up to Masbury at that time. Railway history was being made, and we were making it. So plentiful was the supply of steam and water on the later stages of the climb that Donald, through sheer 'joie de vivre', unleashed 92205 from Winsor Hill Tunnel up to the summit. And the 'Nine' gave an almost frightening display of power accompanied by an exhaust beat from her chimney top that was music to the ear. But nevertheless I was glad to see 'Bridge 38' which marked the top of the bank, for I was feeling physically tired now. Why this run should have taken so much out of me, I don't know, because I have been involved in some even harder efforts of locomotive performance than this since that time, but I have never felt so uttery exhausted as I did after this run. On arrival at Bath shed, we were met by Mr. Harold Morris, the shedmaster eager to learn how the 'Nine' had performed. He was delighted with what Donald had to tell him.

After attending to the needs of the inner man in the mess room at Bath, I felt fit for anything once more. Mr. Morris popped in to inform us that the return load was wired as twelve for 408 tons. "Will that be all right?", he enquired, "Chicken feed", said Donald with a broad grin, and so it was. The

'Nine' walked it and so, surprisingly enough, did I. For this effort, Donald and myself were both proud to receive letters of congratulations from the area Motive Power Superintendent, and on the strength of this performance the load limit of the class Nines were increased to 410 tons unassisted.

It was unfortunate, but true, that our performance did not please everybody. One or two Templecombe crews were rather upset at the loss of the 'Pines Assist' job from their depot, and showed their feelings. They didn't seem to realise, even at this late date, that the axe was delicately balanced over the S&D and that anything that could be done to make the job more efficient was a step in the right direction.

The loss of one turn from Templecombe depot was preferable, in our view, to the closure of the line and everybody being made redundant. Apart from our obvious enjoyment in our work, this was why Donald and I wanted the class Nines to be the success they undoubtedly were.

But fate was now to take a hand, and decreed that Templecombe shed would not lose its unproductive assisting job. The 'Pines' rolling stock was by now made up entirely of BR Standard coaches, somewhat weightier than Midland coaching stock. Also, one or two coaches with 'Commonwealth bogies' were being introduced into the train and so, more often than not, the 'Pines' weighed in excess of the 410 tons laid down, and consequently piloting from Evercreech was re-introduced. Strictly speaking, it was not necessary, the engines being capable of hauling more than the given tonnage. But one must view the situation in its logical sense, the human element entering into this decision considerably. The overriding factor was not the output of the engine, but the input of the fireman, and make no mistake about it, this was a tough job. An engine of this type hauling a gross load of 450 tons over the Mendips had to produce in the region of 1,700-2,000 edb hp, continuously over lengthy periods. Something which they were well capable of doing, if the fireman could stand the strain. Remember, one doesn't always go to work at the very peak of one's physical and mental energy, and to expect a fireman to produce his uttermost six days a week would be asking a lot from any human being. So as a general rule, I think assistance was necessary, if from this viewpoint alone. It was only during the period of the summer service that the Pines was normally loaded in excess of the 410 ton mark, the winter time load usually being in the 10-11 coach range — say between 350-390 tons, well within the capacity of the class Nines. Dispensing with assistance on this train for eight months of the year should have made sizeable financial savings in operating costs. But again it was not to be. No steam heating apparatus was fitted to the class '9's' and despite frequent requests to the management from the engine crews and Bath shedmaster alike for the S&D stud to be so fitted to enable us to keep them all the year round, it was of no avail. So of course, it was back to the class 'Five' haulage during the remaining eight months of the year and consequently, all the year round piloting. It appeared to me that for the modest outlay of money needed to fit steam heating apparatus — and on only four locomotives at that — a very substantial saving on annual S&D operating costs could have been achieved. Why it was not done is hard to define. With this country's climate, it was really necessary that carriage heating apparatus be available on these Bath engines all the year round, working as they did overnight trains from the Midlands to Bournemouth at weekends. The fact that some engines were incapable of heating the carriages must have detracted considerably from the pleasures of rail travel, as I have witnessed passengers emerging from these trains at 6 am in the morning literally blue with the cold. Hardly the way to attract business in the competitive world of the sixties. Perhaps someone, somewhere, had already made up their minds about the fate of this stretch of line, I don't know!

Bath Loco Depot was for years an example of 'organised chaos' on summer Saturdays, with train engines and their pilot engines queueing for the turntable, coal stage, disposal pits, and generally getting in each other's way. But the introduction of the Nines to Bath literally cured this problem overnight. Some pilot engines were still there, but dispensing with just a few of them made conditions on the shed much more tolerable, and gave room to manoeuvre. Except for the 'Pines' itself, most trains weighed in the region of 350 tons tare, and the big 92000s handled these with consummate ease. With the more liberal Saturday Schedules in force, full regulator and 35% was usually ample on the long banks in order to keep time. I was with one driver — Jack Thorne — when he was having his first trip on one of these engines. The ease with which our ten coach load of 330 tons was being handled so surprised him that he could hardly believe it, and on the first long curve that we came to, I saw him looking back along the train trying to count the number of coaches. "Thought we'd left some behind", he explained. I remember the engine was my personal favourite, the doyen of the class, 92000. This engine went the whole way from Bath up to Masbury Summit without ever having to be worked harder than full regulator and 25%. Driver Jack Thorne was vastly impressed. That any engine should dismiss the Mendip Hills so contemptuously, with such a load, was almost beyond his belief!

Mention of 92000 brings to my mind July 14th, 1961, the day that Baron Vuillet of France rode with Donald and myself on the footplate of 92000 hauling the down 'Pines'. In order to show our distinguished guest the true powers of that great engine, Donald requested of Mr. Morris, the Bath shedmaster, that we be allowed to take the train unassisted and he readily agreed. I expect he knew what we would get up to. Before departure from Bath shed, there was a grand get-together of people interested in the 'Nine'. With Donald and myself on the footplate, there were — and all at the same time — Baron Vuillet, Inspector Darrell Smith, (Western Region's Chief Inspector), Mr. Morris, Mr. O. S. Nock the railway author, and finally, last but not least, the head fitter at the depot. Time went quickly however, the talking had to stop and the work commence. Our non-travelling guests left the footplate, leaving Baron Vuillet and Inspector Darrell Smith in our care, keenly anticipating their run to Bournemouth. Baron Vuillet took very complete details of our running which he later sent to Mr. Nock, and he published them in the October 1961 issue of the Railway Magazine, and in so doing fulfilled an ambition of mine, which was to appear in the columns of 'British Locomotive, Practice and Performance'. In fact this run has received wide publication in this country and abroad.

Upon returning to his home in Paris, Baron Vuillet was kind enough to send both Donald and myself a detailed log of the performance of 92000 hauling her 450 ton train, and a brief reference to this shows what manner of engines the class Nines were.

July 14th was a day of high westerly winds and heavy rain, and it was in these severe conditions that we departed from Bath, 12½ minutes late. In view of the weather, I must confess to a slight feeling of apprehension. On the first taste of 1 in 50 the Nines was worked with full regulator and 35-42% cut-off, speed was sustained at 24 mph and I had no trouble in maintaining boiler pressure of 235-245lb per sq. inch and the passage through Devonshire Tunnel was much more comfortable than it normally was with a pilot engine coupled in front. Donald did not press the engine from Midford to Radstock, in order that I could stablise both steam pressure and water level — plus pack a good fire into her. We thus lost 30 seconds on the point to point timings of this winding length, but Radstock was approached in great form for the Mendip gradients.

We then produced what Baron Vuillet described as a 'remarkable climb' to Masbury Summit. It was as usual very hard work for me, but the engine steamed beautifully. As we neared Moorewood, Baron Vuillet pressed a slip of paper into my hand, which had the number 2,000 written on it. "What does that mean?" I enquired. In his very French accent he replied, "Why! It's your drawbar horsepower." "Is it that good?" I asked innocently. "Magnificent," he said, throwing his arms wide in an expansive gesture. Both he and Inspector Darrell Smith seemed to think that we were putting on a special show for their benefit, and were not quite convinced I think when we explained that it was a normal performance, especially in view of the fact that we were late away from Bath and it was Donald's practice to try and recover any arrears.

By using the superb hillclimbing ability of the class Nine, we had halved the 12½ minutes by which we were late away from Bath as we triumphantly passed Masbury Summit at 30 mph. Donald was then able to take the winding descent to Evercreech Junction in unhurried fashion.

Evercreech Junction Station staff carried out their station duties with customary smartness, cutting their allowance by two minutes, and saw us away just under a minute late.

We had a very comfortable run from this point to Shillingstone, the breaks in steaming to accommodate the crossing loops, ensured that our engine was not extended in the least. We did reach as much as 60 mph at times between the slacks to take the loops, and Baron Vuillet made the remark that "the engine rode as smoothly as a coach at this speed." Donald and I exchanged a grin of appreciation at this statement.

We stopped at Shillingstone in accordance with the schedule to cross the

Stanier class "5" No. 45440, piloted by "2P" No. 40564, has just left Combe Down Tunnel, and is crossing Tucking Mill Viaduct as they enter the beautiful Midford Valley with the southbound "Pines Express".

"4F" No. 44102 takes time off from her regular turn of duty on the 6.35am. Evercreech—Poole freight, and has a trip to Bath on a stopping passenger train — here seen enjoying the sunshine as she ambles sedately down towards Midford station.

Class "5." No. 73087 enters S & D territory proper at Broadstone Junction, whilst hauling the 10.35 am. Bournemouth West—Derby.

The New Team

This photograph was taken at Evercreech Junction just after I was made a registered fireman with Donald Beale. The engine is class "5" No. 73050 and we were working the southbound "Pines Express".

S & D "7F" 2-8-0 No. 53808 joins up with the Weymouth—Waterloo main line at Holes Bay Junction with a summer Saturday extra.

One of the poor steaming Ivatt 2-6-0s No. 43047, as originally built with double blastpipe and chimney, shunting stock at Bath Green Park Station.

The "Branch" to Highbridge can be seen carrying virtually straight on in this picture; it is the Bath line which curves round sharply to join the "Branch" at Evercreech North Box. I am firing on rebuilt West Country No. 34039 *Boscastle*, working the Sheffield portion of the "Pines Express". Note the unique S & D crossover signal on the right of the photograph.

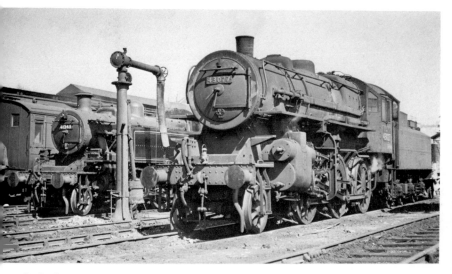

During investigations into the draughting arrangements of these engines in order to try and bring about some improvement in their steaming capabilities, No. 43027 turned up on Bath shed one day with this ugly stovepipe chimney.

Donald and I take to the Bournemouth line at Templecombe No. 2 Box with a southbound express. The line climbing the embankment on the left of the picture led to Templecombe upper station, and the Southern Region's West of England main line.

Bath shed acts as host to Eastern Region class "B1" 4-6-0. No. 61143 seen posing along-side S & D "7F" No. 53807.

Inspector Jack Evans of Bournemouth Central Depot (looking out of the fireman's window) spots Ivo Peters as he accompanies Donald Beale and myself on the Sheffield portion of the "Pines Express" near Chilcompton down distant signal. We were hauled by West Country No. 34041 *Wilton*, and piloted by "2P" 4-4-0 No. 40568.

This view of the entrance to Combe Down Tunnel from the footplate of 73050, gives an indication of the limited clearance of this bore and the similar Devonshire Tunnel. The pilot engine, "2P" No. 40564, looks as though it will fit the tunnel like a glove, small engine though it was. Large engines did. Literally!

"West Country" class no. 34105 *Swanage* acting as pilot engine to a Standard class "4." 4-6-0. No. 75071, nears Masbury Summit on the 10.35 (S.O.) Manchester—Bournemouth express.

Standard class "4" 2-6-0 No. 76005 either has a defective tablet catcher or is not in fact fitted with one, necessitating tablet changing by hand. Midford signalman Harry Wiltshire is about to hand the "large pouch" to the fireman of the 1.10pm. Bournemouth—Bath.

This photograph shows up the clean lines of a Midland "2P" to good advantage — and of No. 40696 in particular.

Skirting Poole Harbour

Standard class "5" No. 73052 finds the 9.55am. Bath Green Park to Bournemouth West an easy task as she starts the 1.60 climb up Parkstone bank. This location is about ¼ mile from where I once lived alongside the line.

Ex-Midland "2P" 4-4-0 No. 40505 works a Templecombe—Bath stopping train near Winsor Hill Tunnel.

The first half of the long climb to Masbury is over for Stanier class "5" No. 44830 and pilot engine "2P" No. 40698, as they breast the final length of 1 in 50 before dipping down to Shepton Mallet, after which the second half of the climb will be tackled. The train was the 9.55am. (S.O.) Bournemouth West to Leeds.

The worst of the southbound climb to Masbury is over once this overbridge has been passed. There are still two and a half miles to go to the summit but the gradients are less severe. The driver's view from the footplate of class "5" No. 73050 on the "Pines".

An historic photograph unfortunately taken in very poor weather conditions. The up "Pines Express" on ex G.W.R. metals stands in Bath Spa Station, during the period of time that this train was re-routed due to the slip in the embankment at Midford on the S & D line in 1960. The engine is "West Country" class No. 34105 *Swanage* driven by Jim Tranter, seen looking out of the cab window.

March 1951, and Bulleid Light Pacific No. 34109 *Sir Trafford Leigh Mallory*, is tested over the Somerset and Dorset. Donald Beale brings her into Bath with the 11.40am. from Bournemouth West. The load was increased daily as the tests progressed.

A Midland "2P" 4-4-0 pilots Donald and myself on "West Country" No. 34041 *Wilton* into Winsor Hill Tunnel with the northbound "Pines Express".

3.40 pm train from Bournemouth to Bath, but she was running late, and the booked time of 3 minutes to cross her was expanded to 5½ minutes and the 'Pines Express' was thus 3 minutes late into Blandford.

We had used 3,500 gallons of water to this point; an average of 66 gallons per mile, and an approximate evaporation of 23,000 lbs per hour. Donald considered that we had sufficient left in the tank with which to reach Bournemouth but nevertheless decided to take a drop here just to make sure.

Getting away from Blandford, Bailey Gate station 6.1 miles from the restart was passed in the smart time of 7 mins. 40 secs. at 64 mph. After easing to collect the tablet at Corfe Mullen Junction Donald opened out for the two mile ascent at 1 in 80. Up this, the 'Nine' sustained speed at 43 mph Baron Vuillet and Darrell Smith were astonished at this performance, as indeed they were with the general severity of the road (neither had been over the S&D previously). At this juncture I pointed out that even with a load of this magnitude, we often had a class '5' on this train; both expressed amazement that an engine of these dimensions was capable of handling such an assignment. Baron Vuillet calculated that 92000 was producing 2700 ihp. during this climb. Be that as it may, we regained 2 minutes between Blandford and Broadstone.

Whilst descending Broadstone bank Darrell Smith mentioned to me how very hungry he was, remarking that during the day he had footplated with Baron Vuillet from Paddington to Newport, returning back through the Severn Tunnel to Bristol, before finally travelling over to Bath for this run on the 'Pines Express' to Bournemouth. I looked in my food box. There were still a few sandwiches left, so I shared them with him as Poole was approached, in an effort to sustain his inner man for a little longer.

A Channel Island boat train from Weymouth to Waterloo checked us outside Poole, and we were 2½ minutes late in. I knew that Donald would go all out to achieve a right time arrival, so despite the fact that there were only a few miles still to go, I maintained a big fire in 92000, and she wanted it all — and more. Once over the level crossings in the town, Donald opened out. There was no notching up, and the engine roared with speed. She was on full regulator and 49% cut-off, and as we got to the point in Poole Park known to local people as the 'Bunny', which marks the start of the 1 in 60 up Parkstone bank, she was dropped out to 52% and the bank was stormed without speed dropping below 41 mph. This tremendous effort regained all but 30 secs. of the lost time still outstanding when Poole was left.

Upon arrival at Bournemouth West Donald and myself were most embarrassed at the praise heaped upon our shoulders by Baron Vuillet and Darrell Smith. But we were pleased that a visitor from a foreign land should eulogise so much over this performance of a British steam engine. Baron Vuillet is probably the most experienced observer of locomotive performance anywhere in the world. His footplate journeys have covered most countries in Europe, and an extensive mileage in the United States of America. Praise of the kind he lavished on 92000 and ourselves was therefore praise indeed. In a letter which Baron Vuillet sent to Mr. Nock concerning this run he made the comment, "This is one of the most remarkable trips I have made on a locomotive, and the class '9' engines are certainly among the very best."

For those interested in the technicalities of the run, I have included in this chapter the log which Baron Vuillet sent me. Study of this reveals perhaps more than mere words can convey, what mastery the Standard 9s had over the S&D gradients — and to think we could have had the services of those magnificent engines all the year round for the sake of a few feet of metal pipe work required to complete the steam heating apparatus.

During the first weeks of operating these engines on the S&D a lot of trouble was experienced with collapsed brick arches. Sometimes an arch only lasted in an engine for three or four days before renewal was necessary. A solution was found to this problem by substituting concrete arches in the fireboxes. These proved to be far more effective, and no more trouble was experienced from that quarter.

With this problem ironed out there were no snags as far as I could see concerning their operation. Maintenance of them on the shed seemed very reasonable, and I cannot recall one breaking down on the road for any reason. They were reputed to be heavy on piston and valve ring wear, but I don't recall this being a source of trouble on any of the S&D 2-10-0s — certainly I never rode on one that was audibly off beat at the front end, or indeed gave any suggestion of trouble in their cylinders. Coal and water consumption was very moderate in comparison with their output of power; and their steaming capacity was superb. They were delightfully smooth engines to ride on, indeed they gave the best ride of any class of engine that I have ever been on; in complete contrast to the other classes of BR Standard engines which gave one a steady, but hard ride, and with a great deal of rattling from cab fittings and side doors when at speed. So steady was a '9' at speed that I think we may have unwittingly exceeded the 70 mph speed limit on occasions, but as speedometers were not fitted to them, it is hard to say with any degree of accuracy. The silky ride, plus the galloping propensity of these locomotives made riding on their footplate an exhilarating affair, especially on the comparatively level stretches of the S&D line, say between Corfe Mullen and Templecombe, where, with gross loads of 450 tons, these engines would scurry along with effortless ease, hardly blowing the smoke off, 160 lb of steam and 15% cut-off being sufficient to keep the load rolling at round about 60 mph. This showed clearly the value, in terms of efficiency of having engines of more than adequate size to do the job, and it was a great pity we hadn't had them years earlier.

When the full power of one of these engines was vigorously applied it sometimes had an amusing sequel, like the day when Driver Eric Elford and I were working the down 'Pines' with engine No. 92245. We were pulled up from about 70 mph to a dead stand at Bailey Gate starting signal. Here the grinning signalman informed us that our guard had failed to board the train after the Blandford stop and was coming on to Bailey Gate by taxi. Later at

Bournemouth West our embarrassed guard explained how he had given us the 'Right away' standing some way from his open guard's van door, but being used to other steam types, had not bargained on the accelerative power of a '9'. Consequently, by the time his van was approaching, he was having two minds whether to jump on board or not — and quickly decided not to, which left him in the embarrassing position of watching his train disappearing into the distance, with him still standing on the station platform. When steam was applied with vigour, the 'Nines' would accelerate like an electric train. This was a very useful asset for making up time, but on this occasion it made us 17 minutes late in Bournemouth West!

The driver of an 'M7' tank engine one summer's day in 1962 could testify to the acceleration powers of a '9'. It was a Saturday afternoon, and he was inadvertently sent out by the Poole signalman to bank us up to Branksome, when we were working the 2.52 pm Bath — Bournemouth West. Actually it was the following train, the 'Pines Express', hauled by an ailing 'West Country' Pacific, that required the banker but the signalman, seeing our class '9', thought that we in fact were the 'Pines'. During the trip down we had been showing off No. 92245's prowess to a group of railway enthusiasts travelling on the train, and decided to deliver the 'Coup de grace' up Parkstone bank.

With only 10 Midland bogies weighing some 340 tons, our '9' went out of Poole Station like a shot out of a gun. She was being worked in a similar fashion to the trip with 92000, and with nearly 100 tons less of train, went like a bomb! I estimate speed was still up to 50 mph as we approached Parkstone Station — on a 1 in 50 gradient.

As we roared around the right handed curve into the station, I glanced back along the train to see how the lads were enjoying it, and was somewhat staggered to see in the distance — some ½ mile behind us — a plume of steam travelling in the same direction as ourselves. "Hey!" I exclaimed to Donald, "We've got a banker on." "What?" he returned in disbelief; then, his surprise turning to determination, "not for long we won't," he shouted, giving 92245 some more stick. "Don't bother, he is about a mile behind us," I hollered back over the tremendous roar of our '9'. But Donald didn't ease her, he was making sure that this 'Southerner' didn't have the remotest chance of catching us up.

Later in the day, a driver walked up to us in the West carriage sidings and commented: "You certainly wanted a banker badly, I must say." It was of course the driver of the 'M7' tank. He continued: "You left me so far behind that when I got to Parkstone up Intermediate signal, it had been returned to danger, so I had to stop there and carry out rule 55 over the telephone to the signalman at Poole High Street Crossing Box. The signalman nearly passed out with fright upon hearing my voice, thinking the section was clear, until I explained how I came to be there."

But then the class '9's' made anything possible.

Chapter Seven

DOUBLE HEADING

The double heading of trains was a regular feature of S&D working over the northern end of the line, and a brief account of the skills and problems concerning engine crews involved in handling these trains would seem appropriate.

The 'Pines Express' was the only train regularly supplied with a pilot engine — between Evercreech Junction and Bath — but on Summer Saturdays practically anything that moved had two engines on it. This state of affairs lasted on the S&D until the arrival of the class '9' 2-10-0s made it possible to reduce substantially this uneconomic working. Southbound goods trains requiring assistance were banked in the rear from Bath Junction up to the mouth of Combe Down Tunnel, and from Radstock up to Masbury summit; goods trains coming North which required assistance had a banker attached in the rear from Evercreech to Binegar.

It was most important that when trains were double headed there was complete understanding between engine crews. The driver on the leading engine was responsible for the braking of the train and the whistle, but this did not excuse the train engine driver from the responsibility of keeping a sharp look out and verifying the aspect of signals. Occasionally the pilot driver might be a shade too enthusiastic and tend to exceed speed limits; it would then be the responsibility of the train driver to draw his colleagues' attention to this by use of the whistle. Failing this he would have to apply the brake himself in order to conform with the speed limits.

This reminds me of an occasion when the up 'Pines' was being dropped down the northern slopes of the Mendips at an ever increasing speed. The train driver, not wishing to upset his colleague up front, resisted as long as possible touching the brake, but as Midsomer Norton was approached at high speed — and with the prospect of a 15 mph speed restriction just beyond the station due to a colliery subsidence, not to mention a 40 mph restriction through the station itself — he had had enough, and reduced speed himself to the appointed 15 mph. Approaching Radstock it was again necessary for him to bring the speed down again to the appointed 40 mph, but this time the effect on the pilot driver was dramatic! He immediately destroyed the vacuum and brought the train to a sudden grinding halt, with the train straddling the busy level crossing, so starting a vast traffic hold-up. The pilot driver dismounted from his engine and strode back to the train engine where he proceeded to give the driver a blistering discourse on whose job it was to apply the brakes on a double-headed train. "It doesn't need two on the brake!" he exclaimed at one point. "No! but it want one b........ on it", the train driver retorted. However, their language was comparatively mild with that being bandied to and fro in the dining-car, where due to the fast descent and erratic braking, chaos reigned supreme. A tide of coffee flowed smartly through the car from end to end, and several succulent dishes had travelled gracefully through the air before being suddenly, and unintentionally, arrested by some poor unfortunate passenger. At least one pair of eyes were seen gazing disconsolately out of a mask of blancmange. When the train eventually arrived at Bath, the entire staff of the dining-car marched as a body up to the leading engine and proceeded to give the driver a monumental harangue, at the end of which the driver's parentage was left in some considerable doubt. I must add that the reaction on the part of the pilot driver on this occasion was not typical of drivers as a race.

Riding on the train engine of a double header could be uncomfortable and even quite dangerous on occasions. When travelling fast it was not unknown for lumps of coal to become dislodged from the tender of the leading engine and to smash into the cab and spectacle plate of the engine behind. Certainly it was prudent to keep one's head inside the cab at speed! When running under light steaming conditions another hazard (though not so serious) was steam and smoke from the leading engine blowing down and smothering the train engine crew with a particularly obnoxious smog. The effect on the crew of the train engine of a double header in a single bore tunnel I have described elsewhere in this book.

Overloading was the usual reason for double heading, but if, as sometimes happened, the engine provided to assist was not in the best of condition, it could prove more of a hinderance than a help — indeed even a possible cause of lost time. If, however, both engines' crews were of top calibre, and could build up an understanding quickly between each other, then it was nearly always possible to keep time.

Donald and I were rostered a class '4F' 0-6-0 one day on the up 'Pines' due to a rare failure of a class '5' on the 2.40 am down mail. No. 44559 was the engine, and with a booked load of 11 coaches, Templecombe depot thoughtfully sent a class '2P' 4-4-0 down light engine to pilot us up to Bath. It was just as well they had had the foresight to do this. By the time Broadstone Station was passed it was evident that 44559's steaming ability was just a bit below par, which was enough to make things difficult on a duty of this nature.

As we neared the summit of the climb beyond Broadstone Station our pilot driver looked back at us and in sign language enquired if all was well. He received the thumbs down signal and his answering nod was all that was required to initiate a perfect understanding between us. An unspoken plan was put into action.

Our '4F' had been worked very heavily from Poole up to Broadstone, and really she wanted a breather — but she didn't get it — not yet anyway. Steam was kept on all the way down Corfe Mullen Bank and we roared, rattled and shook — and did everything else one experienced on a '4F' at 60 mph — to

Bailey Gate, and kept plugging away against the mainly rising tendency of the road as far as Spetisbury. Pressure was back to the 90lb mark by now, but the train was still going well. At this point the line dipped down hill for a short distance then up in switch-back style towards Charlton Marshall. We shut off steam, gave a toot on the whistle, and the Templecombe driver gave a wave in acknowledgement and his '2P', which was steaming magnificently, swept us on into the Blandford stop in great style.

Our boiler pressure had recovered to blowing off point by departure time from Blandford and we needed every ounce for the 1 in 80 climb that lay ahead up to Milldown, but as we progressed northwards up gradually rising gradients, the pressure gauge remorsely crept back and the water level in the boiler got lower and lower despite every effort and constant attention by myself. Beyond Sturminster Newton, with pressure back to 80lbs, Donald remarked, above the clatter, that we were producing just about enough steam to heat the train. At this juncture the regulator was shut, a toot given on our whistle, and the '2P' was opened out to sweep us in to our next port of call, Stalbridge.

These series of short breaks in our steaming enabled us to recover boiler pressure for the succeeding stages, but the class '4F's characteristically slow injectors found us with only a couple of inches of water showing in the gauge glass as Templecombe Junction was passed. With the long climb up to Masbury looming ahead it was imperative that our engine, with its superior tractive effort, should leave Evercreech Junction with a full boiler of water and full steam pressure so as to be able to assume major responsibility for this section. Our pilot driver knew this, and with his '2P' still steaming well, he virtually took over the haulage of the train from Templecombe No. 2 Junction to Evercreech, the '4F' working with just a breath of steam going to the cylinders.

The road was reasonably favourable over this stretch and the '2P' did not have to be extended to a degree which might have jeopardised her subsequent effort over the Mendips — and so it proved. Complete understanding of the situation, and co-operation between the two engine crews on the way in which the train should be run south of Evercreech, ensured that both engines were ready for real work where it mattered most. During the long climb up the southern slopes of the Mendips the '2P' ahead of us plugged away steadily, whilst the water level in the boiler of our '4F' was sacrificed gradually in favour of steam pressure, until at last this valiant pair of veterans forged confidently through Masbury station at some 14-15 mph amidst splendid sounds echoing back from the walls of Masbury rock cutting. Our ultimate arrival in Bath was 5 minutes late, if memory serves me correctly, but without planning and understanding on the part of the two crews, it would undoubtedly have been a much later arrival. Instant management you might call it, because it required on the spot forethought, organisation, planning, and not a little hard work.

It was always most interesting to anticipate what combination of locomotives would be seen on the S&D during those halcyon years, especially in view of the diverse types of motive power used. 'West Country' Pacifics paired with '2P's, '4F's, and '7F's, two '7F's, (though it must be admitted that this particular combination was very rare), perhaps even a 'West Country' and Jinty tank 0-6-0 — in short, any combination of engines was possible on Summer Saturdays.

The most powerful combination that I personally was ever concerned with was an occasion when Donald and I brought an unbalanced working up to Bath with a 'West Country' Pacific and were booked home light engine. But traffic that day was so heavy that the signalman at Bath could not even hazard a guess as to when we would be allowed out on to the main line to travel home. We knew what this meant! Having successfully departed from Bath we would surely see the inside of most station sidings, in order to allow trains to pass (despite pleas to the signalman that we wouldn't hang about). A four or five hour trip back to the Bournemouth seemed a certainty. With this very much in mind, Donald suggested to the Bath signalman that we should pilot the 2.52 pm express from Green Park Station, to which he agreed. This resulted in the powerful combination of a 'West Country' and class '9' 2-10-0, the only occasion as far as I know of this pairing having taken place.

As a spectacle, double heading was impressive, but economically, it was extremely wasteful of men and motive power. Its use undoubtedly contributed to the untimely demise of the S&D line.

Chapter Eight

IT ALL ENDED WITH 'EVENING STAR'

As the year of 1962 was ushered in, so were unconfirmed, but persistent rumours that it was proposed to re-route the 'Pines Express' away from the S&D line.

This was very unsettling indeed for the S&D staff as a whole, because it was a foregone conclusion amongst us all that once this step was taken, it would be only a matter of time before the line would be closed down altogether. Needless to say, it was the common desire that the rumours would prove groundless.

This hope was cruelly shattered one day in April, when upon our arrival at Bath Green Park Depot, Mr Morris, the shedmaster, called Donald and me into his office and gravely confirmed all our worst fears.

He told us that as from the end of the Summer Service, the 'Pines' was to be re-routed via Basingstoke, Reading and Oxford, and confided that he thought that this was the beginning of the end for the S&D line.

Once this news had got around, the summer of 1962 proved to be somewhat of a pilgrimage for railway enthusiasts and railwaymen alike, as many who knew and loved the S&D came for what could be their last trips over the line, rubbing shoulders with others who flocked to make their acquaintance with this fascinating stretch of railway whilst there was still time, for the writing was now plainly on the wall.

Although the line officially closed to traffic on March 6, 1966, September 8, 1962, marked the end of through traffic between Bournemouth, Bath and the Midlands. On this day, the 'Pines Express' was scheduled to make its last trips in each direction over the line.

Looking ahead from the time that we first heard the news, it appeared that Donald and I would be on the northbound 'Pines' on this sad occasion, the southbound train being in the charge of another Branksome engine crew, Driver Peter Guy and Fireman Ron Hyde.

During the interim period some thought was given (unofficially) by the other engine crew and ourselves, as to how we could best mark the occasion by doing something special. One of the local railway clubs suggested that the train should be hauled by a Stanier Black '5' with a '2P' as pilot (if one could be found), over the Mendips, as in the days of yore. But we came to the conclusion that every opportunity, even at this late date, should be taken to demonstrate once more to the Railway Authority that there was a simple way to reduce operating costs. Accordingly we put the proposition to Mr Morris that we should work the 'Pines' on this occasion with a class '9' locomotive unassisted whatever the load was, and make no mistake about it, we meant just that. If the load had been made up to 500 tons, we would have taken it unassisted. Mr Morris not only received the idea well, but suggested that we should use the last steam engine built for BR — 92220, *Evening Star*. He then disclosed that this distinguished locomotive was shortly to be transferred to Bath Green Park, and it seemed (providing she was in good fettle) the obvious choice for this occasion, and so it was.

It appeared to me that the time seemed to fly by during the summer season of that year, as though it was doing its utmost to hasten the last appearance of the 'Pines' on S&D metals. But as September 8th approached, it looked as though I was destined not to take part in this working after all. In my capacity as a passed fireman, I was rostered for driving duties on this day and was being taken off the 'Pines' to work the 5.30 pm to Templecombe. Normally, of course, I would have been very happy to be upgraded from firing to driving duties, but this was one occasion when I was most unhappy about it. But there it was, (I thought), I should have to accept it. I would not be participating in this finale after all.

This thought persisted until the Thursday of that week, when upon arrival at Bath Green Park Motive Power Depot, Donald and I were requested to go to Mr Morris' office, where a local newspaper reporter (complete with photographer) wished to interview us in connection with Saturday's run.

In the office I left the talking to Donald, and was later going to explain that I, personally, would not be taking part on Saturday. But before I could, I was startled to hear Donald's answer to a question concerning his feelings at working the last 'Pines' over the S&D by replying. "You had better ask the Driver that one," and at the same time making a gesture in my direction. I was dumbfounded. "What do you mean by that?" I asked him. "Oh," Donald explained, grinning, "I have arranged it with the list clerk to change our turns of duty on Saturday. I shall be working the 5.30 p.m. to Templecombe, so you will have to work the last up 'Pines'". I protested feebly, being more than a little shocked at what I had just heard. However, not wishing to make too much of a spectacle under the circumstances, I waited until after the interview was concluded, and we had gained the privacy of our footplate, before I tackled him again on the subject.

It was, of course, inconceivable to me that Donald should give up this opportunity to crown his career with the distinction of driving 'Evening Star' on the last 'Pines Express' over the S&D line, a train which over this section, at least was almost synonymous with his name. Donald's reply to this form of protest was typical of his unselfishness, and of his high regard for anybody whom he considered had served him well. "My Son," he said. "I've driven this train on hundreds of occasions, and from time to time have received congratulations for my performance on it. But without your hard work and co-operation, none of it would have been possible. As my thanks to you, I wish you to have the opportunity to drive it in your own right, and Saturday's occasion will be a memory that will never leave you. Enjoy it."

I must admit now that I felt a lump in my throat by the time he had finished his little speech, and very humble too. Admittedly, we had always held each other in the highest esteem, but for a man with 45 years service on the footplate, to give up the kudos of this occasion to me, a mere apprentice, was in my opinion too great a sacrifice for him, and too great a reward for me.

But my further protests were of no avail — his mind was firmly made up, and when Donald's mind was made up on anything, that decision stood.

As usual I drove him home after out turn of duty was over. As he got out, his parting comment to me that evening was this. "Saturday's trip will be a severe test in enginemanship for you. I have taught you all I know over the past years, now go and prove my confidence in you by making a good job of it. I'll be thinking of you, Son!" It was with those words ringing in my ears that I made my way home that evening.

The morning of September 8th dawned with a grey overcast sky, and rain looked imminent, which seemed to fit in perfectly with the general feeling of melancholy that was the hallmark of the occasion. Fireman Aubrey Punter and myself signed on duty at 8.15 am for the last trip that either of us were going to have over the S&D system throughout to Bath. Incidentally, the combined ages of Aubrey and myself did not equal Donald's years of service to date on the railway. There were about a dozen engines simmering on Branksome shed, but *Evening Star* was easy to spot in the line-up on the pit road. She looked a picture of cleanliness, and was a great credit to the Bath cleaning gang, who must have expended a considerable amount of elbow grease to get her like that, especially as she was transferred to Bath depot in a somewhat grimy condition. One of the overnight trains from the north of England had been her previous duty, and her crew had left her on the pit with the fire up one side of the firebox. So Aubrey and myself set about the task of preparing her for hauling the last up 'Pines'.

At about 9.30 am, we backed on to our train at the West Station, and found out from the guard that the load was one of 12 coaches, weighing 426 tons. So even on the final run of this train over the S&D a record was to be broken; 426 tons is the heaviest authenticated load ever taken unassisted over the Mendips, and this record belongs to *Evening Star*, Aubrey and myself, and is of course now unassailable.

A large crowd of well wishers cheered their farewells to the 'Pines' as we pulled away punctually at 9.45 am, and indeed, this was a feature of the entire run. People were waving and cheering at virtually every station, bridge, tunnel and cutting that we passed through. But despite this, Bath Green Park Station provided, I think, the largest gathering of people who wished to say farewell. Train spotters were outnumbered on this occasion by the general public, who gave us a cheer and milled around the engine to talk to us as we came gently to a stand near the station buffer stops. One little boy was carefully carrying a model of *Evening Star,* which he told me his daddy had made. 'Daddy' was with him, and the pair of them proudly showed it to me, obviously thrilled to be standing by the real thing.

For this final trip, I had hoped to pull off a very fast one, but the 9.25 am. to Liverpool, immediately ahead, checked us two or three times, culminating in a dead stand in Cole Station for several minutes. This fouled my plans, and in fact we were eventually late on arrival at Bath, but by now how much I don't know. I forgot to check my watch, so busy was I talking to the crowds of well wishers at the station.

But one question which had so far gone unanswered, was in fact to be resolved on this trip. This was, if a class '9' locomotive, hauling a full load of 410 tons or more, was stopped by signals on the 1 in 50 grades of the Mendip Hills, would she be able to restart this load? No one had ever been stopped with a really heavy load before.

We had got away from Evercreech Junction and were going 'hammer and tongs' at the start of the 7¾ mile climb over the Mendips, when I was dismayed to see the Evercreech New distant 'on'. The 9.25 am to Liverpool — which frankly, I don't think was trying very hard — was baulking us again. On the approach to Evercreech New Station, the outer home came off slowly for us, but as we crept up to the starting signal, it remained obstinately at danger. It flashed through my mind that we should soon know now, whether a '9' could restart 426 tons on this up grade!

The forward movement of the train was barely perceptible, and I was just about to apply the vacuum brake too hold the train on the gradient when the signal was slowly lowered. With full regulator, and 78% cut off, *Evening Star* heaved her train away from the platform, and gradually accelerated to about 10-15 mph, but she knew there was a young town tied on behind her. 60% was the shortest cut off she would accept up the first bank to Shepton Mallet. I tried her briefly in 55% at one point, but she started to slow up, so 60% it had to be. Aubrey Punter sweated bucketsfull in his efforts to keep the firegrate covered. He was down to coal which was little more than dross, and which by now was virtually out of reach of his shovel in the tender, necessitating frequent trips into it to pull coal (dust) forward. His was a gruelling task indeed.

Boiler pressure on this part of the climb averaged 230lbs, but at the expense of water in the boiler. We topped the first part of the climb with about half a glass of water showing on the gauge glass. This train didn't stop at Shepton Mallet on summer Saturdays, so as we eased on to the brief downhill stretch leading to the viaducts over the town and the start of the second half of the climb to Masbury, I was musing as to the best line of action to take — shut off and recover as much steam and water a possible, but loose impetus for the next climb — or keep her going. I had to make my mind up in seconds. I kept her going hard using full regulator and 45% cut off with speed reaching a maximum in the dip of about 40 mph. This setting took us up to the North End of Winsor Hill Tunnel, but with speed back in the low twenties I lengthened the cut off to 50% Aubrey Punter was visibly tired by now and I entered the tender and pulled some coal forward, and did a round of firing while he watched the road.

We approached Masbury Halt working on 55% cut off, and so well had Aubrey stuck to his task that we had no less than 240lbs showing on the pressure gauge. And in this style we triumphantly breasted the summit, though the sudden change in grade from 1 in 50 up to 1 in 73 down caused the water level to fall sharply in the boiler, but the use of two injectors just maintained it in sight in the gauge glass.

It had been a most gruelling climb, but despite being brought virtually to a stand and on a 1 in 50 gradient, with a train 16 tons in excess of the full load and some of the worst coal imaginable, the '9' had still done well, and this on the Northbound ascent to Masbury which was much harder than the corresponding ascent southwards from Radstock to the summit. So we had the satisfaction of knowing that right up to the bitter end, we were still showing the authorities what could be done with a '9'. *Evening Star* also worked the last southbound 'Pines' after being rejuvenated with a clean fire and the tender filled with some good fresh coal at Bath, and put up a magnificent performance in the hands of my shedmates, Pete Guy and Ron Hyde. Altogether a grand finale, although a sad one, for the tiny Branksome depot.

With the departure of the 'Pines' from the S&D metals, it appeared to me as though the very life blood of the line had been drained, and it must be only a matter of time before the Western Region would produce a good case for closing the line. History shows how right that assumption was; indeed, I was surprised the line remained open as long as it did.

Branksome crews did not finish their long association with the 'Pines' completely on September 8th, as it was still rostered to be worked by us over its new route as far as Oxford — a distance of 102 miles. However, this arrangement did not last very long. Bournemouth Central men had long wanted the duty as their own, and took this opportunity to wrest the job away from us. They first made representation to the Railway management, but were told "Branksome men will work the job as usual." Not content with this reply, they got certain sectional council members of the ASLE&F union to fight their cause. Now members are elected onto this Council by ballot, and as one of them frankly implied to a Branksome representative, Bournemouth Central, having a block vote of something like 300 compared to Branksome's 12 members of this Union, it was a certainty that they would back Bournemouth's claim irrespective of the strong case for Branksome keeping the duty; and our case was a strong one. After all, the 'Pines' had not been withdrawn, but was purely re-routed, and there was no real case for making a set of Branksome men redundant and giving Bournemouth an extra turn of duty. But personalities won the day. The outcome of this wrangle, which cast great discredit on some members of Bournemouth depot and to certain ASLE&F officials also, was the transference of the turn to Bournemouth Central's top link in return for which they parted with a Bournemouth-Poole pick-up goods duty. Even out of this situation we found some simple amusement.

Bournemouth's top link men had not had the duty very long before they were complaining of the inability of the 'West Country's' to keep time on the trains and 'Merchant navy' Pacifics were substituted for them, the first regular duties of these engines on the Oxford Road. So what Branksome men had achieved with class '5' locomotives, Bournemouth men required class '8's to do the similar work.

This underlying rivalry between the two depots I have portrayed on occasions during the course of this book. We at Branksome did our best to keep the S&D flag aloft in the face of our nearby neighbours with, I think, considerable success.

In the winter of 1963, Branksome shed was closed, and its duties were transferred to Bournemouth Central, along with the engine crews and shed staff alike, the locomen taking their place in the links of their new depot according to their seniority. But even though we were absorbed in this way, our identity was not lost, we were still referred to individually as "the S&D men," thus proving what an impact our railway and its traditions had left on the Western section of the Southern.

Now of course, the line is closed, most of the track has been lifted, and its meandering course claimed back by nature, but its memory lives on, and what rich memories there are for ex S&D railwaymen to relive, and to relate to others.

When I visit Donald's home in his retirement, our conversation inevitably turns sooner or later (usually sooner, according to my wife) to the old S&D. We remember of course the good times we enjoyed together, and some of the bad ones as well, although the passage of time mellows even these occasions to such an extent that we usually get a laugh out of them also.

We speak appreciatively, for instance, of the odd pheasant that we have found on our engine buffer beam at the end of the journey, and which has provided one or other of us with a very tasty meal. We have nearly bagged golfers in this way on several occasions in the vicinity of Broadstone down distant signal, where is was necessary for them to cross the track to complete their round of golf. Amazing as it would seem, they seldom heard our approach, and a pair of them, no doubt discussing their respective handicaps, would wander slowly over the wooden sleeper crossing trundling their golf trolleys behind them, with rarely an urgent thought in their heads. However, a sharp blast on our engine whistle always produced movement of the utmost alacrity!

I imagine much the same fate must have befallen a certain S&D crossing keeper at Common Lane Crossing, near Templecombe. This worthy was always kept extremely well-supplied with coal by passing engine crews who, under cover of darkness, made their deliveries by the simple expediency of kicking huge lumps off the footplate, just in advance of the crossing. He was well satisfied with this set up until the occasion when one of our firemen on the 6.40 pm Bournemouth West-Bath slightly lost his bearings in the pitch blackness of a Dorset night, and the crossing keeper lost the back door of his house, a huge lump of coal wrenching it clean off its hinges and hurling it backwards into the house, by which time its condition made it eminently suitable for firewood. One can imagine the consternation of the occupants of the house during this brief but effective demolition job.

Mention of demolition jobs is likely to remind us of the comments of a signal and telegraph engineer, who was present at Bailey Gate road crossing on the occasion when an unfortunate Templecombe driver, working the 6.55 am. Bath-Bournemouth, had just crashed through the crossing gates, reducing them to matchwood. A motorist who was forced to pull up and wait while the debris was cleared from the road, enquired of the engineer as to the cause of it. "Termites," came the laconic reply.

The pride and interest that Mr Morris, the Bath Shedmaster, took in his stud of locomotives, despite the constant problem of staff shortage, is something that all S&D locomen appreciated, and none more than Donald and myself.

This quality in him is typified, I think, by his reaction to the arrival in Bath of the much scorched and scarred 34040 on the occasion of the fire referred to earlier in Chapter Four, and the story belongs to Donald, who was of course her driver.

Despite the apparent intensity of the fire, 34040 was found to be quite sound in wind and limb, after a thorough examination had been carried out on Green Park Shed, and perfectly capable of working the southbound 'Pines' back to Bournemouth later in the day. But her appearance! "That will never do," explained Mr Morris. "I am not sending an engine of mine out looking like that." He thereupon dispatched a young cleaner to the town with instructions to buy a tin of green paint from Woolworths, and to hurry back to the shed.

On receipt of the paint, a rapid job of patchwork painting was performed on the engine by two of the more artistic members of the shed staff. The new paint did not quite match up with the existing green, being more akin to apple green than the somewhat darker green of the Southern engine's livery. Nevertheless, the engine ran in this condition for a considerable time afterwards, and gradually the smoke and grime weathered the newly painted sections, and the old and the new eventially combined very well together. Mr. Morris never had sufficient cleaners to keep his engines in the condition that he would have liked to have seen them in. But staff shortage or not, there were certain standards to maintain.

One name that constantly crops up during our nostalgic conversations together, is that of Ivo Peters. Although he was not a railwayman in the strictest sense of the word, he was part and parcel of the S&D scene, and rarely did a weekend pass by that he and his camera were not seen somewhere or other on the S&D system. He was and indeed still is, well known, if not by name certainly by the familiarity of his face, to a great number of ex S&D staff of all grades.

Besides his weekend photographic excursions over the line he somehow managed to be on hand to record the majority of the more unusual occasions or events that took place. Such as 'strangers in the camp' in the form of foreign locomotives working over the line, or sent perhaps explicitly for trial in order to gauge their suitability for S&D work. In fact, in my view, he was the official photographer of this line, and the excellence of his work can be seen within the pages of this book. He has amassed by far the largest and finest collection of S&D photographs that I have ever seen, and I feel very privileged to have had the freedom of this collection with which to illustrate my book. I could do no better.

Another distinction was his feat of photographing the same train on three or perhaps four occasions in the course of its journey from Bath to Evercreech Junction. Certainly he has photographed Donald and myself at such locations as Bath Junction, Midsomer Norton, Morewood, and would then finally photograph us before we departed from Evercreech. This demanded skilled driving, good road knowledge, and a fast car. All of these attributes he possessed. But it was still a performance of some note in my estimation from a character of some note, who added more colour to this already colourful railway line.

In addition to these tales, there are the more questionable exploits that the S&D has witnessed, some of which are so hilarious they make us laugh until the tears roll down our cheeks. I could write a book on this subject alone, but not enough water has passed under the bridge yet. But perhaps a few thinly veiled examples will give an insight into what I mean.

The freedom of the footplate was extended to interested members of the public many times over the years, but the occasion I remember best is a very vivid memory, because I was the fireman when the event took place on the 'Pines Express.'

My driver during this particular week on the 'Pines' (not Donald I hasten to add) had just cheerfully agreed to a request from a local Roman Catholic priest to footplate with us up to Bath and back. But the Priest had with him his rather attractive housekeeper, who, he said, was also fond of 'steam trains.' "Bring her along as well then if you like", my gallant mate answered. So they both climbed up on the footplate, and the lady made herself comfortable on my seat. During the course of this run, it was an education to watch the reaction of various footplate crews, when they spotted our unusual guests on board. Usually their faces wore a look of incredulity, and I could well sympathise with them. The fireman of a Johnson '3F' at Sturminster Newton was sprawled out on his footplate reading a newspaper, when we passed at about 50 mph. He glanced up to wave to us, and nearly fell off the engine when he caught sight of a lady in a green jumper leaning over the side of our cab.

I thought my mate was pushing his luck somewhat with this escapade, and was expecting someone of authority to appear at every station we stopped at, but luck held out, until Blandford that is, on the return journey.

As we entered the station, a locomotive inspector was seen waiting on the extreme end of the down platform, obviously with the intention of boarding us. But my driver, confident and resourceful to the last, deliberately overshot the platform by a coach length or two, and the priest plus his housekeeper were hastily bundled off the engine on the off side, where they made an ungainly, but rapid, retreat down a steep embankment to the safety of the public highway. When the inspector climbed on to the footplate, he was greeted cordially by my driver, who coolly engaged him in pleasant conversation, whilst the two fugitives made their escape. I poured myself a cup of tea from our tea can, although a stiff whisky would have been more appropriate under the circumstances!

Then there was the occasion when the driver of the 6.35 am Evercreech-Poole goods train came by a nanny goat during the course of his journey, and arrived at Branksome shed with it happily looking over the cab side of 44102. The goat was off loaded from the footplate, and the driver walked it home to keep for milking, holding the goat's lead in one hand and pushing his bicycle with the other.

If this turn of duty was rare in producing goats on its engines, the same could not be said of Christmas trees, which it produced annually, round about December time, if memory serves aright! Where did they come from anyway? Well that's another story. What a railway the S&D was, and what characters served on it at different times.

Never again will trains run from Bath Green Park to Bournemouth West, but in my mind, I can still see every sleeper of that 71½ miles. The exhaust beats of hard-pressed engines storming the windswept heights of the Mendip Hills are still loud and clear in my memory and in those of many another Mendips Engineman.

DISTANCES

Main Line

	Miles
BATH GREEN PARK	0
Bath Junction	½
MIDFORD	4¼
WELLOW	6¾
SHOSCOMBE & SINGLE HILL HALT	8½
Writhlington & Braysdown	9¾
RADSTOCK	10¾
MIDSOMER NORTON	12½
CHILCOMPTON	14½
Moorewood	15¾
BINEGAR	17
MASBURY	18¾
Winsor Hill	20
SHEPTON MALLET	21¾
EVERCREECH NEW	25
Evercreech Junction (North)	26¼
EVERCREECH JUNCTION	26½
COLE	29¼
WINCANTON	33½
Templecombe No. 3	36¼
Templecombe No. 2	36¾
TEMPLECOMBE	37
HENSTRIDGE	38¾
STALBRIDGE	40¼
STURMINSTER NEWTON	44¼
SHILLINGSTONE	47¼
STOURPAINE HALT	50¼
BLANDFORD	52¾
CHARLTON MARSHALL HALT	54½
SPETISBURY	56
BAILEY GATE	59
Corfe Mullen Junction	
CORFE MULLEN HALT	62
BROADSTONE JUNCTION (SR)	63¾
Holes Bay Junction	66½
POOLE	67¼
PARKSTONE	69
BRANKSOME	70¼
Bournemouth West Junction	70¾
BOURNEMOUTH WEST	71½

Note: Distances are given to the nearest quarter of a mile.

Locomotives

A list of the diverse types of locomotives which have, at some time or another, run on the S&D line during the period 1949-1966.

British Railways Standard Locomotives	9F	2-10-0
	5MT	4-6-0
	5MT	4-6-0(c)
	4MT	4-6-0
	4MT	2-6-0
	4MT	2-6-4(T)
	3MT	2-6-2(T)
	2MT	2-6-2(T)
Ex LMS Locomotives	8F	2-8-0
	7F	2-8-0
	5MT	4-6-0
	5MT	4-6-0(c)
	5MT	2-6-0(H)
	4MT	2-6-0
	4F	0-6-0
	3P	4-4-0
	3F	0-6-0
	2P	4-4-0
	2MT	2-6-2(T)
	JINTY	0-6-0(T)
	JOHNSON	0-4-4(T)
	L & Y 'PUG'	0-4-0(T)
	SENTINEL	0-4-0(T)
Ex Southern Railway Locomotives	8P.M.N.	4-6-2(B)
	7P W.C./B.B.	4-6-2
	V	4-4-0
	U.I.	2-6-0
	U	2-6-0
	Q	0-6-0
	T9	4-4-0
	M7	0-4-4(T)
	Z	0-8-0(T)
	G6	0-6-0(T)
Ex GWR Locomotives	22XX	0-6-0
	46XX	0-6-0(T)
	56XX	0-6-2(T)
Ex WD Locomotives	W.D.	2-8-0

(C) Caprotti valve gear; (T) Tank Engine; (H) Horwich Crab; (B) Officially banned from the line.

BR 'The Pines Express' 14.7.61 Radstock to Masbury

MP	min/sec	MPH	Cut off %	
10.75	0.00		32	
11	24	37.4		
11.25	53	30.7	35	
11.50	1.21	31		Midsomer Norton
11.75	1.52	29.7		
12.25	2.58	28.5	40	
12.75	4.11	24.7		
13	52	22		Tunnel
13.25	5.30	23.7	42	
13.50	6.09	23.2	44	
13.75	6.45.5	24.7	48	
14	7.21	25.3		Chilcompton
14.25	7.50	30.7		
14.75	8.40	36	28	Top of 1/50
15.25	9.32	34.7	35	
17	12.42	33.1	23	Binegar
17.25	13.7	36		
17.75	14.7	30		Summit

Regulator full open
Boiler pressure maintained at 240 lbs
Water level full throughout
Firing with ovoids: frequent: 4-5 shovels at a time
Maximum power output: MP 10.75 to 14.75: average gradient: 1/56

average gradient compensated for curves: 1/52
speed at MP 10.75: 38 mph, speed at MP 14.75: 36 mph
average gradient compensated for curves and corrected for loss
of impetus: 1/52.5
weight of engine and tender: 133 tons
weight of train 450 tons
average speed 27.7 m.p.h.
resistance formulae: train: BR experiments
resistance loco. and tender: Strahl
Average equivalent draw bar HP: 2000
Average cylinder HP: 2240
Average output MP 10.75 to MP 27.75: Average speed: 29.8 mph
EDBHP: 1840
Cyl. HP: 2100

BR 'The Pines Express' Blandford to Broadstone 14.7.1961

Start with 55% cut off on a down grade of 1/80, soon reduced to 32%
50 mph at Corfe Mullen Jc for tablet exchange.
With 45% cut off, full regulator and 235lbs boiler pressure, sustained 43 mph up 1/80
grade. Estimated Cyl. HP: 2700

Poole to Bournemouth

From start: 1 mile level, then 1.5 miles at 1/60 with a short 1/50 and 1/300 through
Parkstone Station: average gradient 1/64. Passed, the top of the 1/60, 2.5 miles from the
start in 4 min 20 sec, attaining 47 mph at the foot of the grade and only falling to 41 mph
at the top. Cut of: 49%, 52% from Parkstone, boiler pressure 225lb; full regulator.

It is difficult to assess the HP output owing to the shortness of the run and the helping
wind; but calculations point to cylinder HP in the region of 2800 — 3000 during one
minute.

A magnificent example of skilled driving and firing with high sustained capacity and
remarkable outbursts of exceptional power showing the flexibility of the steam
locomotive.

FOOTPLATE OVER
THE MENDIPS

PREFACE

In my previous book 'Mendips Engineman', I set out the story of my own footplate experiences on the S&D over the ten year period extending from 1953-63. Also therein, I mentioned my interest in bygone days on the S&D, an appetite regularly whetted by senior drivers cabin reminiscences. With the realisation that such memories were becoming fewer as time passed, and with it the men who had first hand experience of the line and its motive power all those years ago, I decided to set sail once more onto the unaccustomed task of authorship and commit to paper a few of those memories of a past era, gleaned from some of the men who knew the line intimately over a period of many years. In so doing I have been able to elaborate here on various happenings occurring before my time, some of which I mentioned briefly in passing during the course of my last book, so in some ways this present offering is complementary to my last.

The original intention was to confine myself to events contained in the period of time extending from 1919 to around 1950 – indeed it still is this period with which this book is primarily concerned. But as the story developed, several anecdotes of the 1950's and 60's came to light, one way or another. So in the hope that these will be of interest I have included them here. In consequence, and for the sake of continuity I have inter-woven into the text some of the more important events concerning the line from 1950 up until its closure in March 1966.

This is not a learned history of the S&DJR but a collection of memories and 'inside stories' which I hope combines sufficiently with the important dates in its lifetime to impart something of the atmosphere surrounding this outstanding railway. I can only hope that I have done justice to the nostalgic memories so painstakingly related to me by ex colleagues both past and present.

Poole,
Dorset.

P. W. Smith.
1977.

Chapter One

LAST MEN IN

When Lou Ricketts, 'Nutty' West, Donald Beale and the rest started their railway careers in the locomotive department of the Somerset and Dorset Joint Railway in the years following the 1914-1918 war they could not possibly have known that they would be the last men actually to start and finish their careers on that line, their retirement dates coinciding closely with the eventual closure of the line in March 1966. This was also true of the steam engine for the S&D line was steam worked to the end, so that most S&D men of Donald Beale's seniority had little or nothing to do with the diesel invasion that started to sweep steam locos from the scene on British Railways with increasing rapidity in the late 50's. These men were thus in very truth some of the last in this country who had cut their teeth and spent their entire working lives on steam engines. I came to know well many of the men of this era during my own career as an engineman on the S&D between 1953-63. They were all drivers by then, and as those who have read my previous book 'Mendips Engineman' will be aware, when I was a fireman my own regular driver for several years was Donald Beale — probably the best known of all drivers in the history of the S&D. I used to sit in the various enginemen's cabins enthralled by the stories these older drivers used to tell of earlier days. Over the years I have also spent many happy hours in Donald Beale's home enjoying his reminiscences and the historical facts that these brought forth. So, with this background, let us turn the clock back more than 50 years, to the pre-grouping era in fact. Using as a convenient starting point, Donald Beale's first day on the S&D all those years ago, I will try to recreate the early morning scene at the start of an engine cleaner's day.

It was the August Bank Holiday Monday of 1919. At 7 am the bell in the roof of the loco offices of the Somerset and Dorset Joint Railway at Bath, Somerset, pivoted to and fro, its clangour reaching the mess room, commonly called the 'cabin', situated at the bottom of No. 3 shed road. This was crowded with cleaners who had just come on duty, and humming with their chatter. Mingling with them were half a dozen pale faced and sleepy eyed men who had been on duty since midnight and still had two and a half hours work to do before they would draw their checks at 9.30 am. At the behest of the tolling bell everyone streamed out of the cabin into the smoky interior of the mainly wooden built shed, still laughing and chatting, knocking out pipes and pinching out the glowing ends of their cigarettes for at the bottom of the shed, a large framed notice warned, 'NO SMOK-ING, anyone caught will be fined 2/6d'. The throng wound around the stop blocks at the bottom of numbers 4 and 5 roads, continuing past the cabin of the boiler washers, and that of Sammy Salvidge the boilersmith, who shared it with Harry Waldron and George Hemmings the tubers. The next cabin (or store room really) belonged to Tom Wells, the foreman cleaner. Tom was already waiting in the doorway for his 'lambs' to appear.

Tom Wells must have been about 68 years of age then. Still very upright and with a head of snow white hair, he ruled over his charges with a rod of iron. Donald Beale recalls, "As we crowded around his doorway, five or six deep, my eyes were busy scanning the rows of engines standing in the different roads. Some were small, some large, and some in various stages of repair; and pervading the whole atmosphere was the cleaners scent — paraffin and naphthaline. Today, more than 50 years on, how a sniff of either brings back those happy memories!".

Naming four men at a time, Tom Wells issued each with a half pound of cotton waste rolled into a ball, and to the senior hand of each gang he gave a piece of tallow and a tin of paraffin together with the day's instructions. Donald's first job on the S&D Joint Railway that morning was to clean the leading bogie wheels of No.14, a rebuilt Johnson 4-4-0 and a member of the first series of engines with this wheel arrangement to be built for the S&D and which handled much of the passenger work on the S&D then. Tom Wells continued to issue instructions until the last of the cleaners were despatched whereupon various shouts could be heard coming from different parts of the shed, such as "Come on, she's over here on 2, Charlie". and "Here's 76 top of 5 road". Others would ask a passing fitter or a steam raiser, "Seen 22 about? What! up 9 road? That's good!, we'll be able to see Tom coming from there and can have a quick 'Woodbine' in safety".

So Tom Wells' motley, merry, shining and greasy crew were distributed over, under, and around the travel stained engines. With cloths, rags and scrapers some would be speedily but effectually cleaning off the dirt, whilst others were busy daubing their engines over with tallow, 'just to preserve her complexion' as someone once remarked. Tom Wells usual stance was just inside the shed between numbers three and four roads, but occasionally he would pace across the top of number two road for a check there also. If anything looked amiss — someone not working, or a bit of horse-play going on — Tom would stroll with a stately tread towards the culprit until one keen-eyed lad could cry, "Look out! Tom's coming", and in a flash everyone would be hard at work, and apparently would not even see Tom when he arrived, so industrious were they. Tom would watch silently for a few minutes, then walk to the framing and look in over the top and remark to the cleaner of the link motion "Now then my lad, wipe up along that motion plate, down around that weighbar bracket and don't forget up under the die-block". To the next victim — "and you, my lad, can come down to the store with me and get a 'napfy' (naphthalene) wad and then clean in behind them auxiliary oil pipes to the axle box, and around the valve spindle guides," — and off he would go, his heavy boots echoing off the brick paving, and the cleaner would drop off the footplate and collect his 'napfy wad' with a pained expression on his face. If Tom Wells happened to stroll around and spot a streak of dirt or a smear not wiped off, on an engine on which cleaning was nearly finished, the whole job would have to be gone over again — and, worse still, he would remain to see it done! This was to the great delight of the other cleaners in the vicinity, and when Tom was observed 'eyeing' a job, the grape vine spread the good news to the rest who celebrated in several ways. The favourite was a trip underneath the water tank. This was a stone built structure of some height on top of which was set the storage tank that supplied the S&D loco shed with water. From roughly half way up this lofty edifice there sprang a wooden bridge which spanned a pathway leading up to the adjacent Midland Railway Loco shed — a small stone built structure which was on a higher elevation than the S&D establishment. This bridge afforded access to the toilets which were situated under the tank, and a constant stream of employees would be observed coming and going. The reason? the smoking ban, and the threat of the '2/6 fine'. So for a quick smoke the slogan was, 'Up under the tank', where various peep holes strategically placed, gave a view of anyone approaching the bridge. Panic stations frequently ensued when a cry from the look-out rang out, "Blimey! look out, here's Tom coming". Then came the rush for the exit so as to be the first nonchalantly to appear, as though nature and nature alone had called. Only one man at a time could pass on the narrow bridge, and Tom usually encountered quite a crowd who would have rather welcomed him elsewhere. Hence the freedom for a worry free smoke when Tom was 'eyeing' a job.

The inevitable horseplay amongst the cleaners invariably occurred after 'blacking down the smokebox'. To carry out this part of the job, the dirtiest piece of waste was taken to Tom's cabin, outside which stood an open tank holding about five gallons of used cylinder oil, or 'Black Jack' as it was commonly known. The waste was dropped in and swirled around until fully saturated with the thick clinging oil before it was extracted and given a tossing from palm to palm, each landing emitting a satisfying, squelchy smack. After the smokebox had been 'blacked down', a likely target was sought as a way of disposing of the filthy cotton waste. The 'blacker' was padded from palm to palm once more until it was nicely rounded, and squelching gently, then the surrounding roads and engines were surveyed until an unsuspecting victim was sighted. The instant the 'blacker' left his hand, the cleaner would dive into the pit between the driving wheels, run down its length to the stop blocks, jump out, stroll around the stop blocks and walk nonchalantly and unconcernedly back towards the victim, when if the aim had been true that unfortunate would be wiping 'Black Jack' from his ear and neck, and vowing vengeance on all and sundry. Commiserating with him, the cleaner would even help to wipe the oil further around his neck.

The cleaning of goods and shunting engines was divided into quarters, with one man designated to each quarter of the engine, and allowed two and a half hours to complete it, making a total of ten man hours work. But this was not so for the passenger engines. These had one cleaner appointed to them, and he was known as cleaning for a particular driver, say, Walt Darvil, rather than his engine which was No. 18, a rebuilt Johnson 4-4-0. Whichever turn Walt was on, his cleaner would sign on ten hours before him in order to complete the engine's cleaning before Walt arrived. An S&D passenger engine cleaner was a slightly exalted being. He had practically a free hand, and could stroll around without being told to "get on with his work". He drew his waste allowance in one go — a pound and a half of cotton waste, plus his tallow, paraffin and emery cloth — and in most cases he also had a private store accumulated by his driver who would hand over cotton waste he had purloined in other depots. Passenger cleaners were paid a bonus rate for their work, so when the job was finished it was necessary to find Tom Wells and ask him to examine and sign for the work. Should Tom not sign, the cleaner's work was paid for at the ordinary day rate.

Prior to the first world war, and up to 1915 — when the effects of war were beginning to tell on supplies of men and materials, and the stern discipline began to slacken — Tom's inspection was thorough and lengthy. Passing underneath the engine he would draw a white handkerchief from his pocket, and folding it over the top of his fingers would first examine springs, brake rigging, the inside of the eccentric sheaves as far as possible, and the insides of the big end webs. Thereafter he passed through to the intermediates, checking the work in the same meticulous way before finally emerging from the rear of the tender. If the driver was on duty, and there was room, Tom would have the engine moved a half turn in order to see if the 'pinching' had been done, which term meant shifting the locomotive by placing a pinch-bar between a wheel tyre and rail and using this to lever the engine along the track. This was necessary so that the top parts of the driving wheels, high up under the splashers, could be cleaned.

Somerset and Dorset engines were cleaned to an incredibly high standard in those days. Old S&D men remember with pride the beautiful Prussian blue livery with black and yellow lining with which many engines were attired up until 1930. After cleaning, the blue enamel would shine with a deep lustre, and a glance under the boiler would reveal the spotless bright red paintwork of the inside framing and eccentric rods, with the brass auxiliary oil boxes and their attendant copper oil delivery pipes to the driving axle boxes scoured and shining. Of course cleaning as practised on the S&D then could be better described as an art — particularly when the finishing touches were applied. For instance, when tallowing the splashers, the tallow was manipulated in such a way that a pattern, which gave the appearance of the rays of the rising sun, could be discerned on the finished splasher. Sometimes when finishing off the tender, a circular motion would be applied with the tallow wad, which produced a pattern similar to bunches of grapes, but this could only be done by experienced cleaners after long practice. The engine side rods and both engine and tender buffer plungers were scoured with emery cloth soaked in paraffin. The final finish to the buffers would be applied by horizontal strokes across the buffer heads then turning the corner of the emery cloth down half an inch, the outside edge of the buffer head was circled, and a silver strip produced all around its edge to attract the eye. Tom Wells never praised his cleaners work although at times it was expected. The job had to be done properly — that was all that mattered — and that was what Tom expected to be done. Fair enough! Such was the standard of engine cleaning on the S&D in 1919 and the early 1920's.

After a period of about twelve months on shed, most cleaners took the firemans examination and became 'passed cleaners', so becoming available for firing duties when required. Normally this could be expected to cover the Easter holiday, the Whitsuntide weekend, and the summer season. Then it would be back in the shed until next Easter. Shed work covered not only cleaning, but all jobs connected with loco working. These were very varied, and all cleaners were mixed up with them. Amongst the characters in the shed was Harry Waldron, the tuber, Donald relates the tale of how he had known an S&D 2-8-0 come onto the pits with tubes leaking, and the running foreman wanting her back in traffic two hours later. Harry would be called. He would enter the cab, squat down on his haunches, give a touch to the blower and throw a flaming wad of cotton waste soaked in paraffin into the dark shadows on top of the brick arch. The tube plate leapt into life, the large tube ends glaring back — some with 'tears in their eyes'. Harry's expert eye would then decide. The foreman would look expectantly at him, and Harry would either say, "She'll do another trip", or, "Have the fire out, we'll have to re-expand them". Should it be the latter, then back into the shed the engine would roll. Harry would have his gear ready, and many a time he got into the firebox with 90lb to the square inch, still showing on the steam pressure gauge. The edges of the wooden board he knelt on would char, and the red embers would blow off with the force of the blower. Harry would come out bathed in sweat, and say to the cleaner helping him, "Do that top left one, I've put the tube expander in, you'll be all right kid", whereupon that worthy would turn around, bend down backwards and place his legs inside the firebox. Then he would push against the floor boards until his shoulders passed into the firebox, followed by his head; the heat was intense, and a hot dry suffocating feeling made him feel helpless. "Go on, kid, nip up on the arch". Harry was down by the firehole door watching. The cleaner would start the expander revolving by inserting the tommy bar into the holes and prising downwards. After working for what seemed an age Harry would shout, "Give her a couple more turns", and then, like words from Heaven, "Come on out". And the cleaner was off the arch and head first out of the firehole door to lay gasping on the floorboard. "Hot ain't it, boy!" Harry would say sliding back in again. "Put on the blower a bit more, kid", and his helper watched with wonder as Harry started again, slipping the expander into another tube, the flame of his 'gawky' (an oil lamp that used rape oil, and burned without smoking) lighting up his sweat streaked face. And then it was the cleaner's turn again, until the job was finished. The anxious steam raiser, who had been fluttering around, was at last told, "All right to light her up, Bert", and to his mate, "take the kit back, son, we've got to put a brick arch in 66 next (a Derby built Johnson 0-6-0). She's out, Mail".

Most of these extra jobs came on the night turn of duty. Whilst busy cleaning, the night foreman's voice was liable to be heard suddenly ringing out for whoever he had picked out. "Donald! help Stan Charlton put on a set of brake blocks" or, "Get up the golden stairs and give the coalman a hand", which meant going up on the coaling stage and loading 10cwt. tubs with coal. When the cry "Right for coal" sounded from below, the tubs were pushed out and the coal tipped into the waiting tenders below. Often when a coalman went sick, a young cleaner would be sent solo on this job for a month, at times shovelling 18 tons of coal a shift. Every ton loaded in excess of that figure was paid for at the bonus rate of 6d a ton, but shovelling this tonnage, plus the pushing and tipping of the tubs, and brushing the floors etc. was virtually the maximum a man could do. Neither the body nor the purse got very fat out of that particular bonus scheme – and were they glad to return to cleaning!

The early twenties saw disputes in the coal fields and the cleaners were continually putting down reserve coal stacks, and picking them up again. They found that using a chipping hammer and the job of walling the stack was no mugs game.

The 1920's saw much industrial strife and unemployment; in fact it is doubtful if any other generation of enginemen 'went through the mill' in quite the same way as did the young engine cleaner of the early 1920's. Growing up from schoolboys into adolescence during the 1914-1918 war, and all that that meant, their lives were dogged by the spectre of unemployment and the depression of the 30's which was the culmination of probably the grimmest period to hit enginemen during their history. Men entering the service of the Somerset and Dorset Joint Railway as engine cleaners around that time, took anything from 20 to 30 years to become appointed drivers. During this period of depression, junior cleaners were usually stood off work at the end of each summer service through lack of traffic, and were usually unemployed through the winter until the commencement of the following year's summer season. With many men chasing few jobs, discipline was strict. Consequently the men would rally round to cover for a workmate who had the misfortune to become involved in a slight contretemps – probably through no fault of his own. Because management had no second thought about sacking men at that time a tremendous sense of comradeship and loyalty built up amongst the workers. One of many stories that I heard in the mess room at Bath, illustrates this well.

Bill Lake, the Gasman, looked proudly up at the three new burner lamps he had fitted to the gas pipe hanging down from the shed roof just outside the enginemen's mess room — and the three inverted mantles, peeping through the glass bowl, winked back at him. Bill had received several complaints that this area in the shed was dimly lit. "That should stop the moaning", thought Bill, as he toddled homewards. 'Bill' Walker (or Johnny Walker as he was always known) was the middle turn call boy that day, and one of his duties, when daylight faded, was to turn on the gas lights in the shed. This was done by hooking a long rod into the rings of the pivoted 'on-off' switch, and pulling the rod down, whereupon the mantles would spring into light. Arriving outside the mess room, Johnny's rod went up and felt the resistance as the hook engaged the ring. He gave a slight tug, but, to his utter dismay, the new lamp fell to the ground with a crash, glass and mantles disintegrating in front of his eyes. Johnny looked in horror at the remnants of the circular green bulb holders together with the projecting piece of gas pipe sticking upwards from its centre. His eyes darted back and forth expecting someone suddenly to appear and start a hue and cry, but the shed seemed deserted. In a moment of panic, he grasped the protruding pipe lifting it up like an open umbrella, and headed out of the bottom shed door, down and across to the banks of the River Avon which flowed behind the engine shed. Here, like the sword 'Excalibur', he swung the lamp around his head, hurling it into the centre of the river. However, compared with Arthurian legends, no hand clothed in 'mystic white' rose to receive it on this occasion, but it went under just the same, and Johnny returned to the shed to pick up as much glass as he could find. Whilst thus engaged he spotted a gang of cleaners enjoying the warmth of a footplate. Climbing into the cab, he poured out his tales of woe, whereupon all adjourned to the scene. Hard brooms were secured, and the roadways and pits were brushed clean and the tell-tale debris picked up in shovels and dispatched outside, over the top of the coal road sleepers. Next a hose was obtained to wash away every scrap of evidence. Finally a mixture of fine sand and coal dust was scattered all around, and the intrepid gang tramped around on this for a few minutes, before leaving the scene. But the next morning the balloon went up!

Just after nine o'clock, Bill Lake arrived through the bottom shed door. His workshop was nearby and he glanced up toward the place where his lovely new lamp had once been. His look of pride turned at once to one of disbelief; no spanking new lamp was to be seen. He gave a gulp and hurried to see the cleaners' foreman Lew Chalker — who had recently replaced the retired Tom Wells — to report the missing item. Lew went back with him to look and both examined the brick floor for any signs of the lamp, but nary a sliver of glass or paint was to be seen. "I should report it to the shedmaster", said Lew. "Only thing you can do", Bill replied, and off he went. When Johnny Walker — whose turn of duty started at 11 am — arrived, he was told to report to Mr. Whitaker the shedmaster. On arrival he found Bill Lake already there telling his story. Mr. Whitaker asked Johnny for his version of what happened. Fearful of losing his job Johnny denied breaking the lamp, saying he had not even seen a new lamp. Cross examination brought no results and they both left Mr. Whitaker's office awaiting further developments. As they passed through the shed door Bill Lake, looking as though he would like to eat Johnny said, "You B. . . . . . little liar", and in fact every time he saw Johnny ever afterwards he repeated those words. The cleaning gang now came under the inquisition, and every time they were caught alone by Lew Chalker, he would whisper quietly, "Now lads, what happened to that lamp?". "Don't know", they would reply. "Come on, just tell me what happened, no one will know you said anything, I give you my word". But the stock answer in the finish was, "Don't believe a lamp was ever put up". Both sides in this argument knew that the other was aware of what had happened. But to a man the cleaners would admit nothing. In time the incident was forgotten, but there was no doubt in the cleaners' minds that had the case been proved against him, Johnny would have been dismissed.

The shedmaster at Bath who also held the appointment of Locomotive Superintendent for the S&DJR then, and for some years after, was A. H. Whitaker, he was the son of A. W. Whitaker, who had been the Joint Line's resident Locomotive Superintendent at Highbridge between 1889-1911. Harry Whitaker was a stern disciplinarian but he had a keen sense of humour, which the following anecdote concerning him illustrates — in addition to highlighting the pressure put on S&D motive power on busy summer Saturdays.

In the running foreman's office one Saturday afternoon at the height of a summer service during the 1920's, Driver Jack Wells and his mate arrived to work a down special to Bournemouth. "What engine have we got?" he enquired. "No. 78." (a Deeley 4-4-0 built at Derby in 1907) replied the list clerk Arthur Polden. "I'm not taking her", said Jack emphatically. "I reported her yesterday not fit for passenger work". "Well that's what you're booked", replied Arthur with an air of finality. "We'll see about that" said Jack. "Where is Mr. Whitaker?" "In his office", he was told. "Right", said Jack, dumping his lunch basket on the floor, "I'll soon get this altered". He stumped out of the door and turned towards A.H.'s office. In a few minutes he returned, his face wreathed in smiles. "Come on Chris," he said to his fireman. "Mr. Whitaker told me I can take any engine in the shed". So picking up his basket, he walked out, crossed the courtyard, and entered the shed. The afternoon sun streamed through the shed windows along the full length of number two road, which was empty, as was number three road. But at the bottom of number five road stood a 'Scotty' 0-6-0 which caught their eye, her smokebox door wide open — and stacked against it, a pile of boiler tubes, chalk white with fur. The only hope now left was number four shed road (there was no number one road inside the S&D shed at Bath) and there in splendid isolation stood the one and only engine in steam, No. 78. Jack and his mate sorrowfully made their way towards her.

The S&D Joint lines' locomotive inspector during most of the twenties was Inspector Wells, who had previously worked on another joint line — the Midland and Great Northern. A strong disciplinarian, he rather took this to extreme at times by going out of his way to catch men out during the course of their duties. From the time he stepped into the cab his eyes were everywhere, and woe betide the fireman whose boiler front and cab paint were not spotless and the lamps trimmed and glasses shining. When his roving eyes could find nothing wrong, he would fix them on the screwed thread of the hand-brake, at its base, where it disappeared into the floor of the tender. If the handbrake had been used only two minutes after it had been wiped silver clean, it made no difference. "Fireman wipe that tender brake screw thread, it's a disgrace". The next thing would be rules. "Fireman you are working a goods train, what would you do if you looked back and saw the train was parted?" — and so the mental gymnastics would go on until thankfully the inspector dismounted from the footplate. It was freely acknowledged however that nobody knew the official rule book like he did and he was much respected for that. Another thing not endearing him to the footplatemen was his constantly trying to increase the maximum loadings as laid down for the various classes of S&D locomotives, but with little success — as we shall see later on — the engines being already grossly over-loaded as things were.

In the early twenties the Bath cleaning gangs were mixed up with Inspector Wells quite a bit. The Bedwas coal supplied to the S&D during the 1914-18 war years and paid for by the government had ended in 1921 and had been replaced by coal of various types from many places at home and abroad. In consequence, a period of coal testing now began. One locomotive that was used for these trials was rebuilt Johnson 4-4-0 No. 18, and the method of testing was as follows.

The tender was first emptied and swept clean with a brush. The engine would then be positioned under the coal stage tip, and Lew Chalker would fetch Inspector Wells, who would climb the stairs to the loading deck, and weigh two ten-hundred weight tubs of the coal being tested. This was then tipped onto the tender and used for lighting up. Coal testing was spread over three days as a rule and each morning under the watchful eyes of Inspector Wells the coal was weighed before tipping. The train selected for these tests was usually the 10.25 am passenger train from Bath to Bournemouth West, and the return trip the 3.30 pm Bournemouth to Bath.

On arrival back at Bath the engine was disposed over a pit which had been cleaned of any previous clinker. First the engine was positioned just short of the smokebox ash heap. Then instead of throwing the ashes on to the ground as would normally be done the fireman shovelled them into a large two handled basket. This was carried by two cleaners to a portable weighing machine, where Inspector Wells would record its weight. After the smokebox had been emptied the engine fire was cleaned following which the ashes and clinker in the pit had to be lifted and weighed. On arrival at Bath shed on the last day of the trials the engine would be dropped down number two road under the coal tip, but this time the coaling procedure was reversed. The remaining coal on the tender now had to be thrown upward from the tender into an empty tub positioned above on the stage. Two men in the 'hole' would shovel the coal to the back of the tender from where two men would throw the coal into the tub. Every scrap had to be brushed up before Inspector Wells would weigh the result. The engine was then coaled as in every day fashion, and another coal test was over.

Chapter Two

THE CALL BOY COMETH

It might appear that as yet there has been little or no reference to the working of locomotives out on the road. But many young passed cleaners of this era were doing just about everything except operating locomotives, and the more mundane and less well documented tasks described in these first two chapters were their lot for many years, and as such are worth recording, I feel, as they were certainly part and parcel of the Somerset and Dorset scene.

In the previous chapter 'The Call Boy' was briefly mentioned and he was then an essential part of the railway scene. In the old days it was usual for engine crews to be called — or 'knocked up' if at night — for their turns of duty, and this was the job of the junior cleaners, designated 'call boys'. At Bath shed the night call boy had the busiest shift. Coming on duty at 10.00 pm his first task was to fill the messroom kettles and make up the fire, and then walk up to the nearby Bath, Queen Square station — renamed Green Park after Nationalisation — to get the night guards list from the traffic department. This list contained the names and addresses of the guards and their signing on times. He would then return to the loco shed where the running foreman would supply a similar list of drivers and firemens names together with their addresses and signing on times. The first call was on the midnight banking men, who would be called at 11 pm, and for the rest of the night the call boy would be scuttling backwards and forwards all over the town. At about 2 am there would be time for a cup of tea and a sandwich in the mess room, and then off again.

In the winter, and when it was pouring with rain, the call boy would frequently call into the waiting room whilst at the station and collect all the unwanted newspapers. Then two would be opened up at their centre pages and wrapped tightly round his legs — they never got wet. When the east winds blew, a newspaper similarly placed across his chest and the east wind had to go around instead of through him.

Johnny Walker became, in his way, one of the many characters that the S&D produced, and life was never dull when he was around. He was a call boy at Bath for a long time during the 1920's — in between being regularly stood off work during the winter months because of the seasonal reduction in traffic. Johnny was known to every member of the Bath City police force because he gave the constables news of the whereabouts of their sergeant, plus the information of night prowlers that he may have seen on his travels. One summer's night at about 3 am he came upon a seventeen stone policeman sitting on a low wall, in his bare feet, with socks and boots lying on the pavement. "My poor feet are killing me," said the constable. "Well if they don't, the sergeant will," said Johnny. "I've just passed him in Moorland Road." "Blast the sergeant," said the copper as he reached for his socks. One of Johnny's refuges on wet nights was a shelter situated right at the base of a tall chimney at May's brickyard, (later Bath Victoria Brick and Tile Company) which had a siding served by the S&D. One Freddie Frackell, fed the fires there by lifting some covers that circled the top of the baking chambers, and occasionally dropping a small shovelful of coal down on to the fires. This shelter was in fact just a lean-to structure, but it had an open fire which gave a warm welcome on unfriendly nights. A small table and a couple of forms comprised its furnishings. If it was raining, Freddie would have an old overcoat warming by the fire for Johnny to change into. But some nights he could hardly get into the building by reason of four or five burly policemen being there, sometimes dozing or, more often, having a game of solo. "Seen the sergeant about anywhere, nipper?" they would ask, and Johnny would let them know when and where he had last seen him. Passing the Lower Weston police station one night the sergeant was at the gate and he called out to Johnny, "Seen any of my chaps?" Johnny said "No", but thought to himself, "But I know where they are." "Well" said the sergeant, "If you see any of them, tell them to come at once, I've just had notice of a burglary." He then went back inside as his telephone started ringing. Johnny hurried to May's brickyard, and sure enough, there they were all stretched out. "Come on," said Johnny, "the sergeant's hopping mad, there's been a burglary over at Weston and he wants you". "That's a fine tale" said one, "I know what he wants," said another meaningfully. It was Freddie Frackell who persuaded them that Johnny was in earnest, "I know when the nipper is joking and when he isn't; if I were you I would hurry over to the police station and find out what's up". This they reluctantly did, and admitted next night that Johnny had saved their bacon. The 'Sarge' had just about threatened to report them.

On another occasion when Johnny went to call the midnight banking men he found he was running ahead of schedule and decided to shelter for a spell in the Drill Hall entrance situated in the Lower Bristol Road. It had been a very hot summer's day, and its warmth still radiated from the brick wall that Johnny rested against. He was about to move off again when he noticed Charlie Southwood, mine host of the Newbridge Inn, situated in a street named Brougham Hayes (a turning off the Lower Bristol Road) come to the front door. He was the epitome of mine host. Fat, rubicund face, and portly corporation covered by a white apron, under which he tucked his hands flapping it up and down. He also had flat feet, and these gave him quite a waddle when he walked. Glancing furtively up and down the street he walked up to some bushes in a narrow garden, and bent down to each of them in turn. Johnny, much intrigued by this, but with no more time to spare, shot off and called his banking men, and then returned quietly down Brougham Hayes. Arriving back at this place of mystery he felt around the first bush and his hand touched the neck of a pint bottle of beer. The second bush delivered another. Taking his spoils with him Johnny hurried to 'the loco' and found Harry Waldron, the tuber, in his cabin. "Want a drink Harry?" asked Johnny. Harry's arm was already outstretched, and a half a pint had gurgled down his throat before he enquired, "Where did you get them?". Johnny told him. "Ho! Ho!" guffed Harry. "I'd love to see the copper coming down and looking through those bushes!" and his laughter only stopped to let the other half pint roll down his throat. "Good boy", he said, as Johnny started to leave. "Keep your eyes open for Charlie putting some more out". Two nights later Johnny watched Charlie go through the same performance; and he and Harry did ditto. Later in the night Johnny was walking quietly down Brougham Hayes when a hand descended on his shoulder and a deep voice said, "What did you do with it?" Johnny squirmed round and saw a burly 'copper' glaring down at him. "Do with what?", asked Johnny. "You know what," said the 'copper', "Out of the bushes". "Bushes? I don't know anything about bushes", said Johnny. "Look, I've to call a set of men for the 4.40 am goods". "Now look here", said the copper, tightening his grip on Johnny's shoulder and shaking him like a terrier with a rat, "If I catch you near here again you'll be sorry you were ever born", and with a thrust which nearly dislocated Johnny's neck, he sent him with a flying start down the road. From that night onwards Johnny Walker passed Charlie Southwood's Inn on the opposite side of the road. The policeman got his pint, and Harry Waldron went back to drinking tea.

Talking of tea, Johnny would regularly make his way into the bakeries; particularly the establishments of the 'Co-op', and 'Viners', usually just about the time that the bakers had made their tea in the middle of the night. He was always invited to have a jar, for in the bakehouses there were no cups; and an old earthenware 1 lb. jar was the vessel used, and very nice too. Donald Beale often told me how thankful he was for this information.

After the end of the 1926 general strike, and with the S&D authorities gradually re-engaging its men, Donald Beale voluntarily assumed the job of call boy for a while, thus placing himself in a lower grade than when he started work on the S&D seven years earlier. How this came about was that Donald and 'Pongo' May were reinstated together, Donald as a bar boy (an assistant to bar men whose job it was to clean tube plates, brick arches and renew grate firebars) and 'Pongo' as call boy. But 'Pongo' was not at all keen on all the walking about this job entailed. He was an ex

Grenadier Guardsman, and had been a prisoner of war during the last year of the 1914-18 war, and this experience had left him with bad feet. He and Donald therefore obtained the sanction of the S&D management at Bath to exchange jobs. Donald said he found calling pretty lonely compared with shed work, but on the other hand there were very few idle periods unless driver and fireman lived reasonably close to each other. Crews had to be called an hour before their signing on time and whilst some only wanted the letter box rattled, and seemed to be waiting behind the door, other individuals wanted a brass band to raise them from their slumbers, and it was sometimes quite five minutes before a gas light or perhaps the flickering flame from a candle appeared from within, and one ended up waking not only the intended person, but neighbours on either side as well who would tell the call boy where to go. In some cases the driver lived one side of the town, and his fireman a twenty minute walk on the other, and they would grumble to the running foreman if one was called five or ten minutes early. But one of Donald's colleagues came up with the solution to ease the situation. "Know what you want to do, Don?" said Lou Ricketts one day. "No" he replied. "Get a bicycle" said Lou. "I haven't got a bike and can't afford to buy one", Donald replied. "Ha" said Lou, "but I know where there is one. Do you know Welch's paper shop at the bottom of Livingstone Road?" he asked, "Yes" Donald answered, "Well the delivery boy's bike is left out all night up in the corner, I know because I've borrowed it before now." The next time he was out on nights 'calling', Donald sailed around comfortably on a bike displaying the sign, 'Welch Newsagent', and now found ample time to dive into the Co-op bakery and Messrs. Viners, for early tea and cakes. Donald said "I was just getting the hang of the job when further men were re-instated". Donald went back cleaning in shed and Johnny Walker came back and took over as call boy again — plus Welch's bike, naturally.

One of the jobs allotted to the call boys was keeping the coal bucket filled in the office of Mr. Whitaker, the Shedmaster. On one occasion Mrs. Stainer (who was the last of the woman engine cleaners employed by the S&D during the first world war) whose duty it was to clean Mr. Whitaker's office and light his fire, complained bitterly to Donald about her difficulty in getting the fire to burn properly. This was not really surprising as the coal used was usually obtained from the nearest engine, and the Somerset and Dorset was supplied with slow burning Welsh soft coal which Mr. Whitaker's fireplace was evidently not suitably draughted to burn. However, engines in the adjacent Midland Railway shed burnt hard North country coal eminently more suitable for warming the cockles of any superintendent's heart, so henceforth it was from this source that the call boys obtained coal for Mr. Whitaker's office fire. However that gentleman was quick to notice the improvement in the general warmth of his office and realised that this was due to the 'brightly burning North coal' in his grate. He obviously knew where the coal was coming from, but as it was tantamount to stealing from the Midland Railway Company, he thought he had better put a tentative question to Mrs. Stainer with the eventual aim of reverting to his own company's fuel. Catching her in his office one morning he asked "Where is all that North coal coming from, Mrs. Stainer?" But her reply was to cause him sober reflection. "If I were you, sir," she said, "I wouldn't ask that question until the summer comes." With the question of his bodily comfort in the balance, Mr. Whitaker realised that the matter required tactful handling. "I suggest", he said, eyes twinkling, "that it would be fair exchange if for every bucket of North coal obtained from the Midland, we reciprocate with a similar amount of our Welsh." Well the North coal kept coming all right, but I am afraid that what Mr. Whitaker didn't know was that the first bucket of S&D Welsh that went in return, was the last.

Chapter Three

REMINISCENCES OF SOMERSET AND DORSET LOCOMOTIVES
FROM THE FOOTPLATE

In the early twenties the engines on which cleaners at Bath received their firing instructions, and later their first firing turns, were the Fox Walker 0-6-0 saddle tanks, first introduced in 1874, and much rebuilt in later years. In addition to shunting, these engines were used for banking trains from Bath up to the Combe Down Tunnel entrance, and from Radstock up to Masbury Summit. The 'Bath Banker' was the preserve of the 'old boys', as it was considered a light job for them to finish their later years of service — the retiring age being seventy. Jack Rainey, Bob Baker, George Darke, and Freddie James were drivers in the banking gang during the early twenties, and they introduced many a young man to his first, probably illicit, but ever memorable experience on the footplate, including the rigours of passing through the infamous quarter mile long single line bore of Devonshire Tunnel during the 1 in 50 climb out of Bath.

One 1920 summer's day Donald Beale overheard Freddie James's fireman — Alfie Banks cursing his luck at having to prepare his engine for duty up at the extreme end of 'No. 9 road', and having to walk so far in order to fill the sand boxes. "I'll do them for you", Donald piped up, "if you will ask Freddie James if I can come and ride up behind the 7.55 pm goods". "You're on," said Alf, and at 7.45 pm, Donald was inside the Midland stone built coal stage, waiting for the banker to draw the 7.55 pm goods train out of 'the Dorset' marshalling yards, and down the siding far enough to clear the crossover road points and exit to the main line. In a few minutes he heard the whistle of the banker — Fox Walker 0-6-0 No. 3 — as she whistled for the ground signal which protected the entrance to the S&D loco, and the ground signal on Albert Road bridge which gave right of way into the Midland loco shed and carriage sidings. When Donald mounted the engine Freddie James was still looking out over his side watching the guard unhook No. 3's coupling. With a clang it fell, and in the same instant came the 'right away crows' from the train engine. Freddie grasped the whistle handle and the piercing 'crows' that answered the train engine nearly deafened Donald. Sliding his hand from the whistle to the regulator, Freddie opened it to the first valve, then looked across and saw Donald for the first time, and a grin appeared over his face. "Hello, you coming with us then?" and without waiting for a reply, quickly shut the regulator and brought the reversing lever back four notches towards mid-gear, before restoring the regulator onto the first valve position. Donald voiced the feeling of many a steam man's first ride on the footplate when he said, "the sensation of the motion was wonderful: the exhaust from the chimney was beating down with that distinctive smell of smoke, warm steam, and a whiff of hot oil. The thump of the motions and the vibrations in the floorboards had me enthralled, and the passing scenery as viewed from a moving footplate seemed so different".

Whilst Donald was thus filling his gaze, Alfie Banks, the fireman, had been busy. At the first exhaust beats he had turned to the back of the cab and taken down the pricker which lay horizontally across the back of the bunker on two large brackets. These also supported the dart, and clinker shovel. Then he opened the top door of the firehole and slid the pricker through the fire, breaking up any coal that had plimmed and caked. This done he withdrew the fire iron and replaced it, glowing red hot and filling the cab with hot fumes. By now they were turning southwards away from the Midland and onto the S&D single line, and as they approached Bath Single Line Junction Box (this box and a Midland Junction box were replaced in 1924 by Bath Junction box) Alfie stepped across the cab to catch the banking staff, which he did with ease.

The banking staff allowed bank engines to assist goods trains as far as the entrance to Combe Down Tunnel, the summit of the climb out of Bath. Here, having seen the rear brake van disappear into the tunnel, the bank engine returned to Bath Junction to surrender the staff. Fourteen minutes were allowed for the bank engine to depart with the train and arrive back light at Bath.

Freddie James grasped the regulator and gave the little tank second valve, and the blast from the chimney made the fire dance and develop into a white heat. Periodically Alf sprayed four shovelfuls of coal, one in each corner of the firebox, and with each shovelful a burst of smoke appeared from the chimney and disappeared as quickly, leaving just a slight grey haze at the chimney top, an indication of good combustion. As they passed May's brickyard Alfie told Donald to "Slip four round her, Kid". Opening up the firehole door, Donald's first glance into the firebox nearly blinded him for the fire was now a sheet of white hot flames dancing like a field of daffodils in a breeze. Swinging the shovel, he lacked the flick of the wrist that Alfie possessed and the coal fell in a solid mass in the small firebox, and boiler pressure soon began to drop. Donald began to suspect that firing a locomotive needed more than muscle. Approaching Maple Grove bridge they were beginning to slow, so Freddie James dropped her down a 'couple of nicks' and the engine's exhaust increased in power. Meanwhile, Alfie was drawing his handkerchief from his pocket and told Donald to put his over his mouth. Shortly afterwards they were enveloped in the dreaded Devonshire Tunnel and the exhaust was suddenly muffled as though a blanket had been placed over the chimney.

The glare of the fire reflected off the back of the cab, and almost immediately smoke was crowding in. Freddie was indistinct over in his corner, and the heat was now getting more oppressive, with sulphurous fumes filtering through Donald's handkerchief, beginning to sear his throat. Alfie motioned him to crouch down in the corner by the damper handle and he found this a little easier, all the same his skin was beginning to prickle with the heat, and he began to wish he had not been so keen to ride on 'the banker'. CLANG! from the other side of the cab, and a louder almost deafening muffled bark — Freddie had dropped the reverser into full forward gear. All that could be seen on the footplate by now was a river of smoke pouring into the blazing furnace through the firebox opening between the top and the bottom doors. The atmosphere was one of acrid smoke and stifling heat and Donald, not being used to it, was beginning to feel quite desperate — when suddenly the muffled bark of the exhaust changed to four clear beats, and amid the swirling clouds of smoke belching out from the tunnel's mouth, daylight streamed into the cab. Donald, rising from his knees, and saying a prayer of thankfulness on the way up, leaned over the cab side and gulped in lungfuls of fresh air, whilst wiping the sweat from face, neck and ears. "Well, how did you like Devonshire Tunnel?" shouted Alf. "Not much", Donald replied. "You ought to ride with us when we get a real hot one", said Alf "it wasn't at all bad this time". Freddie looked across and said sympathetically, "Never mind, you'll get used to it, the first time is always the worst". As they passed underneath the overbridge in the beautiful Lyncombe Vale, Freddie closed the regulator, and opened the steam brake valve, bringing them gently to a stand. As they watched the train disappearing into Combe Down Tunnel. the guard came out onto his platform and gave them a parting wave, as he vanished into the smoke filled blackness again.

Freddie swung the reversing lever into back gear, closed the steam brake valve and the merest touch of the regulator sent them rolling back down the 1 in 50 towards Devonshire Tunnel, where he turned on the blower, and closed the regulator. The injector was working at full bore, for the water in the boiler was low, Alfie having mortgaged it to keep the steam pressure high during the climb. This could be done in safety as when Freddie had stopped the engine still just on the 1 in 50 gradient, the water in the boiler flowed back over the firebox end and thus saved the lead fusible plugs in the crown of the firebox from becoming uncovered. Smoke was still pouring out of Devonshire Tunnel, visual evidence of their passage a few minutes earlier. With a shrill warning note of the whistle they entered, but what a difference from the up trip! As the engine gained speed, Donald watched the daylight disappearing from the end of the tunnel as it curved away. When the last flicker of daylight disappeared he turned and looked through the bunker spectacle plate and saw the first gleam of daylight gradually enlarging until the engine shot out into the open and coasted down the straight length to Claude Avenue Bridge, round May's curve, and over the GWR London — Bristol main line and back to the shunting Yard at Bath Single Line Junction, surrendering the banking staff in the process. The young Donald Beale thanked Freddie and Alf for the ride, and stealthily made his way unobserved past the running foreman back to his mates.

The Fox Walker tanks did most of their duties at Radstock, banking the through goods trains at night, and working the collieries at Writhlington, and Midsomer Norton, plus the stone quarries at Moorewood, Binegar and Winsor Hill. These engines were liked by their crews, and in fact some preferred them to their replacements, the S&D 0-6-0 tanks of the LMS standard '3F' design. Seven of these, Nos. 19-25 were obtained from W. G. Bagnall Ltd. between December 1928 and February 1929, although in fact the last Fox Walker tank was not withdrawn until 1934. But like all things in life, the Fox Walkers were not perfect, the positioning of the steam brake control valve in the centre of the cab being a poor feature, and their replacements were far more convenient in that respect. Naturally the driver had to have his head over the cabside during shunting operations in order to see the shunter's hand signals properly. But on a Fox Walker, when receiving the stop signal, although the driver was able to reach the regulator and close it satisfactorily he had to turn inwards and lean right over to operate the steam brake control valve. Bearing in mind the care required to brake loose coupled wagons — each seemingly with a mind of its own — without causing a 'breakaway', plus the need for constant observation outside the footplate, the driver's dilemma when shunting with one of these engines can be better appreciated. Some of the more thoughtful and experienced firemen used to operate the steam brake at the driver's behest for which the 'old boys' used to be most grateful.

Young S&D passed cleaners quickly had experience on the 'Scotties'. These were Johnson 0-6-0 goods engines and were nicknamed 'Scotties' because the first batch was built by Neilson of Glasgow in 1878: all were rebuilt during their lifetime. Besides freight duties they did much main line work on fast trains. Now, there was a ride for a young passed cleaner, and even now there are some ex-S&D enginemen who still shudder at the memory of being coupled from Bath to Evercreech Junction to the down 'Diner' as it was unofficially named by S&D men, the forerunner of the Manchester — Bournemouth 'Pines Express'. There were two superheated 4-4-0s of standard Midland class '2' design (483 class) operating on the S&D line in 1919, Nos. 70 and 71. They were normally berthed overnight at Branksome shed with one of them working the 10.20 am up 'Diner' from Bournemouth West over the 71½ miles from Bournemouth to Bath, and returning in the afternoon with the corresponding down 'Diner', whilst the other engine worked the 11.40 am up and the 4.00 pm down passenger trains. Assisting No. 70 on the down 'Diner' to Evercreech Junction, a 'Scottie' seemed dwarfed — it must be remembered that these blue 4-4-0s were big passenger engines by S&D standards then. Their exhaust seemed to roar down on the crew of the 'Scottie' up front, and their puny efforts to keep away from the 4-4-0 seemed hopeless as they charged out of Bath. The 'Scottie's' driver would shut off steam after entering Combe Down Tunnel, and a little while after, the driver of No. 70 did the same, whereafter they coasted briefly down to Midford to give up the single line tablet. But from here both engines would be opened up again. The little 'Scottie', lurching and rocking, would scuttle along the winding undulating stretch from Midford to Radstock, shaking up its fireman so much that every other shovelful of coal missed the firehole, and the speed of the train whipped the small coal off the tender into the eyes and ears of her crew. One attempt to combat this was to open the injector feed water valve, lean over the side with a bucket dangling on the end of a piece of wagon sheet tie, and hold it under the injector overflow pipe until full, when it was drawn up and the contents flung over the tender. Unfortunately, when the firemen started to draw the bucket up, there was often a violent lurch from the engine, and the bucket would strike a chair key or rail, and bounce and bump around spilling the water, so the tie was drawn in and a fresh attempt made. Climbing the long bank up to Masbury Summit was not too bad, but (assuming the assisting engine was not detached at Masbury Station) the fast descent to Evercreech Junction — which was the first stop — was like a trip on the 'Giant Racer'. It was a case of hanging on for dear life as the 0-6-0 lurched first one way and then the other around the curves during the headlong flight down the long 1 in 50 bank. Invariably as they shot into Winsor Hill Tunnel, the floorboards would be displaced by the air pressure inside, accompanied by an unpleasant shower of coal dust, after which almost immediately they would be speeding down and across the high curving Charlton viaduct into Shepton Mallet, with the crew looking down into the green fields far below, and only a small brick wall between them, and wondering if the 'Scottie' would come out of the curve all right, or go over the top into oblivion. But before there was time to think about it they would be off the viaduct, and tearing through Shepton Mallet station at 60 mph the signalman at the end window of his box watching their swaying progress with grave interest. Then into the final stage as with ever quickening speed they came bucketing down through Cannards Grave and into the 'S' bend at Prestleigh viaduct. But despite all this the crew of the 'Scottie' had tasted victory as they came to a stand at Evercreech Junction, to unhook quickly whilst No. 70 took water. And when they came back across the road to stand alongside the 4-4-0 the smiles of the train engine crew were for the two black faces which grinned back at them. But the young cleaners cum firemen enjoyed the glory of working the 'Diner', and later, back in shed cleaning again, they described their exploits as though they were old hands at the game.

Due to a shortage of freight locomotives on the S&D in the early twenties, various ideas were tried out to increase the effectiveness of the available motive power, particularly of the six 2-8-0s then operating on the line. One such idea, put forward and subsequently tried out by Inspector Wells, was for the little 'Scotties' to work some of the Bath — Evercreech Junction duties rostered for the 2-8-0s. For example a 'Scottie' would set off from Bath Goods Yard with a full 2-8-0 load of 172 quarters on which rather imprecise conversion scale would equal around 550 tons, and a 2-8-0, instead of heading the train, reversed its role and banked it, not merely up to Combe Down Tunnel as was normally the case, but all the way to Masbury Summit some 18 miles from Bath. Thereafter the 2-8-0 would return light to Bath ready to repeat this procedure as necessary on southbound freights. Less banking was required on northbound freight trains up to Masbury since in the make-up of these there were more empty mineral wagons than was the case with southbound freights. However, banking assistance was normally available from Evercreech Junction up to Binegar if required, which was more often the case with the night freights. By deploying its motive power in this way, the S&D authorities hoped to move a greater number of heavy freight trains more economically over the Mendips.

The driver of one such trip was Walter Smith, of Bath shed, a dapper little churchman, with lovely white whiskers. On the footplate he would sing like a lark, hymns and such songs as, "He's a fine old English gentleman". His fireman on this occasion was Stan Shellard, a young passed cleaner. Well, they got up to Masbury all right and were approaching Prestleigh on the 1 in 50 descent to Evercreech Junction when Walter realised his brakes were not holding the train back, even though an extra vacuum fitted brake van was attached next to the 'Scottie' to give increased brake power, so he opened the whistle full and left it open. Stanley went over to his food box and took out his sandwiches and to Walter's astonishment, started eating. He said afterwards, "I thought I might as well eat them, as let them get wasted". Fortunately their 'whistle' had been heard at 'the Junction' and the road cleared through to Wincanton and Walter came safely to rest somewhere near Cole, some three miles past their intended destination — and so did this idea. With S&D freight trains it was not just a question of load haulage. The 'Scotties' brake power when descending the hills proved insufficient resulting in the 2-8-0s being speedily restored to their former role.

Almost as uncomfortable in their riding as the 'Scotties' were the rebuilt Fowler 0-6-0 goods engines originally built in 1874. Their Stirling 'Great Northern' type cabs sloped down rather steeply at the sides, and tall men like the 6'2'' Donald Beale suffered headaches galore from standing up too quickly and bumping their head on the cab roof. However, these engines were rarely seen at Bath after 1920, being mainly employed between Highbridge, Templecombe and Bournemouth. The 'Scotties' were preferred for the arduous Mendips section due to their superiority over the Fowlers with regards to steaming and braking power on unfitted freight trains.

A larger and more popular 0-6-0 at that time were the 'Bulldogs', as they were known by S&D crews. The first batch of these Derby built Johnson engines came to the line in 1896 and the second batch built by Neilson and Company arrived in 1902. Compared to other S&D engines they had a large firehole, and when firing, the heat radiating from the firebox would scorch the fireman's hands and face — but they taught them to fire quickly! All these engines were rebuilt at various times and Donald remembers vividly when one of the 'Bulldogs', No. 66 returned from Highbridge works after being rebuilt, in 1920. He told me, "I can see her now as she dropped down on number four ash pit road at Bath shed, in her spotless coat of blue paint. The first of the class to be fitted with a Belpaire firebox, she was one of the best, and very free steaming". In fact in this form they were similar to the Midland standard class '3' saturated steam goods engines and were very popular with engine crews. Some men preferred them on all but the heaviest jobs to the Fowler standard Midland class '4' 0-6-0 design that largely succeeded them on the main line in 1922. Primarily goods engines, they nevertheless performed usefully on passenger trains when required. During the 1920's and 1930's if Bath Shed's rather limited stock of passenger engines had given out during the busy summer season, a 'Bulldog' would go off quite gaily with a seaside day excursion bound for Bournemouth 71½ miles away or even Weymouth which was over 90 miles off. These splendid Johnson loco's showed an unforgettable doggedness on heavy freight trains. When launching themselves on to a bank, the Woof! Woof! of their exhaust would gradually sharpen to a pound as they were opened out, and often one of the four beats per revolution was almost inaudible. At night under conditions of heavy pounding, continuous streams of tiny sparks could be seen issuing from the chimney, and a lurid glow coming from the ashpan. The fire would be white-hot, sending a blinding shaft of reflected light shooting into the night when the fireman was at work. The 'Bulldogs' thrived on this treatment. With the regulator shut these little slide valve engines would coast along freely and comfortably — an attribute noticeably missing in their piston valve-fitted Fowler successors.

Of course the largest locomotives at work on the S&D in the early twenties were the six highly individual Derby built 2-8-0 freight locomotives, designed especially for the line by Sir Henry Fowler, C.M.E. of the Midland Railway. Introduced in 1914 they were numbered 80-85 and were followed in 1925 by a further five of basically similar design, built by Robert Stephenson & Company, Nos. 86-90. This second series was instantly recognisable to lineside observers by virtue of being fitted with 5'3" diameter boilers compared with 4'9⅛" of the Derby built engines. However in due course the 1925 engines required reboilering, and as their 5'3" diameter boilers were non standard, they began to acquire 4'9⅛" boilers similar to those of their older sisters. This change over was completed by the end of 1955 and thereafter the outward appearance of all eleven engines was very similar. But on the footplate the 1914 series were driven from the right hand side and the 1925 engines from the left hand.

As built, the original series were fitted with tender cabs to facilitate the high proportion of tender-first running then necessary with these engines between Templecombe and Bath (to which section they were normally confined) due to the lack of adequate size turntables to accommodate them. This problem was not finally resolved until 1935 when the inadequate turntable at Bath was replaced by a 60ft version, although, however, the tender cabs had all been removed by 1920. The usual explanation for their removal — unpleasant draughts on the footplate and the liability of the cab to fill with smoke and fumes in the tunnels — requires some amplification. In fact it appears there were several factors weighing against them. Firstly there was difficulty in handling fire irons on the footplate. To get any fire-iron down off the tender, through the small tender access door in the tender front and into the firebox, needed considerable manipulation. The fire-irons were necessarily lengthy to cope with the 2-8-0s 9' long firebox, and this feature, coupled with the restricted space available on the footplate due to the tender cab, made their handling a laborious procedure. It was even more difficult replacing them on to the tender, red hot a quarter of the way up the shaft after use in the fire. Exclamations, none of them biblical, were wont to rend the air at times, especially when steaming was poor, as it often was towards the end of the day's work when they were returning tender first to Bath on an up freight from Evercreech Junction and with the fire getting dirty. In addition to this, great care had to be taken when out on the road to avoid hitting obstructions when getting down or replacing fire-irons on to the tender, due to the need to poke part of their length out through the cab side during the manoeuvre. The second factor against the tender cabs was the very small access door high up in the tender cab back plate. This was barely sufficient to get a head and arm through so making it difficult to pull forward fresh supplies of coal from the back of the tender whilst the engine was on the move and causing frustration and worry to S&D firemen.

During the 1920's the 2-8-0s had a reputation amongst footplatemen of being 'erratic steamers'. But following some hit or miss experiments with various blast pipe proportions during the 1930's an acceptable compromise was arrived at, and this criticism was rarely heard in later years when engaged in working the heavy freight and mineral trains for which they were designed. (Plus the fact that after nationalisation their maximum rostered freight loads were slightly reduced). But on the express passenger trains between Bath and Bournemouth to which they were often drafted on busy summer Saturdays after the second world war the 2-8-0s wanted very careful firing, and even so, there was often a tendency to some shortage of steam towards the end of the climb to Masbury Summit with their permitted maximum unassisted load of 10 coaches (310 tons). Indeed, this loading limit was imposed by their continuous steaming ability rather than tractive effort and their performance on these passenger trains was rarely sparkling. They also suffered throughout their lives from various problems of lubrication especially highlighted when working fast passenger trains, and evidenced by hot boxes, hot big ends, and the unearthly groaning noises sometimes heard eminating from oil starved cylinders. But that is not fair criticism really, because they were not designed for such duties and on the freight trains run over the northern half of the line where this traffic was much the heaviest, they were unsurpassed. Their ability to stop unfitted mineral trains was first class — particularly when in later years they were fitted with Ferodo brake blocks in place of the usual cast iron type originally supplied.

It was this chronic S&D complaint of 'poor braking' on heavy freight work which over the years rendered many steam types unsuitable, and indeed, lengthened the eventual life of the S&D 2-8-0s themselves. An S&D posting demanded — particularly of the larger types — that they be competent in handling both heavy passenger and freight trains. This mix of duties was ever part of the daily round of most S&D engines. For example, the 'West Country' Pacifics during their unhappy sojourn at Bath from 1951 until 1954 were never at home when working the balancing turns encountered before and after working the up and down 'Pines Express'. These were an early morning mixed freight and mail train between Bath and Bournemouth West, and an evening unfitted freight from Poole Yard to Bath. The inability of the Pacifics not only to start, but once underway to stop their trains on these duties caused several "near things" — more particularly on the normally heavy 9.25 pm Poole-Bath freight — when several times their trains all but took control of the Pacifics whilst descending the steep banks. This so unnerved some Bath drivers that after relieving Templecombe men (who had worked the 9.25 pm goods up from Poole) at Templecombe No. 2. Junction ready for the continuation of the run to Bath they would, upon finding a full load behind the tender, refuse to continue on with the train. This occurred on a good many occasions at which time the train was shunted and left behind in Templecombe Lower Yard, the Pacific continuing on to Bath either light engine or engine and guards van only. This unhappy situation contributed greatly to the decision to remove the light Pacifics from Bath shed and off everyday S&D work in 1954. Later on during the summer months of 1960/61/62 the BR 2-10-0s also regularly worked these two balancing freight workings after their 'Pines Express' duties and though vastly superior to the 'West Countrys' in braking ability were nevertheless inferior to the S&D 2-8-0s in this respect.

With regard to the use of the S&D 2-8-0s on passenger workings the first instance of this kind occurred in the mid 1920's when Driver Henry Jennings of Bath shed took one through to Bournemouth on an express passenger train. This was done to alleviate a shortage of suitable motive power. Prior to departure, Mr. Whitaker spoke to Henry, telling him not to adhere to the point-to-point timings and to take things easily. But although

Henry complied, it was still too much for the 2-8-0, and she landed up on Branksome shed with two hot big ends. Before the last war these engines were often used on heavy pigeon specials from Bath through to the Bournemouth area, but never on purely passenger work if this could possibly be avoided because they would as like as not be out of service until the hot boxes or big ends had been repaired. But as mentioned, during 'the 1950's the pail was often empty', and they were regularly employed on such trains during the summer service on Saturdays. The problem then was as much one of finding additional footplate crews as engines. These 2-8-0s were a godsend in both respects due to their ability to take 10 coaches over the Mendips unassisted. Their use in this way delighted railway enthusiasts, most of whom were unaware of the problems and worries their drivers could face, or of the increased maintenance incurred by using the 2-8-0s on such duties. The maximum speeds attained by the 2-8-0s on the summer holiday trains rarely exceeded much over 50 mph at which pace their footplate was becoming a decidedly lively environment. Of the Derby series all six engines attained over a million miles during their lifetime. The later series averaged 70,000 miles short of the million mark. To have accomplished this sort of mileage was no small achievement when the heavy nature of the work which was their daily round is considered.

The two 7'0½" superheated rebuilt Johnson 4-4-0s of Standard Midland class '2' design on the S&D, Nos. 70 and 71, were joined in 1921 by three more members of the class, Nos. 67, 68 and 69 thus virtually ousting the smaller 4-4-0s from the best passenger trains. The new 4-4-0s were made to work very hard indeed, their toughest duty by far was the working of the through Manchester — Bournemouth restaurant car express which they were rostered to haul unassisted in both directions between Bath and Bournemouth. Its normal winter loading was six coaches, which tonnage of around 190 tons, even including a restaurant car, was below the rather impractically high figure of 212 tons rostered for these modest sized high wheeled locomotives unassisted over the Mendips. But when made up to seven coaches as this train sometimes was, the tonnage generally exceeded the magic figure by just ten tons or so, whereupon the hard pressed driver requested a pilot engine from Bath to Masbury station if going south, or Evercreech Junction to Binegar on northbound runs. (During the 1920's and 30's special stops were frequently made by express trains at these locations to detach assisting engines if they had no balancing working, whereafter they returned light to Bath or Evercreech Junction respectively. This was unlike the operating practice of later years when pilot engines normally remained on the front throughout in either direction on the Bath — Evercreech Junction section, although on the very busy summer Saturdays of the early 1950's shortage of motive power sometimes occasioned a reversion to the common practice of yesteryear on northbound trains). The alternative to having a pilot engine on the 'Diner' when made up to seven coaches, was to substitute an 'Armstrong' 0-6-0 in place of the rostered

111

4-4-0. However, since seven coaches only exceeded the laid down maximum load for the 4-4-0s by just a few tons, and conveniently ignoring the fact that even at that figure the engines were already overloaded over the Mendips, our old friend Inspector Wells wanted them to do even more, and take seven coaches unassisted over the Mendips when required. This was very much despite the contrary views expressed by S&D engine crews. However in the early 1920's one of the 4-4-0s was involved in a test run between Bath and Bournemouth hauling seven coaches weighing approximately 220 tons tare and provided the opportunity for Inspector Wells hopefully to prove his point.

The driver on the southbound test run with number 68 was Jack 'Cocker' Chamberlain (so called because one of his eyes appeared to be higher than the other, giving him a cockeyed appearance) and his fireman was Bill Darke, both of Branksome shed. Prior to the departure from Bath, 'Cocker' Chamberlain and Inspector Wells — who was accompanying the crew on the footplate — had exchanged a few heated words, as they finally put their respective points of view about the practicalities of what was being asked of these small engines. Both were fiery characters when roused, and here were the perfect ingredients for a first class explosion. Despite 'Cocker's' contrary opinion Inspector Wells was adamant that the engine could do it, and 'Cocker' being overruled was in a state of high dudgeon by the time he received the guard's 'right away'.

They went away "hammer and tongs" with the seven coach train. The start out of Bath called for a high rate of steaming right from the beginning of the journey for down trains, and with many more miles of adverse grades to follow, heavy trains needed exceptionally skilful firing. They managed the climb up to Combe Down Tunnel all right — albeit on full regulator and full forward gear for much of the way — and 'Cocker' had to utilise the easier Midford — Radstock section in order to refill his boiler after this hard climb. But now came that most severe of locomotive battlefields, the Mendips: seven and a half miles of climbing up to Masbury Summit, with much of it inclined at 1 in 50. 'Cocker' poured on the power — or such as there was. As on the climb out of Bath, the engine required full regulator and practically full forward gear throughout in order to keep the train moving, let alone keep time.

With the blue 4-4-0 blasting away, the big ends banging remorselessly on the crank pins, Bill Darke worked assiduously on the fire to keep the needle of the pressure gauge up to the rated 160lb per square inch as the engine toiled away at around 12 mph on the worst stretches of this gruelling bank which seemed to go on for ever at times of stress. Doubtless in regular rounds at every two minutes or so, the firehole door was opened, firehole flap pulled down with the back of the shovel, then one shovelful of coal in each corner of the firebox, one under the door, where the fire was maintained at its thickest, and two half shovels of small coal sprayed with a flick of the wrist across the front of the box where the fire tapered to its thinnest depth: then flap up, doors partly closed onto a small piece of coal placed on the runners to prevent the firehole doors from closing completely and admitting additional secondary air to the firebox. With small coal or with an engine shy of steam, the firehole flap would usually be left up and firing done over the top. This required real artistry with the shovel. The standard method of firing the class '2's on heavy trains went very much like that, with slight variations for quality of coal or personal preference of individual firemen. Every inch of the firebed was maintained white hot and the slightest drop of the pressure gauge needle would bring about some corrective measure from a very attentive fireman.

But alas, notwithstanding such dedicated handling as just described, on the run in question, by the time Binegar was reached the locomotive was in a pretty poor state as regards steam, and the water level was low in the boiler. Inspector Wells ordered 'Cocker' Chamberlain to stop and regain some steam and water and this was the flashpoint. 'Cocker' said, "No fear! you said she could take them and take them she will." All of Inspector Wells' commands to stop were brushed aside and, with well separated exhaust beats, over the top of Masbury they went. With the gradient changing from 1 in 73 up to 1 in 50 down, into the bottom nut of the gauge glass went the water, with the regulator kept well open to save what little water there was from draining from the crown of the firebox and causing the lead plugs to fuse. All appeals to 'Cocker' to shut off or brake fell on deaf ears until after Shepton Mallet was passed by which time the use of both injectors working at full bore had restored the boiler water to a safe level. One can only imagine the sort of ride endured by the crew during that hectic descent. Like most Midland engines these 4-4-0s usually had plenty of 'knock' about them at speed, and were prone to roll somewhat at the slightest track imperfection. Still, doubtless 'Cocker' knew what he was at. One imagines also that the passengers in the train must have had a pretty stormy ride as they were hurtled down from the heights on this sinuous length — especially those in the rear coach getting all the 'wag'. Although the inspector was present, and smoking on the footplate was strictly forbidden, fireman Bill Darke took out and lit a cigarette. He said later, "I thought it was the last one I should ever have". Regarding their high speed entry into Winsor Hill Tunnel, Bill said "I thought we were going to miss it, 'till all the floorboards flew up". And by the time they were back in position 'Cocker' was at Evercreech Junction — so ended another 'good idea' and the loading for these engines was reduced from 212 to 190 tons.

Even this was a high figure for these engines to work reliably. In the winter months when gale force winds came straight off the Bristol Channel, blustering and storming amongst the Mendip Heights, hitting the sides of the train and screaming through the carriage ventilators, these 4-4-0s would sometimes be brought to a complete standstill on the harder northbound climb to Masbury, occasionally by slipping, but usually through the sheer weight of the train. If this occurred between Evercreech and Shepton Mallet, the Shepton signalman — once the running time had expired and with no 'Diner' in sight — would guess what had happened. So if an engine was available there, he would make out a wrong line order form for the driver, instructing him to run out light engine on the down line and pick up the 'Diners' fireman who would be walking towards Shepton Mallet with his driver's wrong line order form requesting assistance for his stalled train. Thereafter the light engine returned on the 'wrong road' to Shepton where the 'Diners' fireman would go to the box with his wrong line order form. Meanwhile, the light engine would cross to the up line and then be piloted by the 'Diners' fireman back to his stranded train. It only remained to couple up and double head the train over Masbury Summit to Binegar.

The choice of these Midland engines, slightly modified as an LMS standard design, led to further engines of this type being allocated for S&D main line work. Although I have attributed these details to the rebuilt Johnson 4-4-0s, they applied equally well to the post grouping development of these engines — the Fowler standard 6'9" superheated class '2P's Nos. 44, 45 and 46 with 180lb boiler pressure which were introduced on to the S&D in 1928. The Fowler engines were generally preferred to the Johnsons by most enginemen and for their size did magnificent work, but they were not a significant advance in power over the S&D passenger engines then in use, and they too had little to spare when hauling their maximum loads which were very similar to their predecessors. Both versions were loaded so impractically near to their limit that a modest drop of 10lb per square inch in boiler pressure whilst climbing the steep banks was immediately reflected by a slight falling off in speed. A drop of 15lb per square inch and there was a real risk of stalling, particularly in bad weather, despite the engine being worked with full regulator and full forward gear. Under the best of circumstances it was the norm when working the 'Diner' or the 'Pines' to turn over the top at Masbury with the boiler water level bobbing in the bottom nut of the gauge glass as the engine dipped down hill, and such boiler water as was left flowed toward the front of the boiler. There was nothing whatsoever to spare.

I have not mentioned cut off positions because the reversing gear indicator on the class '2's — and certain other screw reverse Midland types — was positioned under the driver's seat and difficult to read accurately. Therefore S&D drivers did not talk of cut off percentages in connection with Midland engines, but of working in 'the third' or 'the fourth', etc. representing the number of nicks on the indicator back from full forward gear to the mid gear position (or vice versa if working in back gear of course).

For years the Midland 4-4-0s and their LMS derivatives were the largest express passenger locomotives on the S&D. As a result the engines had to be worked very hard indeed. Only the utmost *esprit de corps* amongst footplate and maintenance staff enabled a service such as the through

Bournemouth — Manchester restaurant car express to be worked with reasonable reliability.

Loading conditions on the S&D were somewhat at variance with normal conditions existing on the Midland where rigid limitations ensured that Midland locomotives did not normally undergo the same sort of thrashing endured daily by their S&D based counterparts. I have mentioned how heavily these engines were loaded over the northern end of the line but south of Evercreech too, much hard work was demanded of them at times. The Midland 7'0½" engines were rostered to haul 290 tons between Evercreech and Corfe Mullen Junction and 260 tons thence to Bournemouth West. (The 6'9" variety were allowed slightly more over each section). But if necessary, game engine crews would take the full 290 tons, or more, unassisted throughout from 'the Junction' to Bournemouth. I have a most vivid memory of my own of mid 1950's vintage in British Railways days when, from the vantage point of my own home situated alongside Parkstone bank, I witnessed one of the 6'9" 4-4-0s No. 40634 (ex S&D 45) on one summer Saturday afternoon confidently tackling unaided the mile and a half of 1 in 60 up towards Branksome whilst hauling no less than ten LMS corridor coaches, which must have meant a gross load of around 340 tons. Banking assistance was usually readily available from Poole up to Branksome, but the 4-4-0's driver had evidently discounted this. In any case to take a banker here whether overloaded or not was "infra dig" amongst S&D engine crews excepting only dire emergency. It just was not done to take assistance from the Southern. With half a mile of 1 in 60 behind her the '2P' was going strongly past me, showing the 'white feather' at the safety valves and roaring like a grampus. Although speed was gradually falling I heard old 45 triumphantly top the bank a minute or two later at a good 10-12 miles per hour. Naturally I was interested as to how the engine came to be assigned to such a job so when I next booked on duty I made some enquiries. It transpired that the 4-4-0 had earlier left Bath in tandem with a '4F' 0-6-0, both rostered throughout to Bournemouth with this 'Saturday relief' from the North of England. But the '4F' had to retire at Evercreech with a 'hot box', and most meritoriously the Bath driver of the '2P' elected to continue the journey unaided, thus avoiding the delay that would have been occasioned by waiting for a relief engine for the '4F'. Not surprisingly the 4-4-0 lost a few minutes on schedule. I imagine this was on the faster and relatively level stretches of line such as the Blandford Forum to Corfe Mullen Junction section for instance, where in their time locomotives designated as mixed traffic or freight such as class '5's, 'West Country's' and class '9's roared along with 12 coach trains at speeds up to 70 mph and even more. Express trains were tightly timed on this section and a '2P' with 10 on would be out of its depth here in any case. Paradoxically the '2P's despite their label of passenger locomotives and possessing the large diameter driving wheels once considered *de rigueur* for high speed work, rarely aspired to such rapid progress unless substantially aided by gravity, even when lightly loaded, thanks to their unenlightened cylinder design and short travel, short lap valves. On the other hand in relation to size and notwithstanding their high driving wheels, their pulling power at slow speed on the banks was very reasonable.

The various designs of similarly proportioned 4-4-0s which worked regularly over the line at different periods, such as the Southern 'T9's, gave little indication that they could improve on the Midland 4-4-0s in the matter of hard pulling at slow speeds. Indeed, experienced engine crews doubted the ability of the Southern engines to take 200 tons daily over the Mendips on the 'Pines' schedule. With regard to a 'T9' hauling 10 bogies unassisted up Parkstone bank — from observation from my home over a period of some 15 years following the second world war, I never witnessed such a thing attempted; but whilst hauling Southern trains, several times I saw them stalled in the cutting beyond Parkstone station with loads of seven or eight, blowing off hard at the safety valves — so shortage of steam was not the cause. Yet the class '2's regularly and happily took such loads here, including the stopping and starting away up the 1 in 60 from Parkstone station, as I experienced in a practical sense on many occasions during my own footplate days. On the other hand the 'T9's had the legs of the Midland 4-4-0s on the faster lengths and showed that the nickname of 'Greyhounds' with which they were dubbed on the SR was well justified.

It is fashionable nowadays to decry the Midland class '2's. In most respects it must be admitted that much of the criticism levelled is inevitably true and yet, feeble as these engines were reckoned by some to be, their work on the S&D main line — particularly over the Mendips — must be classified as first class up until 1938 when they were largely superseded on express work. Just about every S&D engineman familiar with their work will accord them little else but praise for the excellent way they performed in relation to their modest dimensions.

The S&D 'Armstrongs', built to the standard Midland superheated class '4' 0-6-0 design, came in 1922 — a batch of five, Nos. 57-61. They were nicknamed 'Armstrongs' by the S&D men because they were built by Armstrong Whitworth and Company, and thereafter all engines of this class that came to the line — irrespective of where they had been built — were referred to indiscriminately by this name. In terms of tractive effort, they were powerful engines compared with the motive power then on the S&D, excepting of course the 2-8-0s. And with the increase in holiday traffic from the North to Bournemouth they were soon heading many of these trains. They usually powered the Easter, Whitsun and August bank holiday excursions from Bath to Bournemouth West and back. These trains were advertised to the public as 'The Bournemouth Rapides'. This terminology implied at the very least swift travel and the probability of a right time arrival in Bournemouth giving the maximum time for the trippers to get a good day at the seaside. If this is what the customers thought, then often, I am afraid, they were in for a disappointment. The term 'Rapide' used to cause howls of laughter in the enginemen's cabin at Bath, when crews considered the prospect of, or remembered in retrospect, the battle of taking one of these 0-6-0s loaded to its maximum to Bournemouth and back. It was nothing unusual for them to stop for steam perhaps once or twice in each direction frequently interspersed with some rather pedestrian running and with the consequence of a late arrival often causing caustic comment from some of the — by now — not so merry travellers about the so called 'Rapides'. Bearing in mind these factors it might not seem so strange that immediately after arrival at the terminals of Bournemouth West on the outward trip or Bath on the homebound leg, and before the first passenger had chance to detrain, most drivers seemed to find that their locomotive was apparently in need of some urgent mechanical attention from themselves, necessitating their presence at track level — and as far as possible from the station platform and frustrated passing passengers and their likely pithy comments as they hurried belatedly past the engine, dragging in their wake, bored, tired, gritty children, clutching buckets and spades.

But the 'Armstrongs' — nominally goods engines — were always inclined to be sluggish performers on smartly timed trains, and not really suitable for such jobs. In consequence their timekeeping was not always of the best particularly on the faster stretches of the S&D south of Evercreech. It was virtually impossible to maintain full boiler pressure on them when prolonged hard steaming was required.

There was a lot of talk amongst the men that Inspector Wells had had the blast pipe caps enlarged on these engines in order to soften the blast and save coal. Whatever the truth of the matter, whether poor coal or enlarged blast pipe cap, practically every driver, fireman and passed cleaner, carried a 'pin' in his basket, to encourage their steaming. The 'pin' was of the type used in the lids of the old grease axle boxes on goods wagons. After being purloined from the carriage and wagon repair shops they were altered so that they would fit over the blast pipe and could be anchored in position by a wagon brake block. This highly irregular operation, known as 'cutting her throat', effectually sharpened the blast on the fire and increased coal consumption somewhat.

In later years the 'pin' was superseded by the 'chopper' (some men called them 'jimmies' or 'razors') a more massive piece of blast pipe equipment. The owners were loath to part with them or disclose their method of construction. At first they were confined to the drivers of the 2-8-0s — a class that also frequently needed this assistance to steam freely in those days — and no one, except their crews, knew when they were inserted, or taken out. But relief crews when disposing of 2-8-0s on shed and going to clean out the smoke box would sometimes find traces of smoke box ash on the framing and would remark to their drivers, "Hello! they have had a 'chopper' in here".

The 'chopper' was in fact, as its name implies, shaped very like the blade of a chopper. Its top edge was drilled and tapped, and a threaded rod screwed in, to which was attached a butterfly nut and a large wire ring to prevent the 'chopper' falling down the blast pipe if it became slack. The edge of the blade was fitted across the top of the blast pipe cap, and the butterfly nut screwed up tightly to hold it in position.

With the growth of the holiday traffic in the twenties and thirties and much of its haulage entrusted to the 'Armstrongs', the growth of the 'chopper' industry increased in proportion, and the blacksmith at Bath, Albert Manley, made a profitable side line, turning out these devices in the S&D Railway Company's time, using the company's materials and pocketing two shillings and sixpence each. He had no lack of customers, they did make steaming easier and enginemen — and indeed the S&D — had every reason to be grateful to him for his business initiative. The discerning ear could detect an engine so fitted and as yet another 'Armstrong' started belting away from Bath Station, men working around the loco yard or on the bankers, would remark to each other, "Hear her exhaust whistling? she's got a 'chopper' in", and as if to answer in the affirmative the Ramsbottom safety valves — or Ross pop from the 1930's onwards — would lift and laugh back in glee.

In LMS days the sorely tried S&D engine crews often resorted to yet another and highly illegal method of improving the steaming capacity of the 'Armstrongs', (or '4F's as they were officially designated under the LMS). This involved tampering with the continuous blowdown apparatus with which these engines were fitted in the late thirties in connection with the installation of a number of Lime Soda water softening plants, authorised by the LMS. In order to avoid excessive concentration in the boiler water of dissolved solids which resulted from water softening, and which beyond a certain concentration caused priming, a continuous blowdown was fitted to most LMS engines (which by now encompassed the S&D stud) so that a small measured quantity of water was drained from the boiler continuously, either whilst the regulator was open, or whilst the injectors were working. Boiler water was discharged into the ashpan at the rate of some 1-1½ gallons per minute. Not an excessive amount on the face of it, but when engaged on S&D express passenger working the 'Armstrongs' couldn't really spare it, and some enginemen considered the water would be more usefully utilised in the boiler than on the track, and various ways were employed of rendering this blowdown apparatus temporarily inoperative for the duration of a trip when faced with the prospect of working a heavy express train. Although this practice and the use of 'choppers' was highly irregular, there was never any move by authority to ban them. It was more a case of passive resistance, "Don't let us catch you", summed up the situation. But I suppose everybody was happy really because their use helped the engines to achieve work beyond their normal capabilities.

Saying this reminds me of an anecdote concerning the use of a 'chopper'.

It occurred in the mid twenties when a person of some eminence happened to be travelling over the S&D line to Bournemouth. The train was to be hauled by one of the S&D's (then) new 'Armstrong' 0-6-0s and Mr. Whitaker was out in the shed yard watching with an eagle eye the crew prepare the engine, because it was imperative that no time should be lost on the trip: he therefore wanted personally to make quite certain that the engine left the shed in 'apple pie order'. However, his presence was more likely to cause loss of time rather than obviate it. The engine crew were very much aware that without a 'chopper' in situ, as like as not the engine would lose time. But the very presence of the watchful Mr. Whitaker made it virtually impossible to get it fitted unseen. Fortunately however Mr. Whitaker eventually 'got the message' when he realised that the driver and fireman were watching him as closely as he was them — just waiting for him to look away long enough for them to slip in the 'chopper'. Thus it was at length that Mr. Whitaker somewhat furtively sidled alongside the fireman and whispered out of the corner of his mouth in a resigned voice, "Oh all right then laddie, put one in her if you must", and for the next few minutes Mr. Whitaker's gaze roved anywhere but near that 'Armstrong's' smokebox — and the deed was done!

At first the 'Armstrongs' were rostered to haul 230 tons unassisted between Bath and Evercreech Junction, later increased to 240 tons. Between Evercreech Junction and Corfe Mullen the figure was officially 365 tons but often — particularly on Summer Saturdays following the second world war — they were saddled with heavier loads. Now these loads were much more than those rostered for the class '2's being based on tractive effort figures which, when speed was in excess of say 20 mph, became secondary compared to boiler output which was really the limiting feature — particularly on the long haul compared to a short all out effort. The boiler on the '4F's was interchangeable with the Midland class '2' 4-4-0s and, in consequence, their loading on passenger trains logically ought to have been the same between Bath and Evercreech and if anything slightly less than the class '2's on the much faster Evercreech to Bournemouth section due to the internal friction of the 'Armstrongs' when running at the higher speeds demanded here. But the powers that be chose tractive effort alone as their yardstick to allocate loading to these engines hence enginemen taking their own steps to increase the steaming capacity of the 'Armstrongs' which, from their inception in 1922 through until 1938, shared with the class '2's the hardest express passenger duties on the S&D — including the 'Pines Express'. However by hook or by crook it should be said the 'Armstrongs' served the S&D line with great loyalty and were stalwarts for over 40 years performing usefully and reliably on freight, local and semi-fast passenger trains on which the intermittent demands for steam allowed them ample time to recover their breath.

Ergonomically speaking an 'Armstrong's' dust-invaded footplate left much to be desired, added to which their riding when working fast trains was at times very rough. This was caused by knocking in the driving and coupled wheel axle boxes, and could be most uncomfortable for those on the footplate. Even after shopping, these engines got rough again very quickly, a condition speeded no doubt by the hammering they got by virtue of their being regularly used as express passenger engines on the S&D, particularly during the 1922-1938 period and fairly frequently thereafter.

This rough riding was once admirably described by (then) fireman Cecil ('Smokebox') Waldron when upon arrival at Bath with No. 58 one day someone asked, "Had a good trip, 'Smokebox'?". "Good!" he retorted. "Huh! she was so rough I couldn't tell if we were on the rails or the sleepers and the axle boxes sounded like someone playing on the castanets". "But", he continued, "one thing I will say for her, she's a friendly soul. She bowed to every cow grazing alongside the line, all the way from Templecombe to Bath". This was a direct reference to the wild side to side swaying of these engines (and most other 0-6-0s) at speed; often quite noticeable from the lineside, but leaving their crews in no doubt as to its presence when watching the antics of the smokebox from the footplate.

In this connection I recall an experience of my own when No. 44557 (ex S&D 57) was pilot engine to Donald and myself on the 9.35 am Sheffield – Bournemouth. The Templecombe driver of the '4F' had given us better than average assistance up to Masbury and was obviously in a great hurry to get home, because he dropped us down the southern face of the Mendips at a tremendous pace. Well before Evercreech New, our speedometer was registering over 70 mph and the antics of the 0-6-0 as viewed by us looking ahead from the comfort of a BR class '5' footplate was really something to behold! The engine and tender were rocking and yawing violently and I watched the driver with interest. With cap yanked down nearly over his ears to prevent it flying off he was perched uncomfortably on his tiny wooden seat, right arm locked firmly over the swaying cab side to anchor himself in position. Any attempt at standing up on that footplate must, I think, have been practically impossible. Actually it was Donald who first applied the brake somewhere near Prestleigh having decided that he had seen enough, concluding that the two spartans on the '4F' were allowing their keenness to get finished and booked off to interfere with their better judgement. I personally never saw a '4F' travel faster than this. And my verdict on this performance is – cannot be recommended!

The locomotives written about here were not the sum total of S&D engines operating on the line during the 1920's and some, such as the Johnsons 0-4-4 tanks which after their introduction in 1877 were, until 1891, the S&D express passenger engines, and the three lovely little 'Bobby Dazzlers' which shunted mainly at Radstock, have not been mentioned here. But the engines about which I have written – all of which actually bore S&D numbers – provided the liveliest recollections amongst the S&D enginemen with whom I was closely acquainted on the Joint line.

120

Chapter Four

CHANGING TIMES

I
1923 – 1930

The period of time from the 1923 grouping until 1966, the year the S&D line closed, inevitably saw change and heard rumour of change, although to be sure, not all of these transpired in fact. How these events, which are now mainly dates in railway history, affected the daily working lives of S&D railwaymen between those times may be of interest.

By the time of the grouping the post war recovery of S&D passenger services was almost complete, and in addition, many extra trains ran over the line to and from the Midlands and the North at weekends during the holiday season. But with the accent on economy, the S&D locomotive authorities did not carry sufficient staff to cover this seasonal passenger traffic and for some years resorted to the expedient of taking on extra men during the summer months and standing them off through the slack winter period. But freight activity north of Templecombe remained intense throughout the twenties, and the shunting yards at Templecombe and Evercreech Junction could hardly cope with the volume. At almost all times of the day goods trains could be seen stored around Evercreech North up yard waiting to be dealt with.

After the passage of the last northbound passenger train to Bath at night, a veritable procession of freight trains would trundle up the main line from the direction of Templecombe. A train with about forty empties on would arrive at the Evercreech Junction South up home signal and take water at the column. This accomplished and the signal pulled off, the train would pull forward over the level crossing and through the station to stop at the North box home signal. In the crowded goods yard an engine was forming its train: the minutes would tick away and an hour soon slipped past. By this time another train would be behind, waiting at the Evercreech Junction South up home signal. The fireman suspecting a lengthy wait, closed the damper and filled the boiler; and the driver — especially if it was a cold wet night — would say to the fireman, "I'll go to the box and sign the book", (rule 55) whereupon his mate would clamber over the top of the tender and shovel down sufficient coal to take them through to Bath. This finished, he snuggled down cosily in his corner of the footplate and dozed the time away till the clang of the signal arm dropping warned him to open the damper a nick, and with the driver climbing aboard he reached to release the tender handbrake. By this time another train would be waiting at Wincanton (Cole box was switched out after the last up passenger train) and quite possibly Templecombe No. 3 Junction. Sometimes in order to clear trains standing on the main line, crews would be given the tablet for Pylle by the Evercreech Junction North signalman, and told to stand out on 'the branch' until their train could be accepted in the up marshalling yard.

The transfer freights from the S&D's Templecombe Lower Yard to the South Western's Upper Yard, and vice versa was a turn of frustration for engine crews. It often took several hours to complete this trip of a little over a mile. Indeed, sometimes things were so congested that after being on duty for anything up to twelve hours, engine crews were often relieved on the footplate without them leaving the respective yards due to no pathway becoming available during their turn of duty. Such was the volume of freight traffic over the S&D line during those times.

Due to this increase in freight traffic, Mr. Archbutt, the resident Locomotive Superintendent at Highbridge, decided to increase the numbers of staff at the motive power depot at Templecombe, and declared vacancies for several drivers there. The outcome of this was to cause a great deal of feeling among some enginemen at Bath. Promotion on the railways of Britain then as now, was based on the principle of seniority, and it was therefore expected that the senior unregistered passed firemen at Bath — as it was much the largest motive power depot on the S&D system — would apply for these jobs. But on the contrary there was some resistance amongst these men to breaking up their homes and moving to a tiny village completely lacking the amenities that they currently enjoyed, and with problems of accommodation. Therefore, even though Inspector Wells attempted to pressurise some of the passed firemen to applying for these posts, he received a unanimous refusal to do so. Meanwhile the staff shortage at Templecombe was becoming critical, and Inspector Wells was forced to petition the next men down in order of seniority and here he met with some success. Using bait of considerable attraction he asked the men, "If I put you through your driver's test and you pass, will you agree to transfer to Templecombe?". Here was an opportunity to lop off several years of the hard and arduous task of locomotive firing, before the exalted position of driver could be reached. One of the first men to agree to this was fireman Len Counsell, who successfully passed his driving examination and was made a Driver at Templecombe in February 1924. Thus he and several more were made drivers some years before senior colleagues who were reluctant to make this move.

Later on rumours began to circulate amongst the men about a projected development of Templecombe loco, making it the main S&D depot. Furthermore, there were equally strong indications that Evercreech Junction North Yard was to be closed and its activities removed to Templecombe Lower Yard which in turn was to be greatly enlarged for the purpose. It was also envisaged that the spur in the lower yard, which at one time was connected to the **L&SWR** (Salisbury and Yeovil line), would be connected once more, and re-establish this link to the West of England main line and facilitate freight working here. One enterprising Templecombe engineman, Driver Courtney, was so sure that this was the pattern of things to come that he purchased a field alongside the lower yard which he hoped later to sell to the railway company at a considerable profit to himself. There is no doubt that a considerable saving could have resulted from such a scheme. Goods trains working into Evercreech Junction North Yard from Bath were broken up, shunted, and reformed before proceeding to Templecombe — for the process to be repeated all over again. The same applied in reverse to northbound freights. However, the scheme in fact did not materialise, and eventually the aforementioned driver became an early member of the 'do it yourself brigade' and built himself a house in his field, and freight trains continued to block the yard at Evercreech Junction and the main line for some miles around for many a year.

Also in the early 1920's, there was something of a perpetual crisis at Templecombe due to problems of water which was in very short supply. There was hardly any piped water in the village, and in the loco shed the supply was also very limited. All engines rostered to be berthed at Templecombe were required to take on water at the last water column before going on to shed. Engines working up from Bournemouth filled their tanks at Sturminster Newton, and those from Highbridge or Bath, at Evercreech Junction.

To assist in overcoming this difficulty Mr. Archbutt formed his 'water trains' to supplement the engine shed supply, and to this end eight old loco tenders were converted, each having a valve in the bottom of the tank which could be opened and closed by means of rodding connected to a wheel on the tender footplate.

At first, these water trains ran from Edington Junction to Templecombe, but salt water started creeping into that supply causing priming trouble with engines using it. Alternatively water was obtained from Glastonbury and also from Wells, where an old fashioned water wheel was used to pump water into the water tower. Sometimes the tenders were used to transport water to Highbridge loco where sea water was also liable to contaminate supplies. Because of traffic congestion around Evercreech Junction water was on occasions collected from either Shepton Mallet or Blandford, whichever was more convenient according to traffic conditions.

There was quite a neat arrangement at Templecombe to transfer the water from these trains to the loco shed. On the spur line which climbed up between Templecombe No. 2 Junction and Templecombe Upper Station a sump was installed between the track. When a water train — which normally comprised four tenders — arrived full, the tenders were positioned over the sump into which they disgorged their water. A pipe then carried the water by gravity to the loco depot's water tank, perched above the steamraiser's cabin near the turntable. However, later on a mains supply to the whole of Templecombe was established and this made life in the loco shed easier for everyone. As engines became due for 'washing out', this could now be done at Templecombe instead of working engines especially to Bath or Highbridge for this purpose.

S&D enginemen ranged their system to a somewhat larger extent in the 1920's than they did in more modern times. One interesting Bath duty was the 3.45 pm daily pick up goods (called the 'road box train') through to Wimborne, taking the original line from Corfe Mullen Junction to Wimborne, the use of which had been greatly diminished following the opening of the 'cut off' line to Broadstone in 1885. The men lodged overnight at Wimborne where the S&D had its own lodging house and engine shed returning to Bath during the following day. However at the end of 1922 the lodging house was closed, and the manning and schedule of the train was modified on this account. Later on in 1933, the Corfe Mullen — Wimborne section of line itself closed, except for a section of track left in situ extending from Corfe Mullen Junction up to Carter's clay siding.

Another turn of interest was the early morning Bath — Bridgwater goods which Bath men worked over the Mendip Hills to Evercreech Junction. Here they turned their engine — usually a 'Scottie' 0-6-0 — on the turntable, and then coupled up to the other end of the train and set off across the level moors of the Highbridge line. After passing Glastonbury, and the hallowed land of Arthur and Avalon, they finally took to the seven and a quarter mile Bridgwater branch at Edington Junction and commenced climbing the 1 in 72 Cossington bank over the Polden Ridge. Once over the summit it remained only to cross the King Sedgemoor Drain, to gain their destination at Bridgwater, where they lodged during the day before returning to Bath in the evening with another goods train. Personally I find this working of particular interest, because during my career on the S&D there were no regular through rostered workings for engine crews from Bath or Branksome to destinations on 'the branch'. This section of the S&D, after closure of the Wells and Bridgwater branches together with their attendant engine sheds, was entirely in the hands of Templecombe and Highbridge enginemen.

At the grouping in 1923 the Southern and the London Midland and Scottish Railway companies — as successors to the L&SWR and the Midland Railways respectively — had become jointly responsible for the S&DJR. However in practice there was little change in the day to day running of the line and its former S&D administration remained, and in consequence the system retained much of its old character, individuality and charm. Indeed this was always one of the most endearing features about this railway which even subsequent nationalisation did not succeed in eliminating. During the period that the Southern Region was responsible for the operation of the whole of the S&D line, the various weekly and fortnightly notices, working timetables, and their appendix thereto issued to operating staff was headed, BRITISH RAILWAYS, SOUTHERN

REGION, SOMERSET AND DORSET LINE, and issued as separate publications, instead of being incorporated within the general Southern Region publications as might have been imagined. I recall the local signals and telegraph inspector approaching Donald Beale and myself at Bournemouth West one day brandishing a copy of one of our 'fortnightly notices' saying: "What's so special about your line that you have separate operating books from the rest of us. I thought we were all British Railways now?". But the S&D was always a railway apart, even its own distinctive headcode — one lamp at the base of the chimney and one above the left buffer for all passenger trains, and for freight trains one lamp at the base of the chimney and one above the right-hand buffer — survived up until the line's closure. Indeed, even when under Southern Region control, headlamps were used on locomotives to distinguish the train rather than the white discs normally used in Southern Region operating areas during daylight to signify its route.

By the late twenties the former Midland depot at Bath (a sub depot to Bristol Barrow Road) was taken under the control of the S&D Locomotive Superintendent. Also around this time Sir Josiah Stamp President of the LMS was appointed, like an early edition of Doctor Beeching, to carry out his ruthless economies which in turn had their effect on the S&D. Whatever benefits were brought about as a result of his actions, it certainly was not to the advantage of the external cleanliness of the locomotives operating on the S&D. One of his first edicts was, "Cleaning engines is a luxury we cannot afford". So dirt and squalor started to become the new tenants. Strong disciplinarians such as Inspector Wells and Tom Wells the old cleaners' foreman at Bath were by now retired and many of the main line drivers too were fast approaching retirement; the standard of cleanliness on the S&D dropped alarmingly from the admittedly exceedingly high standards prevailing hitherto. As from January 1930, the S&D locomotive stock was taken into LMS stock and on 1st June 1930 as an economy measure the LMS assumed control of the line's operation whilst the Southern took over the track and civil engineering generally.

These changes resulted in the S&D's locomotive and carriage works at Highbridge being closed, the disappearance of the famous blue livery, the new order being black for both passenger and freight locomotives, and their receiving LMS numbers and power classifications. To quote some examples of altered power classification, the 'Bulldog' and 'Armstrong' 0-6-0s previously classified '3P'/'3G' and '4P'/'4G' became '3F' and '4F' respectively. Similarly the superheated 4-4-0 passenger engines and 2-8-0 freight locomotives previously '3P'/'2G' and '5P'/'5G' now became designated '2P' and '7F' respectively. 1930 also marked the end of what could be termed the true family spirit of the line, although it never lost this atmosphere completely. Now, under these changed conditions, enginemen belonging to the new combined S&D and Midland sheds at Bath, instead of confining their activities to their own lines as before, began to work over each others routes. Former S&D crews from Bath shed were eventually to be seen over the years working regularly to such places as Birmingham and Derby on freight and passenger trains — indeed, right up until the 1960's in BR days, Bath men had a nightly job to Birmingham taking over the 8.25 pm Templecombe — Derby perishable train at Bath and returning on the 12.37 am down Leicester parcels train.

From 1930 onwards, all loco depots on the S&D system came under the LMS Sectional Council No. 2. and the area for promotion amongst the staff stretched from Branksome shed — now an LMS outpost right in the heart of the Southern Railway — up to places such as Saltley, Walsall and even beyond. Soon, some S&D men moved to various LMS sheds for promotion, and several vacancies occurring at Bath, Templecombe and Branksome sheds were filled by men from depots such as Saltley, Stoke and even Crewe. I remember that during the period of my own footplate career at Branksome, there were two drivers from Templecombe, one of whom had previously been a fireman in the top link at Crewe North shed working express trains between Crewe and Euston, and Crewe to Glasgow or Perth, firing to Stanier 'Duchess' Pacifics mostly. I recall him in the enginemen's mess room at Branksome one day when it was also occupied by a Southern top link crew from Nine Elms, off the down 'Bournemouth Belle', the engine of which was serviced on Branksome shed prior to working the up 'Belle' back to London. These particular 'cockneys' were rather flamboyant characters and soon struck up an argument by inferring that the Waterloo to Bournemouth main line express trains required superior locomotive work than was necessary anywhere else, and that the 'Merchant Navy' Pacifics were the finest express passenger engines in the country. Both arguable propositions, particularly the latter, since at that time (around 1954) the 'Merchant Navy's' were still running in their original and rather unpredictable state. After listening to these boastful assertions for a while, the ex Crewe man innocently interrupted politely asking "How far is it to London from here?". "112 miles Mate, wiv only two stops, and 12 Pullmans on", said the London driver proudly. "Oh, is that all?" said the Templecombe driver in exaggerated surprise. "I thought you said it was a long way. When I was firing at Crewe on the 'Duchess' Pacific we used to reckon the first 100 miles, with 16 coaches on was just warming the engine up before we really got going". Well, I don't know about warming up the engine but this ego deflating comment certainly warmed up the conversation and caused plenty of spirited rudery between this ex LMS and ex SR crew, but it all ended amicably.

Actually this sort of thing was rather typical of the professional jealousies of enginemen in steam days when, even if stationed at the tiniest depot, they liked to glorify and, perhaps, slightly exaggerate their exploits often eliciting amusing side retorts from the retinue. Like the time when a gathering of S&D enginemen from several depots occurred on the sad occasion of the funeral of a colleague who most unfortunately had been crushed between some buffers at Bath shed, and died as a result. After the harrowing business of the burial service, the lads — looking for some light relief — gathered in a public house for a drink, and inevitably the conversation turned to railway work. One of the Bath contingent, Dick Evry, then a fireman, started talking about some of the harder turns of duty worked from his depot. But 'Basher' Pearce, a portly fireman stationed at the tiny Wells depot down on 'the branch', whose usual job consisted of shuttling up and down the 5½ mile stretch from Glastonbury to Wells, probably on No. 28a (a rebuilt 2-4-0T originally constructed by G. England in 1861) hauling one coach, was in the gathering and, not to be outdone by his colleagues, butted into the conversation saying, "You blokes on the main line don't do it all you know, there's some hard work done on the Wells branch mind". "So there might be", Dick replied, then pointing at 'Basher's' corpulent figure added, "but you don't do any of it by the look of you".

II
1931 — 1938

Some of the "new arrivals" in the thirties, soon found the gradients of the S&D line a different "kettle of fish" from that which they had previously been used to. Alfie 'Buddy' Moore came to Bath shed from the Midlands — he was a happy-go-lucky sort, and at first was far from at home on the difficult S&D gradients. He was rather heavy handed with the brake, and in consequence was initially often concerned with breakaways and buffer-locking derailments. One day after another of Alf's "fireworks" fellow driver Bert Kear commiserated with him saying he was sorry to hear he was in "the soup" again. But 'Buddy' just laughed at him saying, "Don't worry about me Bert, look at it this way, if your name came up at Headquarters in Derby, they would say, Kear? who's Kear? never heard of him, but when my report gets there they'll say, Hello! Moore's been at it again, thought it was about time we heard from him!"

Actually the working of unbraked freight trains connected by three link couplings was always difficult, but never more so than over the 26 miles between Bath and Evercreech Junction. This stretch contained all the worst hazards connected with working heavy unbraked mineral trains and drivers, when thus engaged, had to exercise great forethought and attend not only to the signals concerning them, but also to the gradient to be encountered, the state of the rail, and to the effectiveness of the brake power available on the train. Also the technique of keeping the couplings strained out on a down grade prior to the next rise or, if operating conditions required, getting the slack out of a long loose coupled freight without breaking away or the guard measuring his length on the brake van floor required great skill. All these things had to be considered to a greater extent on unfitted freight trains than was the case on passenger work. To the enginemen at Bath goes most of the credit for handling this difficult service. Incidentally the Midland combination vacuum and steam brake control valve fitted to S&D, Midland and LMS engines was a rather poor device where finesse in the operation of the steam brake was required. The combined vacuum and steam brake valve with an independent graduable steam brake valve as fitted on the BR standard locomotives proved a great boon to S&D enginemen engaged on goods work in later years when the various BR standard engines worked the line.

As the thirties progressed the tallow for cleaning engines gave way to paraffin jelly and the practice of 'blacking down' the boiler and firebox front on the footplate and the cleaning of the paintwork inside the cab began to die. Promotion at Bath shed was slow in coming during the thirties and several Bath passed cleaners, including Donald Beale and Johnny Walker, moved to Branksome, the S&D depot at Bournemouth for fireman's jobs.

Branksome shed of timber and asbestos construction, with a history dating back to 1896, was a very small depot compared to Bath. Up until 1922 it had eight turns of duty, but after the 1923 grouping these were reduced to five which number was retained until its eventual closure in 1963. Branksome — a sub depot of Templecombe until 1958 — had no allocation of locomotives, the motive power for its regular turns of duty was provided mainly from Bath shed. Small engine sheds — particularly sub-depots — usually consisted entirely of easy and light duties. But Branksome shed, despite its diminutive size, was from the time of its opening to its closure, the 'top of the tree' passenger train depot of the S&D, its footplate crews were always associated with the crack Bournemouth — Manchester 'Diner' and its successor the 'Pines Express' and made a reputation all of their own for their handling of this duty.

In S&D and LMS days, men who were being transferred from other depots to Branksome in the capacity of Driver or Fireman, were always given a pep talk by Mr. Davis the chief clerk at Bath shed on behalf of the Locomotive Superintendent prior to going. They were informed that Branksome shed unlike most others was not subject to on the spot supervision and that, by and large, the depot ran itself with the minimum of interference from management — and that was how they wanted things to continue. The chief clerk would usually finish his talk by saying — "Off you go then", adding as an apparent afterthought, "and for God's sake don't lose any time on the 'Pines'!". During summer Saturdays practically all Branksome drivers, passed firemen and passed cleaners, would be engaged in working heavy express passenger trains through to Bath and back, handling a wide variety of motive power, particularly after nationalisation. Branksome generally had the reputation of excellence amongst its footplate crews, and of being a homely happy depot. Obviously there were disagreements from time to time, human nature being what it is, but basically it was always a happy shed and much laughter was generated in

A group of engine cleaners and shed workers photographed at Bath in September 1919. Donald Beale is in the back row standing third from left. Note the SJC cap badge worn by Somerset & Dorset footplatemen denoting 'Somerset Joint Committee'

The engines on which many an S&D engineman of the teens and twenties had their first experience were the Fox Walker 0-6-0 saddle tanks. Here photographed at Radstock is No. 3 as rebuilt with extended saddle tank.

Photo: Real Photos Ltd.

'Scottie' 0-6-0 No. 47 photographed standing on the "Boat Road" in Bath shed loco yard at around the mid 1920's. Passed Cleaner Donald Beale then about 24 years of age is on the footplate, and note also the neat wall of reserve coal stacked behind the engine.

Photo: Real Photos Ltd.

Donald portrayed as I shall always remember him. Ivo Peters took this superb picture of a "top link driver" during a footplate trip he had with us on BR class '5' No. 73050 hauling the southbound 'Pines Express'.

Photo: Ivo Peters.

Rebuilt Fowler 0-6-0 No. 19, heads a short southbound goods train at around 1900 near the site of what has now in 1928 Clondara March 'Halt.

S&DJR 2-8-0 as originally built. The cramped tender cab can be clearly seen, including the small access door (here seen open) to the fire irons and coal storage space in the tender. The tender cabs fitted only to the first series of these 2-8-0s were subsequently removed.

Photo: L. T. George Collection.

For many years there were shedded at Radstock three diminutive shunting engines dimensionally suitable for passing through the low Tyning Arch located nearby, known locally as "Marble Arch". Enginemen called these neat little engines "Bobby Dazzlers" due to the highly polished state in which they were normally kept by their crews. Pictured above is "Dazzler" 0-4-2 tank No. 25A. These engines were replaced in 1929 by two Sentinel 0-4-0Ts Nos. 101 and 102.

Photo: L. T. George Collection.

A member of the first and smaller series of rebuilt S&DJ 4-4-0s No. 45, heads the 11.58 am Templecombe – Bournemouth West local passenger train off the 1 in 50 section of Parkstone Bank and into the station in 1925. Parkstone signal box, seen in the background, was abolished on 9th July, 1933.

Photo: L. T. George collection.

Small rebuilt 4-4-0 No. 16, leaving Broadstone with a down local around 1920.
Photo: Kelland Collection: Bournemouth Railway Club.

An engine familiar to S&D enginemen of the 1920s who worked on "the branch" or its various offshoots was this rebuilt G. England 2-4-0T No. 28A.

Photo: L. T. George collection.

Superheated 4-4-0 No. 68, inside the S&DJR shed at Bath, the wooden construction of which can be clearly seen. Standing behind the 4-4-0 is 'Armstrong' 0-6-0 No. 57, with its front end stripped for attention to valves and pistons.

Photo: Real Photos Ltd.

Prior to their replacement by 4-4-0 tender engines in 1891, Johnson 0-4-4 tank engines worked the main passenger expresses between Bath, Wimborne and Bournemouth. Thereafter they were relegated to local passenger work. No. 55, heads a northbound local up the 1 in 75 gradient near Broadstone at around 1920.

Photo: Kelland Collection: Bournemouth Railway Club.

The first S&D 'Bulldog' to be rebuilt with a Belpaire firebox was No. 66, seen here newly rebuilt at Wellow in 1920.

Photo: L. T. George collection.

Standard Fowler 'Jinty' '3F' 0-6-0 No. 7152 (ex S&D No. 21) at Bath in February 1931. This engine was further re-numbered 7312 in 1932. The stone built ex Midland locomotive shed is in the background and that company's coal stage – demolished in 1934 to make way for an enlarged turntable – is just visible on the extreme left of the picture.

Photo: L. T. George collection.

Photographed soon after the 1930 LMS takeover; superheated 4-4-0 No. 326, (ex S&D No. 69, later 43) waiting to pilot saturated 4-4-0 No. 320 (ex S&D No. 77) out of Bath, Queen Square.

Photo: L. T. George collection.

Down Bournemouth express passing Moorewood during the 1930's double headed by '4F' 0-6-0 No. 3875 and '2P' 4-4-0 No. 633 (ex S&D 44). This engine was fitted with an experimental Dabeg feed water heater visible on the locomotive framing adjacent to the smokebox.

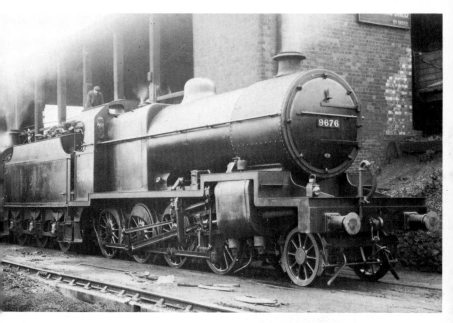

No. 9676 (ex S&D 86) — one of the handsome 1925 series of large boilered 2-8-0s — with the LMS number carried by the engine from 1930 - 1932, photographed under the coal stage at Bath.

Photo: Lens of Sutton

Prior to 1935 the S&D 2-8-0s spent a fair proportion of their time running tender first (hence their being fitted with tablet catching apparatus on both sides of the tender) normally working chimney first from Bath to Evercreech Junction or Templecombe, and returning tender first. No. 13806 (ex S&D 86) is heading an up train of coal from the Somerset collieries near Wellow in March 1934.

Photo: L. T. George collection.

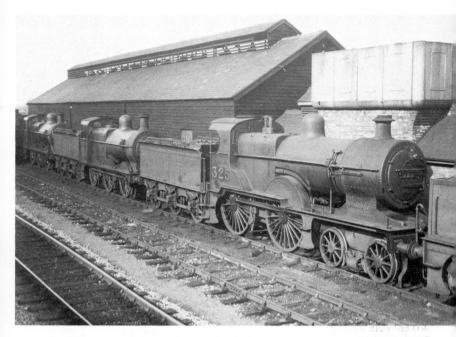

Ex S&D superheated 4-4-0 No. 325, (ex S&D No. 68, later 42) poses in a locomotive line up alongside Templecombe shed in 1935. This wooden built structure was replaced by one of brick in 1950 under the auspices of the Southern Region of British Railways.

Photo: L. T. George collection.

During 1935 trials were held over the S&D with an ex London, Tilbury and Southend 'Intermediate' 4-4-2T No. 2103, following which it was used for a time on the Bath – Bristol service. No. 2103 was engaged on the latter service when it was photographed at Bath Queen Square station on 16th July, 1936.

Photo: Rev A. G. Newman.

Three out of the 'big four' are represented in this picture taken on Saturday 7th August, 1937 at Broadstone. Two LMS '2P' 4-4-0s pulling out of the station with an S&D line train are passing in the yard SR 'M7' 0-4-4T No. 21, coupled ahead of GWR 'Saint' class 4-6-0 No. 2916 *Saint Benedict*. The latter had been shunted here whilst in the process of turning on the Holes Bay Junction, Hamworthy Junction, Broadstone triangle. The GW engine had worked a through train from Wolverhampton to Bournemouth Central, the empty stock of which was berthed at Hamworthy Junction.

Photo: G. W. Puntis.

A fine action shot of the locomotive tablet catching apparatus about to pick up the tablet from the lineside standard for the Broadstone – Corfe Mullen Junction single line section on 27th September, 1939. The locomotive is Stanier 'Black Five' 4-6-0 No. 5023.

Photo: G. W. Puntis.

Prior to the last war LMS engines off the S&D line were fairly frequent summer visitors to Weymouth and Swanage with excursion trains or pigeon specials. Here '2P' 4-4-0 No. 628 is being turned on the Swanage turntable after working a

The empty stock of the Royal Train working of 14th May, 1940, coming off the S&D line and entering Broadstone Station hauled by 'Black 5' 4-6-0 No. 5289 . . .

Photo: G. W. Puntis.

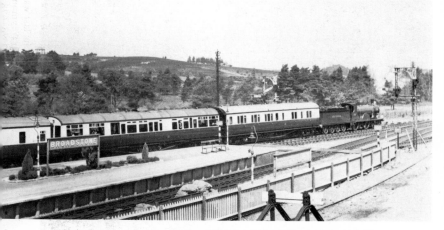

. . . here the LMS engine unhooked and 'T9' 4-4-0 No. 119 coupled on at the other end for the resumption of the journey, here seen departing from Broadstone in the direction of Wimborne.

Photo: G. W. Puntis.

Compound 4-4-0 No. 1046, which saw service on the S&D during the last war, pulling away from Broadstone with the 5.15 pm Bournemouth West – Bath on 5th June, 1940.

Photo: G. W. Puntis.

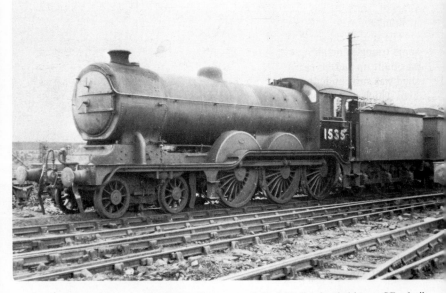

During the last war ambulance trains traversed the S&D line headed by ex GE rebuilt 'B12/3' 4-6-0s. A member of the same class was No. 1535 (just renumbered from LNER No. 8535) seen here at Stratford in 1946.

Photo: R. C. Riley.

its mess room over the years, some of which I was privileged to enjoy during my time as an engineman there.

In 1934 Donald Beale was paired at Branksome with a driver by the name of Albert White. He was 'one of the old school' whose seniority on the S&D dated back to 1896, and who insisted on the 'old standards', including having a clean boiler and firebox front on the footplate with every copper pipe and all the brasswork gleaming like gold, and the inside cab paintwork reflecting 'spit and polish'. At this time 'Bert' was the chairman of Branksome 'Mutual Improvement Class' – run by the men in their own time for the benefit particularly of firemen preparing themselves for the driver's examination. These classes normally took place on Sunday mornings, which seems appropriate enough; footplate work was something of a religion in steam days. Being an LMS depot there was always a natural rivalry between Branksome men and enginemen on the Southern, however, this did not assume the proportions of pointless rivalry. Thus Branksome M.I.C. class was thrown open to Southern men from nearby Bournemouth Central shed mainly for the convenience of those who lived in the vicinity of Branksome. Every Southern man who attended this class – and quite a number did – passed his driver's examination with credit. Inspector Bullard of the Southern, who then conducted the Southern men's examinations once told 'Bert' White, "I always ask a candidate prior to the driving examination if he has attended a 'Mutual Improvement Class', and if he answers Branksome, I know I shall have no trouble in passing him." With this background, and firing to such a man as 'Bert' White, Donald naturally had no problems in passing his driving examination in 1936, anymore than I did in passing my own driving examination in 1962 after a number of years of firing for Donald. Such were the traditions that were perpetuated at Branksome until its closure.

The tiny Branksome Motive Power depot was situated within the Branksome triangle and alongside Branksome coal sidings. The surrounding area was built up and quite heavily populated but on railway property itself the shed was surrounded by what could be described as 'a moat' of railway lines which at night when traffic was sparse gave it a somewhat 'remote feeling'.

Probably as a result of this seeming remoteness, Branksome shed was reckoned by some to be haunted. I personally cannot claim to have seen or felt any ghostly presence during my time there but I did hear several hilariously entertaining accounts. One tale dating from the 1930's concerned the little humpedback man, wearing a black raincoat and bowler hat (a long gone locomotive inspector maybe?) who some steamraisers on 'nights' claimed to have seen in the smoky and dimly lit interior of the shed. It appeared that on odd occasions when the night steamraiser, during his round, climbed onto the footplate in the small hours of the night, this figure would be seen in the part shadow and flickering firelight, sitting on the driver's or fireman's seat. The few observers who had apparently seen the apparition promptly fled the scene. Indeed some would not go near that engine for the rest of the night, "not even if she drops her plugs", one was heard to remark. But those who did venture back for a further sighting failed to make one that night. The (in)spectre, had flown, to appear again perhaps some months later — or so the story goes.

One imagines that these stories were very much in the mind of the then 17 year old passed cleaner Ron Hyde one dark morning years later in the 1950's when he arrived on shed for the "6 am to 2 pm shed duties" turn, at the height of a violent thunderstorm with lightning flashing across the sky at frequent intervals. All the electric lights had gone out inside the shed and the loco yard, so he walked carefully up through the pitch dark shed, taking care not to blunder painfully into the several water hydrants poking up out of the shed floor, past the deserted but gently hissing engines standing inside towards the engineman's mess room. Entering he was most surprised to find not a soul in sight. The only sign of life — or at least proof that someone had been there — were two lit candles, standing in bottle necks and four steaming cups of freshly poured tea on the table. But where was everybody? A further check round the shed with the aid of light from a flare lamp revealed nothing and Ron thought that the story of the 'Marie Celeste' had occurred all over again — only on dry land this time. It was quite ten alarming minutes before all was revealed to him.

Donald and myself had arrived on shed at about 5.30 am that morning to work the 6.57 am Bournemouth West — Bath to find Albert Toop the night shed steamraiser sitting alone in the candle lit mess room. Lightning had struck the main electricity supply cable to the shed, thus blacking it out. Soon afterwards another cleaner for the 6 am - 2 pm turn arrived early for duty, made a can of tea and poured out a cup for each of us. But before we had time to drink it, a pyjama clad figure came lurching out of the blackness through the mess room door breathlessly informing us that the small Cooperative Coal Office in the adjacent coal yard was on fire and would we assist him put it out. His home overlooked the railway line alongside the sharply curved Bournemouth West Junction — Gas Works Junction section of the Branksome Triangle and he had been woken by the thunder and upon looking out of his bedroom window had spotted the few flickering flames which were the fire's beginning. Overcoming our momentary surprise we all dashed out to the coal yard to find a broken but still live electric cable dangling onto the office roof and some associated timber which was smouldering badly. The live wire was gingerly moved aside and wet coal sacks lying around the coal yard were purloined and used to beat out the fire. Someone charged the office door down, and a similar beating exercise ensued inside the smouldering smoke filled building. It was whilst all this was going on in the yard that Ron Hyde had arrived on the shed and fully explains the absence of anyone actually inside the shed at that time. The fire was effectively extinguished and upon our return to the shed we soon found Ron who was most relieved — to say the very least —

to see our flare lamps and hear the cheerful badinage as we walked up through the shed, and it was perhaps a good thing that the little bowler hatted man in the black raincoat did not see fit to visit Branksome shed in the early hours of that morning.

For sheer friendliness, humour and loyalty, the Somerset and Dorset line as a whole must have been difficult to beat, and this was not confined to any particular time in history or to the footplate staff. Take Fred Toller, an ex-Midland Guard, who transferred to Bournemouth West during the thirties and took over for a time the position of regular guard on the 'Pines'. He soon caught the friendly mood of the line. One day just after leaving Bath Fred was walking up through the train, when he was called into a first class compartment containing three rather prosperous looking gentlemen. One of them who turned out to be a Lord of the realm said, "Care to come in and make up a four at solo?" "Sorry", said Fred, "I can't leave my van unattended for too long". "Tell you what then", his lordship replied. "We'll come back with you" — and so they did. Back in the van a suitcase was used as a table, and others as seats, and the game proceeded nicely, interrupted only by station stops where Fred saw the luggage in his care on and off and thereafter 'flagged' the train on its way again. Every time after this whenever his Lordship travelled to Bournemouth he rode in the Guard's van if Fred was in charge.

However it must be admitted this friendliness could be taken to excess. After the second world war there came to Sturminster Newton a signalman who being friendly and gregarious by nature, found time hung heavily on the night shift and applied his own solution to the problem. He would wait for the up 9.20 pm Bournemouth Central — Bath night freight to pass and he had received the section clear signal from Stalbridge. There was then a lull in traffic from 11.40 pm until 3.00 am when the 1.40 am Poole — Bath freight was due so, leaving his box, he would go to the small shed where the platelayers motor trolley was stored. The shed was kept locked, but this held no fear for the intrepid signalman. Opening it somehow, he would place the trolley on the rails, start the motor and have a run up to Stalbridge or down to Shillingstone as the whim took him. On arrival he would enjoy a chat and share the comfort of some hot tea in the warm oil lit mellowness of the interior of his colleague's signal box before returning through the darkness of a North Dorset night, to the loneliness of his own box. This went on for a while until one night the crossing keeper at Hammoon woke up and heard him pass. Next morning he met the permanent way inspector walking the track and enquired what the trouble was in the night to fetch the trolley out; thus the balloon went up and the signalman went out! so to speak.

But friendly as things were on the line between men of all grades, this rapport was strained from time to time. For instance Sturminster Newton cattle market caused the embankment in the goods yard to be considerably enlarged with sweepings from the cattle wagons in the yard, which were tipped conveniently over the edges of the embankment. This proved very fertile, and local platelayers used to plant marrow seeds in the matter and from their adjacent hut would lovingly watch them grow. However, enginemen eventually got to know about this and more than once under the cover of darkness, a fleet-of-foot fireman, whilst station duties were being carried out on the last down passenger to Bournemouth, would dash across the yard, rustle amongst the leaves groping for two marrows before a speedy return to the engine with one tucked under each armpit. Despite accusations from the gangers of "robbing their patch", the enginemen's denials were emphatic, and never actually having been caught in the act, they grinned and commiserated with the platelayers in their loss.

Another timeless feature of the joint line — particularly on 'the branch' — was the leisureliness of its local passenger trains. Main line trains were usually comprised of three or four coach sets — although two coaches usually sufficed for the branch — with relatively easy work for engine crews when thus engaged; and running late or not, the guard would have his little chat with the station staff. One summer's afternoon Bert White and Donald Beale arrived at Henstridge two or three minutes late on an 'up local' hauled by a '4F' 0-6-0. Bert, keen to regain the lost time, had his hand on the regulator, all ready to start as soon as he got the "tip". Donald peered back along the platform to where the guard was leaning contentedly against his van door, green flag down by his side, chatting to the porter, when suddenly, the green flag was vigorously waved above his head. "Right away Bert", shouted Donald, an almost immediate tug on the regulator from Bert, and they were off. But looking back along the train once more, Donald saw the guard still on the platform dancing up and down excitedly, giving them the stop signal. "Whoa!" Donald yelled. Bert brought the train to a grinding halt, whereupon the guard resumed his chat. Later, on arrival at Templecombe Upper, the guard came up to the engine and laughingly told them his right of way signal had in fact been caused by a wasp buzzing around his head too close for comfort. What a contrast then, this tranquillity in working, compared with working the 'Pines Express' where engines, loaded right up to their capacity, (some might say above it) regularly battled it out with fierce gradients, often adverse weather, and against the clock on a schedule leaving little to spare. The 'Pines Express' was as hard to work as the local trains were easy. The S&D was indeed a line of contrast in many respects.

At the end of 1935 an ex London, Tilbury and Southend 4-4-2 tank, No. 2103, was tried on the system working out of Templecombe shed to both Burnham on 'the branch', and over the main line to Bath. None of the drivers of my immediate acquaintance had any dealings with it though one overheard the comment in Bath shed one day of a driver who did. "What's the 'Tilbury Tank' like then?" he was asked. "'Tilbury Tank'! so that's what they call it" he growled. "I'll give it Bl. . . . . . 'Tilbury Tank'". he muttered as he stomped off up through the shed grumbling away to himself. So in this case one can only make of that what one will. But in general terms this engine was not particularly successful on its S&D line diagrams and following a further period of trials during 1936 on the Bath – Bristol service it was transferred elsewhere. A high coal consumption, a tendency to prime badly when worked hard and unreliable injectors were its downfall as far as the S&D line was concerned.

During the 1930's the S&D rebuilt Johnson '2P's were transferred elsewhere on to the LMS system and the last of the older S&D class of engines were scrapped including the Fox Walker 0-6-0Ts, the 'Scottie' 0-6-0s and the Fowler 0-6-0s. (In fact all these were withdrawn by 1928). But other familiar locomotives arrived, mainly in the shape of more Midland types comprised of '2P' 4-4-0s, and '4F' 0-6-0s and some additional Johnson '3F' 0-6-0s. Heavy express and excursion trains run during holiday periods were usually hauled by a '4F' and '2P' in tandem or perhaps any combination of the two depending on train loading but the normal midweek and winter load of the 'Pines' was six coaches hauled by a Fowler '2P' unassisted. With loads weighing up to 210 tons, this was a formidable task over the 1 in 50 Mendip gradients – as it had been in the past for the rebuilt Johnson engines on the 'Diner', and day after day these engines were thrashed to their limit during the climb over the Mendips.

Relief came to the S&D motive power situation in 1938 with the arrival of a number of the ubiquitous and extraordinarily capable Stanier 'Black Fives'. This was made possible by the rebuilding of several weak bridges on the Mangotsfield – Bath line thus giving the 4-6-0s access to the S&D line. These bridges had long proved troublesome necessitating certain types of locomotives prior to traversing this stretch having to have their side rods removed and be towed along at reduced speed. A Horwich 'Crab' 2-6-0 was tested on the S&D during 1927, the axle loading of which was too heavy for the bridges on the Mangotsfield – Bath line and thus the engine reached Bath in the way described.

The first Stanier 'Black Five' to traverse the line was No. 5228 on trial in March 1938. The engine was driven by Bert Lee of Bath who was quick to appreciate the all round superiority of his mount over the engines he had hitherto been used to over this road. It was not just the superior steaming and pulling in the banks, but the very free running on the level stretches by the six foot 4-6-0. The 6'9" class '2's were rather leaden footed by comparison. Such were the benefits of the modern front and design endowed on the Stanier 'Black Fives'. Following a test run Bert Lee told an admiring audience in the locomen's cabin at Bath how on the journey up from Bournemouth he had passed Sturminster Newton at speed and three minutes later and some four miles further on he was whistling for the Stalbridge up distant signal which was displaying caution.

The tests successfully concluded were followed in May by six of this class being allocated to Bath shed. Once the 'Black Staniers' got to grips with S&D main line passenger trains they soon began to show their paces

133

as evidenced by the mention of their exploits in 'The Month's Best Runs' articles featured in the February 1939 edition of 'The LMS Magazine'.

For S&D crews it was pleasant to traverse with passenger trains Southern Railway territory in the Bournemouth area in charge of an engine that due to its modern purposeful appearance allied to an obvious outstanding ability with regard to heavy load haulage and speed, commanded the respect of Southern enginemen. The class '2P's and '4F's hardly made much impression when viewed against the background of 'Lord Nelsons', 'King Arthurs' and 'Schools' class locomotives which were then the pride of the Southern main line fleet.

As was the case in many parts of the LMS system — and years later virtually throughout the BR system as a whole — no other class of locomotive that ever came to work on the S&D was so generally reliable and useful to shedmasters as the class '5's. Besides being able to work and keep time with the heaviest express trains unassisted between Evercreech Junction and Bournemouth West, they were equally capable of making up for any deficiency of '7F' 2-8-0s on the heavy freight trains operating between Bath and Evercreech Junction — moreover without requiring too drastic a reduction in train load. Their brake power proved satisfactory on these jobs and they could be accommodated on the turntable at 'The Junction' a feature incidentally not possible with the class '9F' 2-10-0s when used on the line in later years which precluded their use on these particular freight services.

The advent of the 'Black Fives' ushered in a new and very welcome era of motive power on the S&D line and at long last its enginemen learned for themselves the true meaning of the expression 'free steaming and free running'. Here was power, and to spare. Not only did the '5's have the power to do the job in all winds and weathers but they also provided S&D enginemen for the first time with spacious comfortable cabs, affording adequate protection from the elements. Their rostered load over the Mendips of 270 tons — roughly eight coaches — was practically based compared to what had gone before and did not tax them so severely as the maximum loads rostered to previous passenger engines. Nevertheless once the enginemen realised what really excellent machines had been put into their hands then the official loading limits for the class '5's were not considered sacrosanct and in later years the 'Black Staniers', and more particularly their counterparts the BR standard class '5's, which arrived to join the Stanier engines on the S&D in 1954, regularly hauled loads greatly in excess of the loading limits laid down. The BR engines in particular performed some remarkable work on the 'Pines Express' during the late fifties and early sixties when that train was formed of some very heavy rolling stock and loads approaching five hundred tons gross were sometimes encountered. But their power and superb steaming capabilities made this a more reliable transgression than was the case with their gallant 4-4-0 and 0-6-0 predecessors.

The class '5's remained in effect the mainstay express passenger loco-motives on the main line from 1938 until the end of through traffic in 1962.

In connection with the introduction of the 'Black Staniers' into the Bournemouth area off the S&D line — I once heard an amusing story in the mess room at Branksome concerning the lifting road bridge at Poole Quay, which today still opens its span to allow ships or smaller craft with insuf-ficient head room to pass through on receipt of three blasts from a ship's siren, thus causing much delay and frustration to local road users. South-bound trains running towards Poole marshalling yard — situated about a mile from Poole Bridge — were instructed to whistle on their approach and when on one of their initial trips to Bournemouth a Stanier '5' obeyed this rule whilst heading the 2.40 am Bath — Bournemouth West mail train, with its Caledonian hooter breaking the dawn silence across the town, Poole Bridge was raised, the bridge operator mistaking the '5's hooter for a ship's siren. In fact there was not a ship of any size in motion on the Poole side of Brownsea Island. It was some while before the error became apparent by which time there was a considerable traffic hold up either side of the bridge even though road traffic then was but a fraction of that pertaining today.

Chapter Five

THE WAR YEARS AND AFTER

I
1939 – 1947

Relief for the locomotive department of the 'Somerset and Dorset' with the welcome arrival of modern and adequate motive power in the shape of the 'Black Fives' in 1938 was brief, for after the outbreak of the second world war in September 1939, most of these hard won engines were gradually transferred elsewhere – much to the chagrin of S&D enginemen. By the end of 1941, 5023, 5194 and 5389 had gone to Perth shed and 5289 and 5432 to Leeds, leaving only 5440 and 5029 at Bath for S&D services.

Thus the war came and in its path the black-out and shortages of men and materials – in fact just about everything. The main line passenger service was reduced to an emergency one of four trains each way and all through trains to the North ceased for a time, but before 1940 was out this situation was eased and a fuller service restored. The most notable was the restoration of a through service from Bournemouth to Birmingham, Derby and Bradford running as a semi-fast over the S&D and which thereafter continued to operate throughout the war period. The Northbound train departed from Bournemouth West at 9.45 am and there was a corresponding down train from the North departing from Bath during the afternoon. Bath shed's two remaining 'Black Fives' were generally employed on the service, but there was a brief spell around 1943 during which the line was without this class of engine. Then a combination of '2P's, '4F's or Horwich 'Crab' 2-6-0s in the main took up the reins on the through service. This was not to the advantage of timekeeping and it was not long before a couple of 'Black Fives' were brought back to the line for this job. By late 1944 No. 5440 had returned to Bath and was joined soon afterwards by 5056 (of which more in a later chapter) and newly built No. 4844, others coming after 1945.

Freight traffic was heavy day and night, and the 2-8-0s contributed greatly to the war effort, moving many tons of goods and wartime equipment over the line. In fact the 1914 series of these incomparable freight locomotives saw out two world wars during their lifetime and rendered yeoman service during both.

Troop trains were often run over the line and some of these were vast ensembles. For example it was reported in a wartime issue of the 'Railway Observer' that one Sunday in November 1942, one of these specials was observed leaving Bath southbound with a train consisting of eleven LMS corridor coaches, a restaurant car, a bogie van, two LMS four wheeled vans and two SR four wheel vans – seventeen vehicles in all. This huge train was hauled by 'Black Five' No. 5440, piloted by an SR 'S11' 4-4-0 and doubtless the crossing of the Mendips made the pair cough more than a bit that day. The line's motive power resources were – as ever– stretched to their limits, and the Southern railway agreed to allocate some of its locomotives to S&D sheds to help out. Most of the engines involved stayed from 1941 until 1945. All elderly types, they were: one 'T9' class No. 304 – although others of the class visited the line, before, during and after the war – 'T1' class Nos. 1 to 6, and 'S11' class engines Nos. 395 to 404. Occasionally other SR types found their way onto the line. For instance 'K10' 4-4-0s did a short stint early in the war and an ex SE&CR Stirling 4-4-0 No. 1188 was once noted during 1941 heading the 3.30 pm Bournemouth West to Bath passenger train, and Drummond '700' class 0-6-0s (nicknamed 'Black Motors') were sometimes seen on the Southern end of the line. However for several ergonomic and mechanical reasons the Southern tender engines were not generally liked by the enginemen. To a lesser extent this was due to the cab design which was rather more spartan and narrow than the more spacious Midland and LMS designs with which they were familiar, and devoid of such refinements as cab roofs extended back to protect the fireman from the elements whilst shovelling. Neither were there cab side doors between engine and tender, (a criticism applying equally well to some ex Midland designs), the provision of which not only improved crew safety but made the footplate much more comfortable by excluding draughts. In addition the sanding gear on the SR engines proved not very efficient and there were some serious bouts of slipping at times up in the hills. Yet another problem with the Drummond designs was priming. They displayed a marked tendency to this trait when worked hard with anything over a half a glass of water. But the most frequently voiced criticism was of the fiddling uncertainty of the steam reversers fitted to some of the exiles. Mostly these were unreliable in the extreme, difficult to set in the required cut off and sluggish in operation, a failing brought rapidly into focus on this difficult line. This was particularly so when these engines were required to start away from station stops situated on adverse gradients. They seemed rather frequently to stop on a 'dead centre' and have to set back, on occasions two or three times before finally getting under way.

Each time the reversers required considerable coaxing before the engines could be reversed, and usually several minutes were lost on schedule before the engines at length finally got their trains away.

The 1914 series of S&D 2-8-0s had steam reversers as first built but because of difficulties in daily operation they were later replaced with screw reversers. It was much the same story in later years with the 'West Country' Pacifics when operating over the S&D in their original form, though in this case the steam reversers were rather more powerful –

though just as unreliable in their way — and drivers could do considerable damage in all sorts of ways if these reversers were not handled with care.

Steam reversers were never popular on the S&D where engines had to be 'driven', and on heavy trains more finesse was required in locomotive handling compared with (say) the Bournemouth — Waterloo main line where once under way the reverser (and regulator) would be set in a suitable position and the driver could often leave it untouched for many miles.

LMS visitors on the line during the wartime period included three Stanier '8F' 2-8-0s briefly, and a good number of Horwich 'Crab' 2-6-0s. This was not the first visit of these massive looking 2-6-0s to the line. Following trials with a Midland '990' class, No. 995 in 1925, Horwich 2-6-0 No. 13064 was given trials over the main line in 1927 and was well thought of by the men. But much to their disgust — having particular regard to the underpowered locomotives then in use — nothing came of the trials. However, as mentioned some of these 2-6-0s visited the line during the war borrowed mainly from Saltley and Burton sheds — indeed they continued to do so up until 1949 — performing some very useful and at times quite sprightly work on passenger trains. On a northbound wartime trip No. 2766 was once reliably timed to reach a maximum speed of 74 mph at Sturminster Newton on an up express. These engines were admired by S&D enginemen for their sheer pulling power in the banks but, in qualification, the effort tended to be transitory for when pushed hard it did tax their steaming capacity somewhat.

On the footplate of these engines the driver's seat rather resembled a piano stool. As they yanked open the regulator, drivers would sometimes remark, "Let's see if we can get a tune out of the old girl". But useful motive power units though they were, a 'Crab' was no Beethoven of the locomotive world. The design was hardly tuned up to concert pitch and though rated then as class '5's they had nothing like the steaming capacity of the Stanier 'Black Five', and a discordant note could sometimes be discerned if one found itself at the head of a train such as the 'Pines Express'.

Midland Compound 4-4-0s made very occasional forays over the Somerset and Dorset from time to time including No. 1046, which was in fact allocated to the line for a time during the second world war. It was employed mostly on local passenger trains like the morning when Branksome crew, Driver Bert Freakley and his mate, the ubiquitous Johnny Walker had it as far as Templecombe on the 6.48 am Bournemouth West to Bath. Bert was noted for 'chopping them off a bit' and true to form before the engine had hardly drawn breath, Bert got his shoulder under the regulator and yanked it wide open. This would have been all right on a simple engine but this action changed 1046 over to full Compound working immediately. With the train barely moving and in the grip of the 1 in 90 gradient out of the West Station 1046 made some very distressed sounds and the train all but stalled. "Close the regulator and open it in the first valve position" shouted Johnny. "No! she won't pull 'em there", said Bert, who it should be said was quite familiar with the method of driving Compound locomotives with their special design of Deeley regulator, this gleaned from earlier days spent at Stoke. But at the time of this run he had not been on a Compound for some time, therefore it can only be assumed that in a moment of mental aberration Bert thought he was on a '2P'. However Johnny gave him a lightning teach-in on the correct driving procedure for a Compound and Bert was persuaded to revert the regulator to the first valve position whereafter the Compound started to gather speed again, and no further problems were experienced.

In mentioning No. 1046 it is interesting to recall briefly that the first engine of this type to traverse the line occurred in December 1924 when No. 1065 was given trials between Bath and Bournemouth to ascertain whether an engine of that type could work a 230 ton train unassisted throughout and adhere to the existing timetable. Its performance was also compared against S&D 4-4-0 No. 67 hauling 190 tons the maximum tare load for that class. The result in brief showed the superiority of the Compound over its smaller competitor in terms of coal burnt per drawbar horsepower hour. But its inability to develop a high tractive effort at low speeds on the heavy banks made it unsuitable for its intended use on 230 ton trains. In point of interest the aforementioned simple 4-4-0, No. 995, coped very well with a like load and but for problems of fitting it onto the turntable at Bath, all ten engines in the class might well have been sent for use on the line.

A further and most interesting addition to the list of wartime locomotive visitors were ex-Great Eastern rebuilt 'B.12' (reclassified 'B12/3') 4-6-0s. The trains hauled by the 'B12/3' were ten austerity (USA) ambulance trains equipped and staffed by the U.S. Army, formed of British rolling stock and Westinghouse braked. The Great Eastern 4-6-0s were selected because of their wide route availability and also due to their being equipped with Westinghouse compressed air brake, vacuum ejector and vacuum Westinghouse combination valve and proportional valve, giving the engines compatibility with vacuum fitted stock. This was particularly relevant to the S&D line when these ambulance trains required double heading over the Mendips — the pilot engine being vacuum fitted only. Under these conditions the driver of the assisting engine who was in charge of braking had to exercise very special care in the application of the brake. Indeed this mix of Westinghouse and vacuum braking caused such problems in practice that eventually special dispensation was given locally for vacuum fitted engines when assisting these trains to run with their vacuum connection not coupled to the train engine. The pilot engine merely hooked on the front of the 'B12/3' and the coupling was screwed up tightly. Drivers of the assisting engine were instructed to desist from touching their brake valve, the braking of the train being left entirely to the driver of the train engine. This practice was entirely at variance with the official general instructions published in connection with the working of these ambulance trains.

The ten ambulance trains were berthed in a number of places throughout the Southern half of the country and each had a permanent crew who lived on the train; these consisted of two drivers, two firemen, one fitter and two guards. Some of these were LNER men and some were provided by the Southern Railway. One of these trains (No. 36) was berthed at Templecombe. It consisted of fourteen bogies weighing 435 tons tare and had the capacity to carry 252 patients in a lying position with 64 sitting. The engine normally coupled to this train was No. 8549 which was shedded at Templecombe. There were also two of these U.S.A. trains berthed at Bournemouth West carriage sidings (Nos. 27 and 31) the 'B12/3's belonging to which were shedded at Bournemouth.

In the early stages of the war a number of S&D enginemen were drafted into the armed services but with freight trains and troop specials running day and night manpower grew short, and some men were recalled from the services. Mercifully the line suffered little from enemy action. Nevertheless one evening in October 1942, the war did come suddenly to the tiny village of Templecombe.

It was about 9.5 pm and the last Bath — Bournemouth passenger train of the day was setting back in the pitch darkness of the wartime blackout down the spur from Templecombe Upper Station to Templecombe No. 2 Junction before continuing the journey to Bournemouth. Suddenly the engine crew were startled by a loud bang which sounded over the hissing steam and the ringing noise emitted by their 'S 11s' side rods. "Detonators!" exclaimed the fireman. "Detonators be bothered" exclaimed his driver, Bert Freakley, "that was a Bomb!". This conclusion had been amply supported by a brick crashing through Bert's cab front window moments after the first report rent the air, narrowly missing him. Fortunately little further damage was sustained by the train and its occupants, but others in its environs were less fortunate. The bomb blast caused the death of thirteen people at Templecombe that evening of whom five were railwaymen.

A notable and happier occasion during the war was the visit of a 'Royal Train' to the line on May 14th 1940, when King George VI accompanied by Queen Elizabeth travelled to Blandford in order to inspect the troops at the nearby army camp. Several S&D enginemen were involved in the working including the Branksome crew of Driver Jack Flynn with Donald Beale firing for him. This pair worked the train from Broadstone to Blandford.

Royal Trains were fairly infrequent on the Joint Line. Once in 1915 King George V and Winston Churchill visited Blandford Camp to review the naval division before the departure for Gallipoli. Other S&D royal occasions were when King Edward VII came to nearby Iwerne Minster house and alighted at Shillingstone. To mark this Shillingstone was made a 'first class' station and thereafter the station masters cap always sported the gold braid.

For the 1940 Royal Train 'Black Five' No. 5274 in ex-works condition was specially worked down light engine from Saltley to Branksome shed, and another of the same class, No. 5269, was worked from Bristol to Blandford to assist in shunting movements there. This engine also worked the return empty Royal Train from Blandford to Broadstone later in the day.

At Branksome, driver Jack Flynn and Donald Beale booked on duty at 11.30 pm on the night of Monday May 13th to prepare No. 5274 and found Mr. Whitaker in the mess room. He was by now the LMS District Locomotive Superintendent at Bristol. Also present was LMS Locomotive Inspector Hartright. "Hello are you riding with us?" enquired Donald. "No", he replied grinning, "I'll see you later at Blandford. Besides you don't need me, if Jack can drive a train for 364 days a year he can manage on the 365th – even if it is the Royal Train!"

After preparing the engine Jack Flynn and Donald proceeded light to Broadstone, arriving at 1.45 am where they were placed in the up platform of the Hamworthy – Broadstone line to await the arrival of the Royal special from London.

At 2.13 am the Royal Train – having departed from Waterloo at 11 pm – emerged out of the darkness at Broadstone from the direction of Wimborne having taken the Ringwood – West Moors line at Lymington Junction. Here reversal took place and 5274 backed on to the train whilst at the other end 'T9' No. 119, then the Southern Railway's regular Royal Train engine on light formations which had hauled it from London, unhooked. At 2.21 am the 'Black Stanier' sporting the four lamp Royal headcode – one at the base of the chimney and three across the buffer beam – ghosted out into the night onto S&D metals heading for Blandford. Not much over three hours before the King had been in the capital welcoming Queen Wilhelmina of the Netherlands, who had fled her own country from the invading German Army.

When I was his fireman Donald often told me how proud he was to have been chosen for this special working, short as it was in terms of actual mileage run. He recalled how as they climbed up the 1 in 97 out of Broadstone, the realisation that Jack Flynn and himself were at the head of the Royal Train and that the King and his Queen were riding behind suddenly came home to him. As the seven coach train sped down the bank through Corfe Mullen he wondered what the villagers reaction would have been if having awoke from their slumbers, and upon hearing it pass, they had known who was on board; but this train was secret, although not totally unseen. As they roared through Spetisbury at 60 mph Donald saw the silhouette against the night sky of a British 'Tommy' with his rifle over his shoulder standing on an overbridge and he realised the whole route was being guarded and many eyes were watching their progress.

After arrival at Blandford at 2.38 am the Royal Train was shunted into the goods yard on the down side by the combined efforts of 5289 and 5274, one at each end, and it then only remained for the latter engine to steam heat the train for the remainder of the night, still in the charge of Jack and Donald, whilst the King and Queen slept, and all concerned with this working hoped devoutly that 'Fritz' would stay away.

Later on Inspector Hartwright joined Jack Flynn and Donald on the footplate and was chatting quietly to them when they were joined by Mr. Sealy the LMS District Controller at Bath who had travelled on the train. He arrived quite convulsed with laughter and as he had difficulty in controlling himself it was quite a few moments before he could speak. It transpired that whilst watching four platelayers placing galvanized trays under the coaches in order that the waste pipes from the toilets could drain into them, someone inside one of the coaches had 'pulled the chain', and one burly platelayer received the full force of a flushed toilet over his arm. According to Mr. Sealy the poor fellow rose from his knees, his right arm extended as far from his nose as he possibly could, and flicking his fingers up and down staggered away from the scene with an apoplectic face, his eyeballs popping, and stifling his unspoken rage. In playing card parlance — truly a 'Royal Flush!'

Dawn came quickly enough after a quiet night, and Jack Flynn and Donald were relieved by Driver Albert Good and Fireman Harry Jeans of Templecombe shed. But the Branksome crew were still on the station platform standing with Mr. Whitaker and Mr. Sealy when H.M. Queen Elizabeth stepped from the train on her way to a royal engagement near Wimborne, whilst the King himself was at Blandford Camp. Donald told me, "I still carry her picture in my memory, as clear now as on the 14th May 1940. She was every bit a Queen and the smile she swept over us as though to say 'thank you' made our day".

Later that morning — 11.30 am in fact — the Royal Train departed from Blandford running as empty stock to Downton, on the West Moors to Salisbury line. It was hauled by class '5' No. 5289 to Broadstone, and there relieved by No. 119. Later the Royal party re-boarded the train at Downton and departed at 3.00 pm for Waterloo via Salisbury.

Another wartime incident on the S&D — though a much less happy one — was on Monday 13th March 1944 when there occurred at Henstridge a serious accident involving a double headed train. The train was a southbound troop special made up to 10 coaches which had been taken over at Bath by LMS '4F' 0-6-0 No. 4523, piloted by Southern 'S11' 4-4-0 No. 402. Bath enginemen were on both engines — Driver Dave Hadfield and Fireman Reg Gunning on 402 with Driver Harold Burford and Fireman Ted Pauley on 4523. Even before the incident at Henstridge things were not going well with the train, which was steadily losing time as it progressed southwards due, in part, to a fierce gale force wind which up in the Mendips was catching the train full broadside on, but mainly to a marked reluctance on the part of the '4F' to maintain steam pressure, and Harold Burford had to bring the troop special to an unscheduled stop at Binegar to enable 4523 to recover her breath and get some more water in the boiler before going over Masbury Summit. Later on in the journey, with the Templecombe Junctions passed, the train was speeding on favourable gradients towards the overbridge carrying the main A30 road near Henstridge station when the two engine crews saw with horror a heavy army transporter, crashing through the bridge parapet now almost directly above them. The next few seconds caused chaos of considerable magnitude. The falling vehicle struck No. 402 first and then fell neatly between the two engines, in consequence of which No. 402 broke away from 4523 and hurtled on for a considerable distance down the line towards Stalbridge with pieces of the transporter and its load festooned over the engine before Dave Hadfield could manage to stop it. The remainder of the transporter and its load hit No. 4523, smashing the smokebox and derailing the 0-6-0 which careered off the rails into an adjacent field before eventually ploughing to rest. Considerable damage was sustained by the first five coaches of the train, a number of fatalities occurred amongst the soldiers and several were injured. Though severely shaken, Harold Burford and his mate were able to put out the fire in 4523 and so prevent further damage to the boiler and firebox after which both assisted in rendering first aid to injured troops. Whilst doing this Harold himself nearly became a casualty. He was treating a soldier who had sustained a broken leg when another soldier who happened to be passing noticed that Harold's overalls were smouldering at the rear and looking ready to burst into flames, but they were doused before this could happen. Eventually help arrived to take over the task of caring for the injured and an army officer sent 4523's crew to the Henstridge Station Master's house for shock treatment which in fact consisted of a 'good old cup of tea'. But it will be noted that this was not before they had taken care of the safety of their engine and to the best of their ability the well being of their passengers, and by so doing acted in the highest tradition of British Railwaymen.

Later in the day this gallant engine crew plus their equally shaken colleagues, Dave Hadfield and Reg Gunning retrieved off the runaway 402, were able to return to Bath travelling up as passengers on the 'Perishable' train which they boarded at Templecombe. They arrived safely at Bath to the great relief of their colleagues many of whom upon hearing over the grapevine of the crash were under the impression that both crews had been killed; fortunately an erroneous assumption. Incidentally one man who had a grandstand view of this accident was William Jackson a porter at Henstridge Station who at the instant that the collision occurred was up a signal post putting the lamp back in a signal after cleaning and filling it with paraffin. Part of the wreckage hit the signal post snapping the signal off like a dry stick with Mr. Jackson still up top. But he fortunately managed to escape unhurt by dropping into a field — as the signal tilted over.

Branksome shed was temporarily closed from June 1942 until the end of the war and its duties were worked out of the SR Bournemouth Central shed by the temporarily transferred Branksome crews, and a mixture of LMS and SR locomotives. The price of berthing LMS engines on a Southern Railway shed was an occasionial buckled water pick up scoop, by reason of the Southern men before shifting LMS engines on shed erroneously operating the water pick up scoop under the misapprehension that they were taking off the tender handbrake. The scoops did not take kindly to attempts at picking up lengths of rail or even sleepers in the loco yard where the track was uneven and not in good condition. The hand brake and water scoop controls were identical in appearance but the hand brake was situated on the right hand side of the tender, the water scoop controls being on the left. Southern engines it will be remembered were not similarly fitted, no water pick up troughs being situated on that railway — although this had been mooted in the past. Mind you in return a price had to be paid at first for having Southern engines working regularly on the S&D. With Midland and LMS engines it was for years normal practice on S&D sheds when cleaning fires to hook up several fire bars from the grate thus providing a hole through which ashes and clinker could be dropped into the ashpan from which they could be raked out into the drop pit. This was instead of laboriously removing clinker from the firebox out of the firehole door using a long clinker shovel as was normal practice on the Southern — a most distasteful and sweaty job, particularly on those SR engines with ratchet and flap type firehole doors. The very limited gap through which clinker had to be manoeuvred on engines so fitted moved resourceful S&D firemen, who elected to clean the fire by 'the baling out' method, to unbolt and remove the entire firehole door assembly, thus widening the gap considerably. When firebars had been moved, they would be replaced with a suitable fire iron, a task requiring a certain amount of expertise. It was in this area that problems with the Southern engines usually occurred. The firebars in Southern engines were set rather closer together than was the case on Midland and LMS locomotives and it often proved impossible to replace the firebars by use of fire irons even though the firebars had been previously removed without too much trouble by the optimistic crew. This possibly meant an engine failure requiring removal of the fire to allow the 'bar boy' to enter the firebox later and replace the firebars by hand or more likely there was some surreptitious spacing out of the remaining fire bars in the firebox. However incidents like these ceased when Branksome shed re-opened in 1945 after the cessation of hostilities, and resumed its former role. With more LMS engines now available for S&D work including additional Stanier 'Black Fives' the rather feeble Southern engines were returned to their proper homes, unsung and unwanted on the S&D but having nevertheless given valuable help during the preceding troubled period.

After the war there was a steady recovery of S&D train services and the through Manchester — Bournemouth West 'Pines Express' service was restored on October 7th 1946. To be strictly accurate its former title 'Pines Express' was not officially restored until 1949, although S&D staff and regular travellers naturally referred to it by that name — as indeed they had to the resumed wartime Bournemouth/Midland service referred to earlier. To the Manchester portion were added through coaches to and from Sheffield and Liverpool which together comprised a load of ten or eleven coaches during the winter months and twelve in summer which required daily the services of an assisting engine both ways between Evercreech Junction and Bath. This was a regular Templecombe '2P' duty until 1961 when for the last year or so of its S&D routing the 'Pines' assisting job was usually performed by a BR class '4' 4-6-0.

1947 saw Britain in the grip of an arctic winter and with a severe coal crisis. In common with certain other trains elsewhere the 'Pines' was temporarily withdrawn in order to help conserve coal stocks thus causing a number of redundancies on the line. For example Donald Beale as the then youngest driver in seniority at Branksome shed was temporarily put back firing — he had been promoted to driver in 1943 — so 28 years after starting on the railway he was once more back on 'the shovel'. Fortunately this setback did not last for too long before the 'Pines' was reinstated once more.

Earlier in August 1946 owing to the deterioration of the coal situation the then Minister of Transport announced a large scale oil firing conversion programme covering all four main line groups, involving 1,217 locomotives and about 58 locomotive depots at which they would be stationed. Bath shed became involved in this and two class '5's Nos 4826 and 4830, were equipped for oil firing and found great favour with S&D firemen. It was planned for all eleven '7F' 2-8-0s to be similarly dealt with, but this did not come about. Lofty oil storage tanks were built at Bath Motive Power depot. They were located facing number nine shed road, which was to be the refuelling point. The pumping machinery was unloaded and partly erected and then suddenly at the end of 1947, the project was halted owing to the lack of the necessary foreign exchange to pay for the oil and in consequence it was back to coal dust, ashes, clinker, sweat and toil for the firemen who had got used to the soft life on 4826 and 4830.

Mind you this should not be taken to mean that with oil firing, steaming problems for footplate crews were entirely absent. As with coal firing there were certain conditions when a 'rough trip' was assured. Like the occasion that Donald Beale and his fireman Johnny Walker encountered in the winter of 1947 when working a down express. Prior to refuelling their engine— 'Black Five' No. 4830 — at Bath, a fresh oil tank wagon had been shunted into position against the coal road siding stop block — the temporary refuelling site — and there was some delay in connecting up its steam heating pipes to the trailing connection leading to an engine standing in No. 2. shed road whose job it was to supply steam heating to the

145

fuel oil thus keeping it at its correct viscosity. In consequence of this delay the oil was very sluggish when 4830 was refuelled and the oil temperature still some way from its optimum when Donald and Johnny departed from Bath with the 'Black Five' hauling eight coaches unassisted for the return trip to Bournemouth. 4830's oil heating element was fully on but the oil temperature gauge needle was most obdurate in its upward movement. Not so however the downward movement of the boiler steam pressure gauge which dropped back with alarming ease. After a most laborious ascent of the Mendips, Binegar was approached with the train some 15 minutes late, and the boiler pressure gauge and water level vying with each other for the lowest position – indeed the boiler water level was so low that Donald was wondering whether to stop and get some more water in the boiler in case the change in gradient at Masbury Summit from 1 in 73 up to 1 in 50 down should cause water to drain from the crown of the firebox. Then realising the flexibility of oil firing compared to coal Donald shouted to Johnny across the footplate, "As we approach the summit make sure both the injectors are working, and when we go over the top, shut off the oil supply to the burner and close the dampers. We'll drop down the bank without a fire". With boiler pressure back to 140 lb and the water now all but out of sight in the gauge glass 4830 painfully dragged her load at a crawl over the summit. Then, keeping the regulator cracked open to lift the water level in the boiler, they gathered speed down the succeeding 1 in 50, but pressure had fallen further to 120 lb and it was fortunate that the 'Black Five's' vacuum equipment was in good order for she still showed 20 inches of vacuum on the gauge. As they sped down the Southern slopes of the Mendips two pairs of eyes gazed anxiously at the water gauge glass waiting for the first bob of water to wink at them, but it was not until they swept up the brief rise into Shepton Mallet station, before any appeared in the glass. On the continuation of the 1 in 50 descent to Evercreech Junction Johnny affixed some cotton waste soaked in paraffin to a long rod. This was lit and pushed into the firebox. With the oil supply valve opened 4830 burst into life again with a Boomf! as the oil ignited and filled the firebox once more with bright yellow flame. Closing the regulator and the shutting off of one injector caused boiler pressure gradually to rise, and joy of joys, so did the oil temperature in the tender as Evercreech neared. After the scheduled stop at Evercreech Junction – including a deliberately contrived drawn out operation of taking water at the column to allow the engine chance to recover – the boiler pressure in 4830 had risen to 225 lb coupled to a respectable water level showing in the boiler, and Donald and Johnny were back in business. The green flag fluttered from the rear of the train and the 'Black Five' departed from 'the junction' with a savage snap in its exhaust as Donald started looking for those lost minutes on the continuation of the run to Bournemouth.

This was not the first occasion that oil fired locomotives had been used on the line. Several S&D engines were converted from coal to oil burning during the coal shortage of 1921 but the oil firing technique applied then was not so successful as that used in 1947. The combustion was so incomplete at times on the S&D engines that sometimes during a run unburned oil could be observed running off the leading coach roof. However this too was a short lived experiment and with improved coal supplies soon forthcoming, the engines were returned to coal firing once more.

II
1948 – 1966

Nationalisation came to Britain's railway system on January 1st 1948 and thereafter the London Midland Region, Southern Region and Western Region all had a hand at different times and in various ways over the years in the operation and administration of the ex S&DJR, and regional boundaries were re-drawn through the system several times between then and its closure in March 1966. On this account the line's footplatemen most of whom had previously worked under the regimes of either the S&D or Midland and later LMSR now took a turn under the auspices of the Southern Region. But as if this was not enough many were later destined to be shuffled to yet another region – this time the Western. But in many ways these were paper alterations and in essence the line remained Midland cum LMS in character as far as the outlook of its men and the general appearance of its motive power was concerned.

In 1950 the locomotive depots were transferred from the London Midland Region to the Southern Region who assumed responsibility for the motive power on the S&D and it looked at one time as though it was the intention that some Southern types would take over permanently S&D duties from the LMS engines. But the Southern engines that were tried out at various times proved far from at home on this heavy line and the S&D's stock of LMS engines – which were then on loan to the SR – continued to predominate and most were eventually transferred to the Southern Region stock book in 1953.

The aftermath of the second world war saw a tremendous increase in summer holiday travel throughout Great Britain and at the height of the holiday seasons the S&D line on Saturdays was called upon to handle the heaviest volume of passenger traffic between Bournemouth and towns in the Midlands and North of England in its entire history. This situation also reflected the rapid development of Bournemouth (plus the attraction of so much of the beautiful area surrounding it) into one of the country's best and most popular summer seaside resorts. During the early and middle fifties post war summer Saturday holiday traffic reached a tremendous peak and the line's capacity was strained to the utmost.

These were thrilling days for S&D railway enthusiasts. The inward procession of weekend overnight trains from Midland and Northern cities and towns into Bournemouth West started well before daybreak and lasted until around 7.30 am on Saturday mornings. After propelling their trains into the carriage sidings and turning on the Branksome triangle all the engines repaired briefly to an increasingly congested and clinker strewn Branksome shed for servicing, and to await the later exodus of holiday makers returning home. This started at around 8.00 am and reached its climax with a veritable procession of S&D line departures out of Bournemouth West between 9.25 am until 10.35 am after which the northbound traffic intensity gradually eased off. Lastly from roughly mid afternoon until the cool of the evening came the third S&D procession of the day — the incoming daytime holiday trains from the North rumbled into Bournemouth West. In between all these specials were sandwiched the normal S&D passenger service augmented by various empty stock and light engine workings, all of which taxed the line beyond its capacity and strict punctuality was often impossible. Most goods trains however, were cancelled on summer Saturdays thus making available additional engine crews and line capacity on which to handle the extra traffic.

Almost any engine that could turn a wheel was pressed into service somehow or other, and resources of manpower — particularly at Branksome and Bath sheds — were similarly stretched.

The arrival on the S&D of its first (three BR class '5's) but eventually sizeable fleet of BR standard locomotives from May 1954 onwards with their labour saving devices — self cleaning smokeboxes, rocking grates, self emptying ashpans and easy lubrication, which required no pit to facilitate preparative and disposal duties — contributed greatly to keeping things moving. A late arrival on shed with many ex LM or SR types often required a re-shuffling in their order of departure time from shed prior to working back. But a BR engine could arrive on shed well behind time yet depart again on its rostered diagram working. Sometimes they would be in and gone again in barely half an hour, something not possible with many locomotives unless preparation and disposal duties were badly skimped. There is no doubt that these excellent standard engines were not generally used to the best advantage by BR operating authorities or allowed to demonstrate as a matter of policy their more intensive utilisation potential.

Exploring briefly once more the world of S&D "might have beens" — the 1955 building programme of BR standard locomotives originally featured five class '6's 'Clan' 4-6-2s for the Southern Region Nos. 72010-14 named respectively, *Hengist*, *Horsa*, *Canute*, *Wildfire* and *Firebrand*. Rumours eminating around 1954 from certain quarters at Bath suggested that probably three of these engines were destined to replace the Southern Pacifics then at Bath. In the event the ten original BR 'Clan' Pacifics that were built and allocated to sheds in the northern half of the country proved less successful in service than was hoped and apparently were unable to surpass the best performances of the lighter and cheaper class '5' 4-6-0s. Subsequently it was considered that there was no requirement for more engines in this category and the projected building of further 'Clans' was cancelled. Much later on when the ten original 'Clans' were being displaced by dieselisation from their normal duties in the northern half of the country, I heard a whisper at Bath shed one day that some of these redundant Pacifics were destined for S&D line service. But this was a transfer that ultimately never took place. Naturally it would have been of interest to see how these engines — of rather poor reputation according to most lay railway writers though not all professional railwaymen agreed — would perform on such a train as the 'Pines Express'.

The successful operation of the post war summer services depended upon the willing co-operation of the staff, and it was normal throughout the 1950's and early 60's for enginemen to work on their "rest days". Indeed at Branksome shed enginemen engaged in working some of the Saturday Bournemouth — Bath locals as far as Templecombe, did two round trips from Bournemouth to Templecombe and back instead of the customary one. With the shed work — preparation, disposal, shovelling coal forward on the tender etc. — added to the running times this meant anything up to a twelve hour shift. Similarly men working express trains from Bournemouth to Bath and back could expect to log up similar hours of duty, particularly if they had one of the four 'West Country' Pacifics loaned from Bournemouth Central shed on most summer Saturdays and which had to be returned after their S&D stint. Traffic was so intense in the Bournemouth area, even in the late evening, that signalmen had difficulty in finding a spare pathway to get light engines from Bournemouth West carriage sidings either to Branksome, turning the engines on the triangle in the process — or to Bournemouth Central sheds. It normally happened that engines destined for Bournemouth Central once released from the carriage sidings got only as far as Gas Works Junction Signalbox — less than a ¼ mile away — before it was necessary to clear the up main line again. Therefore they were shunted into a siding alongside the up main line near the lofty Bourne Valley Viaducts. This happened to quite a number of engines travelling light to Bournemouth Central from the direction of Bournemouth West or Poole. Eventually having 'snared' perhaps six or seven engines in his net, the Gas Works Junction Signalman would at the appropriate time release them once more now all coupled together, and the crocodile of engines — predominantly Southern types but occasionally including a Bath based standard '5' or a Great Western 'Hall' from Oxford amongst them — would wend their way in the twilight towards Bournemouth Central — and another traffic jam. That depot's disposal pit and approach roads were usually jammed with engines standing amidst mountains of ash and clinker, and it was necessary therefore to store engines waiting to get on to shed, usually in the up through road in the station until there was room on the pit, whereupon an engine would be allowed on to shed. Officially enginemen were not permitted to leave their engine until it had been taken on to shed, placed over the disposal pit and positioned clear of all points and crossings. With the situation thus, Branksome enginemen often booked on duty at around 9.00 am and did not get relief from duty until past 9 pm or perhaps 10 pm that night. After a hot dusty day spent on a Pacific's footplate the memory lingers on of the cup of tea that Donald and I enjoyed in the Bournemouth Central station refreshment room as we waited for a train to transport us to Branksome. Hot, dirty and tired as we were, it was pleasant to relax now and reflect on the trip we had shared that day. This was what the summer service meant to many an engineman, in this case particularly to S&D enginemen from Branksome who had an engine borrowed from Bournemouth Central shed on a summer Saturday in the 1950's. In all the line's history this was probably its most useful and the most fascinating period of all, and with which it was my great good fortune to be concerned, coinciding as it did with my own footplate career at Branksome shed, an experience I would not have missed for anything. However, in my previous book "Mendips Engineman" I have already described in some detail my own footplate life on the S&D from 1953 culminating with the passage over the line of the last up and down 'Pines Express' on September 8th 1962 (in which I had a hand) following which it was re-routed via Basingstoke, Reading and Oxford on its journey to and from Manchester. So with this in mind, and in order to avoid, if possible, the charge of *déjà vu*, I will not dwell overlong on the general day to day events of this period.

All this intense year by year summer activity earlier described ended effectively with the transference of the 'Pines Express', away from the S&D line (along with all other through traffic). This was a decision sorely felt by S&D railwaymen, not only because it marked the beginning of the end for their line, but by virtue of losing the train that was their pride and joy and for which the privilege of working was the culmination of most S&D enginemen's ambition. Thereafter, instead of being a trunk route to the Midlands and North, the S&D now became purely local in essence and remained so until its closure in March 1966. Evidenced not only by the loss of its through passenger service but also by the radically shorter freight trains to be seen on the line, often hauled by Stanier '8F's which started to appear regularly in 1961 to bolster the dwindling ranks of the veteran S&D 2-8-0s due to scrapping. This re-routing severed for the first time since 1st October 1910 — when the Manchester — Bournemouth forerunner of the 'Pines Express' commenced running — Bath and Branksome sheds' hand in the running of this train over the S&D section by virtue of Bath shed normally providing the motive power for its haulage and Branksome the engine crew both ways for much of this period — although during the 20's and 30's Bath shed provided the crew for the 'Pines' in the down direction only. Templecombe shed's contribution by supplying when necessary the engine and crew for the piloting work over the Mendips should also be acknowledged. This situation continued largely unchanged right up until the last time the up and down 'Pines Express' ran over the line, Bath shed providing to haul it BR standard class '9F' 2-10-0 *Evening Star* — the engine having been specially transferred to Bath for this occasion. No. 92220 looked a fine sight tackling twelve bogies unassisted throughout in both directions, the normal assisting engine over the Mendips being dispensed with for this occasion. The reason for so doing and how I came to be the driver of No. 92220 on the northbound leg of this 'last occasion' I have fully described in my previous book. Suffice it to say here then that *Evening Star* gave on September 8th a final demonstration of what excellent locomotives the '9F's were for S&D main line passenger work — though not for all year round use due to their lack of steam heating equipment.

In passing I sometimes wonder what old S&D drivers such as 'Cocker' Chamberlain — whose exploits on a class '2' feature in Chapter Three — and others of his generation would have thought if they could have known that one day massive 2-10-0 locomotives would be working S&D main line expresses that could haul twice the tonnage that made his 4-4-0 struggle so gallantly. Doubtless the prospect would have warmed the cockles of Inspector Wells heart had he lived to see it, though 'Cockers' fireman Bill Dark might have had some reservations. The class '9's were highly efficient steam locomotives — particularly the double chimney version with which the S&D line was supplied — but power is not obtained for nothing, as sweating firemen quickly found out when the 2-10-0s were unleashed. Equivalent draw bar horse powers of over 2000 were recorded with them on more than one occasion on the 'Pines Express' and indicated horse powers but little if at all short of 3000 being obtained on occasions.

For example under full load conditions on the 'Pines' it was often necessary to steam the '9F's at a rate equivalent to over 30,000lb of steam an hour, at times for quite lengthy periods. Certainly the eighteen miles from leaving Bath with the engine "cold" up to Masbury Summit gave the fireman on the Southbound 'Pines' an interesting forty minutes or so. Having done it on many occasions I can personally testify that one was at full stretch throughout and sweating profusely from the effect of keeping the '9F's 40-2 square feet of grate area supplied with coal, sometimes with the engine consuming almost one cwt. every minute. Much of this length was done to the accompaniment of a thunderous exhaust issuing from the chimney which kept the interior of the firebox looking like an electric arc furnace, this in turn threw back almost intolerable heat on to the fireman feeding this inferno. The exhaust injector would be on continuously plus occasional use of the live steam injector to keep the water level up in the boiler. There was little margin for any mismanagement on the part of the fireman or else the effort would collapse. This of course was only part of what was for the 'Pines' fireman a pretty hard day's work involving the working of both the up and the down train plus intermediately carrying out full preparation and disposal duties on the engine at Bath shed. This job certainly sorted out the men from the boys. Historically, engines engaged on S&D express passenger trains had always been regularly flogged to the limit on the adverse sections. But no matter how hard the 4-4-0s of yore were worked on the 'Diner' and later the 'Pines', any average fireman would have little trouble in keeping pace with their demands for coal. But a '9F' working practically all out was a very different kettle of fish. From Bath to Masbury alone they could consume one to one and a quarter tons of coal, an amount which would almost have seen a class '2' through to Bournemouth on the pre-war 'Pines'. The working of these big 2-10-0s when unassisted throughout on the 'Pines Express' between Bath and Bournemouth or vice versa provide the hardest physical task ever normally faced by any previous S&D fireman. When one considers these engines working in 50% cut off, or even more, with full regulator at speeds of around 20/30 mph and sometimes more one can imagine the pandemonium let loose in the hills. Understanding what all this means in the physical sense one can better sympathise with the Branksome fireman who, upon arrival back at the shed one evening in July 1960, tired, grimy and sweating after an 'unassisted' day on the job with poor coal in the tender, and a trailing load well in excess of the 410 tons maximum load limit, telephoned control in some ill humour to express his feelings and during the conversation declared, "If you want super engines on this job you'd better get super firemen to fire them because I'm not". But that was said in the heat of the moment and of course he did fire them on many subsequent occasions. Nevertheless, thereafter the 410 ton limit was much more strictly adhered to and authority saw to it that for any load appreciably over the limit – and the tare load frequently reached and sometimes even exceeded 430 tons at this time – assistance was provided over the Mendips. Thus it was in deference to the fireman's back that basically piloting remained the norm on the 'Pines Express' over the Northern part of the line, notwithstanding the use of the '9F' 2-10-0s which were capable of handling unassisted the heaviest passenger trains normally to be seen on S&D metals and gain substantially on schedule, as Donald and I proved on several occasions. But it must be admitted that whilst steam locomotives remained hand fired, such performances were not reliably obtainable on a daily basis. I am afraid it was more than flesh and blood could regularly stand.

The overall firing rate expected from Bath to Bournemouth with an unassisted '9F' on the 'Pines' was approximately 3000lb per hour, regarded by BR as the maximum to be expected for one fireman to sustain. But overloading of the engine, poor quality coal in the tender, or inclement weather conditions – and how often all three of these conditions transpired to combine – could cause this figure to be exceeded quite substantially.

Chapter Six

KEEP TAKING THE TABLETS

With a high proportion of single-line track incorporated within the Somerset and Dorset system (60 miles out of 105½) the single-line tablet was one of the most important and sometimes troublesome constituents in the daily life of S&D engine crews. The purpose of the single-line tablet was to avoid head-on collisions on the single-line sections. The driver of a train occupying a stretch of single-line had always to be in possession of the tablet (or token) given to him by the signalman at the beginning of the section. If there was an assistant engine the tablet was normally shown to each driver but carried on the rearmost engine. Drivers rendered themselves liable to dismissal if they left a token station without the tablet for the section of line over which the train was about to run. The single-line tablet itself was withdrawn by the signalman from his Tyer electric tablet instrument, and this machine was electrically interlocked with another at the signalbox at the other end of the section, so that once the tablet had been withdrawn from either instrument, both became locked. It was impossible to draw another tablet from either until the first had been replaced.

The names of the signal boxes between which the tablet applied were clearly inscribed upon it, and drivers had to be careful not to overcarry it. Once it was in the driver's possession no other train (under normal conditions) was allowed into that section until the tablet had been handed in to the signalman at the other end of the section.

Tablet exchanging on the S&D main line was normally carried out by means of the automatic exchanging apparatus designed by Alfred Whitaker during his reign at Highbridge works. As fitted on the engine, and at most signal boxes, it was a combined deliverer and receiver. But signal boxes located where the line diverged from single to double or vice versa (such as at Midford) only required a lineside standard for receiving in one direction or delivery in the other. The locomotive catcher as fitted to S&D engines was carried outside the tender close to its side, and was mechanically swung or slid out into position when tablet catching was imminent. But on later engines allocated to the line, such as the Stanier class '5's, Bulleid light Pacifics, and various BR standard types, the catcher was stored in the engine cab when out of use, and it was necessary for the fireman to lift the heavy gun metal catcher outside of the cab, and slide it into a bracket welded or bolted onto the outside of the tender. This was a fairly dangerous and difficult procedure with the engine travelling at speed, but it was a way of life to S&D engine crews who rarely gave this a second thought. However, it could sometimes present problems even to them, but more of this later.

When collecting the tablet, the jaws of the engine's mechanical apparatus engaged with the metal loop of a leather pouch, inside which the tablet itself was carried, snatching it from the lineside apparatus. Outgoing tablets were placed between two spring clips at the rear of the catcher, to be picked up by the signalman's mechanical apparatus. Occasionally engines working over the line were not fitted with catchers, or perhaps the equipment might be in some way defective. In these circumstances the tablet was exchanged by hand using a leather pouch with a large metal loop which necessitated the train slowing down to 10 mph to effect the exchange. This operation demanded considerable skill and judgement on the part of both signalman and fireman, particularly the latter, who required both hands for the exchange and the necessity to keep his balance whilst leaning out of a moving locomotive. Under these conditions it was impossible to keep time on express trains.

With the increase of weekend holiday specials and excursion traffic in the thirties, there developed a need to borrow LMS engines that happened to be at Bath after working in from the North for a "fill in" trip to Bournemouth and back. For these engines, the foreman fitter at Bath, Tom White, evolved a portable "clamp on" tablet catcher, and also a "clamp on" bracket into which a tablet catcher could be placed. These could be fitted quickly and easily, usually to the leading tender handrail, but occasionally to the engine cab handrail. These were designed dimensionally for fitting to ex Midland and LMS engines, the '4F' 0-6-0s and (from May 1938) Stanier Black '5's being the types mainly borrowed. Portable catchers or brackets could not be suitably clamped on to BR Standard engines or the Southern Light Pacifics, extensively used on the S&D line in later years, due to their different dimensions. A bracket welded on to the tenders of these engines was necessary for carrying the catchers, and naturally this was only done on engines regularly working over the line. It was because of their suitability to the clamp-on brackets and portable tablet catchers that "foreign" Stanier '5's in particular, from many distant sheds, could be seen working on the S&D main line right up to the end of through passenger traffic on 10th September 1962, whereas the use over the S&D of "foreign" Midland or Northern based BR standard '5's, which were often available at Bath, was rare. During the '50s virtually all the allocation of Bulleid light Pacifics at Bournemouth Central shed were equipped for carrying automatic tablet catchers thus enabling their use on the S&D when required which was mainly at weekends during the summer working. Incidentally, when additional '2P' and '4F' locomotives were drafted to the line after 1930, some were fitted with these portable catchers, which a number of them retained over a good many years – some in fact right up until their eventual withdrawal from service.

The branch between Evercreech Junction and Burnham, and the Wells and Bridgwater branches were worked by a mixture of electric tablet and 'train staff and ticket' working, all hand exchange.

Having departed from Bath station with a down train, the first thing uppermost in the minds of the S&D crews was the tablet to be picked up at Bath Junction, and of course it would exercise their minds intermediately if they were working south of Templecombe, where the bulk of the single-line on the S&D main line was to be found. Naturally the same thing applied to Branksome men setting off north from Bournemouth with an up train, their first tablet pick up point being at Broadstone, where the Southern metals were exchanged for S&D.

After promotion to a passed cleaner, one had an ever increasing number of firing turns over the line, and the further one went over the S&D the more information would be sought from colleagues who had already performed these trips, regarding the location of tablet sections. I was fortunate in that my own initial trips as a passed cleaner from Bournemouth to Templecombe, and later to Bath, were made in daylight. Not all were so fortunate, and tablet work was far more difficult to the uninitiated when carried out in the dark. Take Donald's first trip from Bath to Bournemouth in the 1920's made during the hours of darkness. He was booked on the 2.45 am 'Down Mail' which put out mail at Radstock, Shepton Mallet, Evercreech Junction, Wincanton, Templecombe Lower Platform, Sturminster Newton, Blandford, Broadstone, Poole and Bournemouth West. In those days this was a "double home" job. The 'Mail' crew slept during the day at a private lodging house, booking on duty again at 8.30 pm that night to prepare their engine at Branksome shed prior to working the 9.40 pm Bournemouth West to Bath goods, booking off at 4.30 am the following morning. Having noted his rostered job Donald, as a precautionary measure, immediately sought out his mate Lou Ricketts, who had done the trip many times. "Where do we collect the 'tab' after Templecombe, and where do I put the tablet catcher out?" Donald enquired. "Easy Don", he replied, "Look for the distant signals, and when you pass them put your catcher and tablet out – you can't miss". At about 5.00 am in pitch darkness on the appointed morning, the down mail hauled by a 'Bulldog' 0-6-0 drew away from Templecombe Lower platform into what, for Donald at least, was foreign country and he was soon staring hard, straining to spot the distant signal for Stalbridge. Then, a green light ahead, and the mental doubt – was it a distant signal or one of the crossing gate signals of which there were several on the Templecombe, Stalbridge section? As the engine came abreast of the signal Donald lifted the top flap of the firehole door. Instantly a shaft of bright yellow light from the fire split the darkness, and there, starkly white against the black sky was a white signal post with a fish tailed arm in the off position. Donald moved to place the tablet in the catcher and in fact he was actually outside the cab placing it in the apparatus when his driver yelled at him over the clatter and roar of the wind, "Come back in, it's not time yet!" "But we have passed the distant signal", Donald protested, and so they had. But that particular signal in fact worked in conjunction with the home signal then situated at Henstridge. There was no signal box there, the signals being worked from a ground frame in the goods yards as required, and this was the one exception to the "tablet out at the distant" rule. Donald said, "I bet old Lou was grinning in his sleep".

The tablet once helped Donald out of quite a spot of bother in a roundabout way, when he was passed fireman in the 1930's. He had a driving turn working up from Bournemouth on the 'Pines Express' with 698, an LMS '2P' 4-4-0, and on arrival at Bath shed went on to the turntable with his engine. Bringing it to a stand correctly positioned for turning, this task was duly performed. But after turning and moving off the table Donald heard a sickening crunching sound emanating from somewhere below. Stopping quickly he got down from the footplate and looked under the tender, and the reason was painfully apparent. The water pick up scoop had worked down into the 'in' position for picking up water from the track water troughs. But what Donald had attempted to pick up was a large nut that sat like a mushroom in the centre of the turntable. This had caused the disconcerting crunch, and in consequence had buckled the scoop, and no mistake! Donald remounted the footplate and looked at the water scoop operating handle. The chain which should have secured the handle when the scoop was not in use, hung limply downwards, and in his subsequent report he had to admit frankly that the damage to the scoop had been caused by this failure to observe the safety chain had been removed.

The following week he was summoned to see Mr. Whitaker who sternly told him he should have noticed the disconnected chain whilst preparing the engine. "But", he concluded, "I am going to say no more about it. Your action whilst firing the up 'Pines' recently cancels out last week's oversight". This surprised Donald considerably as he had forgotten the incident referred to by Mr. Whitaker. What had happened was this; the 'Pines' was approaching the tablet exchange apparatus at Sturminster Newton doing about 55 mph with Donald crouched in the swaying gangway between engine and tender to enable him to watch closely the tablet exchange. But at the moment of impact a most unusual thing occurred. The arm of the engine's tablet exchange apparatus snapped off like a carrot and flew upwards. Donald, reacting like lightning, instinctively shot out his free arm and grabbed the heavy apparatus — complete with the tablet for the Sturminster — Stalbridge section — out of thin air and had it back on the footplate before his driver had even realised what had happened. A well nigh incredible feat. Fortunately it had not gone unobserved. A fitter by the name of George Adams, in the process of making his routine inspection of the tablet exchange apparatus situated along the line, happened to be at Sturminster Newton, and had witnessed the incident. He was so impressed by what he had seen that he told Mr. Whitaker about it, commenting that there would have been a serious delay to the 'Pines' if the tablet had fallen. That was certainly a snatch that paid off for Donald.

Most of the tablet troubles were caused by them falling during the exchanges which were carried out at speeds of up to 70 mph — the maximum permissible speed on the S&D main line. Failure to collect was normally due to mis-alignment of the engine catcher. However, dropping the tablet by an engine shedded and maintained at one of the S&D depots was rare, the equipment being excellently maintained. The clamp-on type catchers fitted at Bath to LMS engines borrowed from "foreign" depots for a trip down to Bournemouth also gave little trouble.

S&D firemen were taught young "never to take your eyes off the tablet during the exchange", as they were liable to fall flat or fly high into the air before bouncing and rolling alongside the track for anything up to 100 yards. They were even known to lodge in the carriage running boards immediately behind the engine. So when the driver brought the train grinding to a halt before sending his fireman back to retrieve the tablet, much time and trouble was saved if the final resting place of the dropped tablet had been pinpointed.

Drivers could get into considerable trouble by reason of forgetting, dropping or overcarrying the tablet. But that was also possible when in full possession of it. For example, back in the late twenties two Class '2' 4-4-0s working the down 'Pines' out of Bath, found their load too much for them, and they came panting to a stand on the 1 in 50 in Lyncombe Vale, roughly midway between the Devonshire and Combe Down Tunnels. The two drivers conferred, and the leading driver instructed his fireman to walk back to Bath Junction to get the assistance of a banker. The train itself could not reverse as setting back through a tunnel with passengers was forbidden. But though this rule was being observed, others were about to be broken, albeit unwittingly.

After a walk of about two miles during which he protected his train by placing detonators on the line and endured a choking walk through the smoke filled and impenetrably black Devonshire Tunnel, the sore footed fireman arrived back at Bath Junction signal box and explained the circumstances to the signalman. Soon telephones were ringing in the adjacent goods yard, and the shunters released their engine which proceeded across the road to the Junction box. The fireman again told his story — this time to the driver of the banking engine. The signalman handed the driver the banking staff who then turned to the 'Pines' fireman and said, "Where's the tablet for your train?" "Back on the train engine" was the reply. Then, delivering something of a bombshell, the banking driver asserted, "You'll have to go back and fetch it then. I'm not entering the section until I've seen it". Rightly so, the driver was acting strictly in accordance with the rule book. The signalman overhearing this conversation with some dismay, took the initiative, and was quickly on the telephone to Bath loco shed from where a taxi was ordered to take the fireman up to Greenway Lane, — the nearest road adjacent to where the 'Pines' was stuck. From there he was able to board the train engine, collect the errant tablet and return with it in the taxi to Bath Junction. Thus satisfied, the driver of the banker proceeded up the bank, conducted by the fireman of the 'Pines', advancing cautiously through Devonshire Tunnel until the banker at last buffered up to the rear of the train. It just remained for the 'Pines' fireman to rejoin his train and return the tablet to the train engine. Thereafter 'two crows' echoed across Lyncombe Vale, and the 'Pines' — now very late — resumed the journey southwards whilst four dismal enginemen were already formulating their excuses for the subsequent meeting with R. C. Archbutt the Locomotive Superintendent at Highbridge.

Proceeding through a single-line section without a tablet was only permissible in exceptional circumstances and then only when an authorised pilotman (usually a station master acting as a human tablet) accompanied the driver on the footplate, or alternatively the driver was in possession of the 'pilotmen's ticket' authorising him to proceed. Nevertheless on one occasion, at least, a driver entered a section without proper authority due to his own cussedness marring his better judgement. It occurred in 1920 on an afternoon train from Bournemouth West to Bath driven by Fred Lock and fired by Harry Miles of Bath shed. Fred was a tall, very quiet man, deliberate in his actions, and was considered the most economical engineman then working on the S&D. In those days a league table was kept, recording the amount of coal used by various drivers — with the one burning the least heading the table. This driver was usually Fred, a fact of which he was justly proud (mind you, in pursuit of the honour, drivers were prone to 'raid' loaded coal wagons conveniently parked in sidings or elsewhere, to supplement the supplies of their tenders). On this day Fred departed from Broadstone with the catcher correctly positioned but at the point of exchange the tablet fell to the ground and Harry Miles shouts of "Whoa! we've dropped the tablet", made no impression upon Fred, who just kept on going. Harry, repeating his cry, begged him to pull up, but to no avail. Fred was probably pre-occupied with thinking how much coal they would consume if he stopped for the tablet, thus causing him to restart his train on an adverse gradient of 1 in 97. So they carried on to Corfe Mullen box — and a red stop signal. The end result of this incident of misplaced priorities was three days suspension for Fred, and one for poor Harry, who was very much an innocent spectator of the affair.

In contrast to the last story is this one where the driver thought he had the tablet on board but had not! In the mid 1950's a BR standard class '4' 4-6-0 was approaching Corfe Mullen Junction heading the 4.25 pm semi-fast from Bath to Bournemouth West. With the familiar 'snick', the tablet, apparently, was collected from the lineside apparatus, and after retrieving it from the engine's catcher the fireman hung it up in the cab. Satisfied that all was well the driver sped onwards up over Corfe Mullen Bank and down to Broadstone where the tablet was given up by means of the mechanical apparatus again, and the train glided to its scheduled stop in Broadstone Station. On arrival the down starting signal at the end of the platform had been in the 'OFF' position, but to the driver's surprise it suddenly returned to danger, followed shortly after by the arrival at the engine of a breathless porter, "The signalman wants to know where the tablet is", he said. "He's got it", replied the confused driver. But he had not. Thus informed, the Broadstone signalman telephoned his colleague at Corfe Mullen box telling him of the missing tablet. There was a moment or two of stunned silence from the other end of the telephone before the signalman replied in a strained voice, "It's here in the box". Then the sequence of events which caused this to happen unfolded. The Corfe Mullen signalman had withdrawn the tablet from his instrument in the box and then reached for a pouch to put it in. But before actually doing so, he had walked down the box and pulled off his signals for the 4.25 down. Then, due to some mental aberration, he fastened up the pouch – minus the tablet – before finally going down the signal box steps and placing it in the mechanical exchanger completely unaware that the all important tablet was still sitting up inside his box. Even after the train had passed, and the signalman had returned to his box, he still did not notice the tablet lying on his instrument. But in any case this did not exonerate the driver on the down train. It was the driver's responsibility to examine and ensure that the correct tablet was being carried – even though in practice the fireman usually dealt with the actual 'handling' of the tablet. But in this case the failure of the fireman to examine the pouch and check that the correct tablet was inside dropped the unfortunate driver 'in the cart' for the ultimate responsibility for was his. Disciplinary action followed.

Despite being situated on a double line section, there was a tablet exchanging apparatus at Binegar – near to the summit of the southbound climb to Masbury Summit. Banking engines on down freight trains picked up the banking engine staff, or key here, which authorised them to return on the 'wrong road' from Masbury back to Binegar, having first seen the rear brake van of the train it was banking, safely over the summit. An amusing incident occurred on the first occasion this system was brought into use on this section. A freight train being banked in the rear, was labouring towards Binegar, and riding on the leading engine was Inspector Wells. As the engine was passing through Binegar Station the fireman happened to look over the side of the cab and saw ahead the tablet set up in the standard for the banker. In yet another of those moments of mental aberrations to which all humans are prone, the fireman slid his catcher out, determined not to miss it. The 'snick' that was heard as the engine's catcher snatched the tablet from the lineside standard caused Inspector Wells' bowler hat to hit the roof – at least metaphorically if not in fact –

and to use an adjective he had never been known to use before.

The rule book stated that when in possession of the tablet on the footplate it should be hung on the hook provided. But although S&D engines were provided with such a hook the more modern engines of later years did not in fact have one specifically provided for this purpose. But this was not a problem, there being plenty of suitable objects on the footplate on which it could be hung. However it was good policy always to hang the tablet in a particular position — according to the class of engine one had — instead of casually stowing it anywhere that happened to be at hand. Amazing as it may seem, in the narrow confines of a footplate, it was possible to forget where the tablet was placed. Then followed several palpitating moments of self doubt, wondering if in fact one did actually have the tablet on board, before finally the eye would mercifully catch sight of it innocently swinging on some or other control valve handle. With this in mind I like the tale that Donald tells of the driver who thought he would teach his fireman to be sure and hang the tablet in the proper place instead of throwing it carelessly on to the lid of the engine's toolbox on his side of the footplate. When the fireman's back was turned he quietly stepped across the cab, picked up the tablet, and quickly lifted the toolbox lid and dropped it inside. When the fireman looked for the tablet to place it in the catcher, the driver read the riot act to him about his carelessness with such an important article and ended up by telling him where the tablet was. "That's where you're wrong", replied the fireman lifting the toolbox lid, "There's no floorboards in this box". The driver looked in the toolbox and to his horror saw only the blur of ballast and flickering sleepers below. However Donald, with an impish grin on his face, finishes the story by saying, "But I don't think that happened on the S&D". However it would not be out of character with the line if it had.

In the September of 1955 a re-arrangement of engine and crew diagrams gave Bournemouth Central men their first ever regular turn of duty over the S&D line. This was on the 6.40 pm Bournemouth West — Bath passenger train which they worked from Monday — Friday as far as Templecombe Upper. Their return duty was with the 9.03 pm from Templecombe (7.00 pm ex Bath). On Saturday nights Branksome men worked the 6.40 pm up to Templecombe returning on a milk train to Bailey Gate, and light engine thereafter to Branksome shed. Bournemouth men worked the 5.18 pm from Bournemouth to Templecombe, but returned on the 9.03 pm down as usual. It was this altered diagram which first introduced the BR standard class '4' 2-6-0s to the S&D line working during part of the diagram the 6.40 pm up and 7.00 pm down. Hitherto these trains were worked by a class '5' 4-6-0 (BR or LMS) and '2P' 4-4-0 respectively.

At first Branksome drivers piloted the Bournemouth men until they were familiar with the road. But right from the start it was apparent that the Bournemouth men's biggest problem was going to be the operation of the tablet catcher — particularly during the dark winter evenings. For

LMS class '5' 4-6-0 No. 4830 fitted for oil burning, heading an up express near Stalbridge in 1948.

Photo: L. T. George collection.

A '4F' 0-6-0 on S&D Express Passenger duty. No. 44236 pounds up the 1 in 55/100 approach grades to Combe Down Tunnel with a northbound summer Saturday extra during the early 1950's.

Photo: Ivo Peters.

During the summer of 1952 'West Country' Pacific No. 34041 *Wilton* failed at Binegar on a down Bournemouth train with valve gear trouble. The engine was unable to move under its own power in either direction. Later in the day 'Black Five' No. 44839 arrived to tow the 4-6-2 back to Bath — but not before Harold Barber the 4-6-0's driver had had a word at the Binegar Station Master's house.

Photo: Ivo Peters.

Should the Bath shed turntable not be available, incoming engines were turned on the Mangotsfield triangle as occurred in April 1953 when 'West Country' Pacifics Nos. 34040 *Crewkerne*, 34042 *Dorchester*, S&D '7F' 2-8-0s Nos. 53809, 53802, and 'Black Five' 4-6-0 No. 44965 were photographed near Mangotsfield during turning operations.

Photo: Ivo Peters.

'4F' 0-6-0 No. 44559 (ex S&D 59) coupled to ex SR 'King Arthur' 4-6-0 No. 30803 *Sir Harry le Fise Lake* are almost abreast of Branksome shed as they reverse towards Bournemouth West Junction signalbox whilst turning on the Branksome Triangle in June 1960.

Photo: M. K. Lewis.

Ex SR 'Schools' class 4-4-0 No. 30932 *Blundells* climbing the 1 in 50 through Lyncombe Vale between Devonshire and Combe Down Tunnels whilst making its way light engine from Bath to Templecombe in connection with an enthusiasts special organised by the Ian Allan group that ran over the line on Sunday 25th April, 1954.

Photo: Ivo Peters.

Following the second world war, trains on the Highbridge branch were normally handled by an admixture of Johnson 0-4-4 tank and 0-6-0 tender engines together with, from 1949, Ivatt 2-6-2 tank and latterly GW 0-6-0 tender and Pannier tank engines. However during 1956, a shortage of locomotives at Highbridge shed resulted in some '2P' 4-4-0s being temporarily transferred there to handle the passenger work. Hence the rather unusual sight of No. 40601 on the turntable at Highbridge on 19th May, 1956.

Photo: P. Pike.

Ex SR 'U' class 2-6-0 No. 31795 drifts down the spur line from Templecombe Upper towards Templecombe No. 2 Junction with a return Christchurch – Paignton day excursion on 23rd July, 1956. At No. 2 Junction the 2-6-0 unhooked from the train whilst another engine coupled on at the other end before reversing the train's direction for the continuation of the run to Christchurch by taking to the track just visible on the extreme left of the picture.

Photo: P. Pike.

Throughout the 1950's and early 60's the '7F' 2-8-0s were regularly employed hauling trains on summer Saturdays between Bath and Bournemouth. No. 53809 (ex S&D 89) is working hard at the head of a down Saturday extra as, in the pouring rain, it labours southwards on the long climb from Radstock up to Masbury here seen approaching Chilcompton.

Photo: Ivo Peters.

An unusual — possibly unique — apparition in the middle road at Evercreech Junction in February 1956 was ex GW 2-6-2T No. 5522 coupled to an engineer's inspection saloon.

Photo: P. Pike

A down summer Saturday extra bound for Bournemouth during the mid 1950s climbing hard at the approach to Chilcompton Tunnel. The train engine is BR class '5' 4-6-0 No.73051 which is being piloted as far as Evercreech Junction by ex LMS '2P' 4-4-0 No. 40700.

Photo: Ivo Peters.

BR class '5' 4-6-0 No. 73047 was deputising for the usual S&D 2-8-0 as it passed over Wellow Viaduct with the 7.18 pm Bath – Templecombe freight in May 1957.

Photo: Ivo Peters.

On 14th July, 1957 'Battle of Britain' class 4-6-2 No. 34110 *66 Squadron* slipped to a standstill on the 1 in 50 gradient at Prestleigh whilst working the Sunday (summer only) 9.45 am Bournemouth West – Bristol (T.M.). Assistance duly arrived in the shape of BR 2-6-0 No. 76026. Now over Masbury Summit the pair are seen coasting down towards Binegar.

Photo: Ivo Peters.

Bath shed purloined just about any type of suitable motive power to cover its S&D diagrams during the intensely busy summer Saturdays of the 1950s, including this Caprotti class '5' 4-6-0 No. 44744, photographed approaching Midford in 1957 with a northbound extra, on a terrible summer's day of high wind and imminent rain.

Photo: Ivo Peters.

Ex S&D '3F' (Bulldog) 0-6-0 No. 43216 (ex S&D 72) blowing off hard prepares to depart from Evercreech Junction with a Templecombe – Burnham-on-Sea Whitsun excursion in May 1958.

Photo: P. Pike.

During July 1958 an ex LMS '2P' 4-4-0 developed a 'hot box' whilst heading an S&D passenger train in the Bournemouth area. Its replacement proved to be an ex L&SWR 'T9' 4-4-0 No. 30120. This engine continued to double for the '2P' for some time resulting in (on July 26th) this most unusual S&D combination of 30120 paired with shed mate, 'West Country' Pacific No. 34041 *Wilton* climbing through Midsomer Norton with the 7.35 am (summer Saturday only) Nottingham – Bournemouth.

Photo: Ivo Peters.

A train of returning pigeon empties composed of no less than 21 vans accelerates out of the short dip which extended from just south of Shepton Mallet station to half way across Charlton Viaduct at which point the gruelling climb from Evercreech to Masbury recommenced. The train was being hauled by two ex S&D locomotives the train engine being a '7F' 2-8-0 piloted by '4F' 0-6-0 No. 44559 (ex S&D 59).

Photo: Ivo Peters.

Part of the aftermath of the Pylle breakaway and subsequent derailment at West Pennard, photographed on 16th January, 1958.

Photo: Peter Pike.

Ex SR 'M7' 0-4-4T No. 30127 was a frequent performer on the Bournemouth West carriage shunter seen here in the charge of ex colleagues (left to right) Fireman Aubrey Punter and Passed Fireman 'Bill' Harford. On the station platform discussing the next move are Shunters 'Billy' Grainger and Rex Dyke, whilst SR Pacific No. 34040 *Crewkerne* simmers quietly waiting to depart with the 1.00 pm to Waterloo.

Photo: G. A. Richardson.

The main event of 1958, as far as the S&D was concerned, was the takeover by the Western Region of the northern half of the line. This change brought about the regular use on the S&D of a number of ex GW locomotives. On 17th December, 1958 ex GW 0-6-0 tender engine No. 2215 coupled to two Pannier tank 0-6-0s Nos. 3604 and 8451, was undergoing clearance tests at Evercreech Junction.

Photo: P. Pike.

Visual proof of the Western Region interest in the northern half of the S&D from 1958 is evidenced by an ex GW 0-6-0PT No. 3742 (instead of the usual LM '4F' 0-6-0) pushing hard at the rear of a southbound freight as it climbs the 1 in 50 out of Bath and is swallowed up in Devonshire Tunnel.

Photo: Ivo Peters.

Nearing the end of their days a line of Johnson '3F' 0-6-0s stand dejectedly stored in a siding in the Templecombe shed locomotive yard during October 1960.

Photo: M. K. Lewis.

400 tons hauled over the Mendips by a '9F' single handed was very hard going for the fireman, and was altogether a fitting arena to display the skills of engine crews. With twelve on, 2-10-0 No. 92206, and its fireman, are hard at it on the 1 in 53 approach to Chilcompton Tunnel with a southbound summer Saturday express bound for Bournemouth in 1960.

Photo: Ivo Peters.

After their arrival in 1960 the '9Fs' quickly proved themselves invaluable during the summer months for hauling the holiday expresses which loaded up to between 300/ 400 tons which the 2-10-0s could comfortably handle unaided over the Mendips. A typical 2-10-0 summer Saturday roster was hauling the 7.35 am Nottingham − Bourne-mouth West seen here climbing the 1 in 50 out of Bath towards Devonshire Tunnel headed by No. 92205 in the charge of Donald Beale with myself firing.

Photo: Ivo Peters.

'2P' 4-4-0 No. 40634 (ex S&D No. 45) gets briskly away from the Parkstone stop with the 5.30 pm Bournemouth West − Templecombe local during the summer of 1961.

Photo: A. Trickett.

Donald and I are in charge of BR class '4' 4-6-0 No. 75027 as it approaches Corfe Mullen Junction doing about 60 mph with the 11.12 am Bournemouth West – Sheffield on a summer Saturday in 1962. The track on the left was the remains of the original Dorset Central line to Wimborne which was retained to provide access to Carter's Clay siding.

Photo: Ivo Peters.

The last active '2P' 4-4-0 on the S&D was, surprisingly, an ex Midland one. Nearly at the end of her working life No. 40537 pulls away from Branksome station with the 5.30 pm Bournemouth West to Templecombe local in May 1962.

Photo: M. K. Lewis.

After driving *Evening Star* from Bournemouth to Bath on the last up 'Pines Express' over the S&D, my return working was with the 7.40 am Bradford – Bournemouth West here seen between Moorewood and Binegar with Fireman Aubrey Punter and myself now in charge of rebuilt 'West Country' Pacific No. 34042 *Dorchester*, piloted from Bath to Evercreech Junction by BR class '4' 4-6-0 No. 75023.

Photo: Ivo Peters.

The first week of the 'Pines Express' re-routing away from the S&D line. The up train was departing from Southampton Central on 14th September, 1962 drawn by rebuilt 'Battle of Britain' class 4-6-2 No. 34085 *501 Squadron*, in the charge of driver Peter Guy with myself firing.

Photo: R. Puntis.

S&D '7F' 2-8-0s were involved in a number of special workings during their final years. No. 53808 was well away from its normal habitat when it was photographed passing Dorchester South on 22nd September, 1962. The engine was working through from Weymouth to Bath via the S&D line with an enthusiasts excursion organised by the Ian Allan group.

Photo: Ivo Peters.

Following Branksome shed's closure and transfer of staff in 1963, engines were no longer stabled there overnight. Thus Bournemouth Central shed became the regular overnight stopping place for locomotives off S&D line duties. On 6th June, 1964 two ex S&D engines '7F' 2-8-0 No. 53807 and '4F' 0-6-0 No. 44558 were reversing on to Bournemouth Central shed prior to working an enthusiasts special over the S&D next day.

Photo: A. Trickett.

quite a while thereafter some men would not exchange tablets using the apparatus, claiming the practice was dangerous. Instead they arranged, before leaving the depot, for the large pouch to be used instead, thus necessitating reduction in speed to 10 mph for the tablet exchanges. However others did use the catcher, but utilised all manner of unorthodox ways of positioning and collecting tablets from the apparatus when the train was at speed. I even heard of one fireman who used to lie flat out, face downwards on the footplate, and from this position hang over the side, feet hooked into some convenient object, to accomplish the operation. From this it can be seen that some Bournemouth Central men were far from happy on the S&D line at that time, and the upshot was something of an enquiry into the system of tablet catching on the line. The Southern Authorities decided to watch a practical demonstration of the technique on a fast and heavy train, where the fireman would already have plenty to get on with, without the added burden of tablet catching. It was a very fair test because the train chosen for the demonstration was the up 'Pines Express' which was by far the hardest turn of duty for a fireman on the S&D line. The crew were as usual Branksome men, but the train for some reason was hauled on this occasion by a 'West Country' Pacific instead of a BR class '5' normally diagrammed at this time. Despite the onerous task of firing the twelve coach load over this mountainous road, the Branksome fireman maintained boiler pressure expertly, and in addition, was able to assist his driver in sighting signals, keep the footplate swept up and the coal dust damped down, and attend to tablet catching with a panache that made the watching locomotive inspector glow with pleasure. But it must be borne in mind that S&D men were born and bred to the difficulties of the line, and that Branksome crews in particular worked the heaviest and fastest passenger express trains on the line and were well used to those arduous tasks.

The test result was deemed satisfactory, which was just as well, because the S&D crews were preparing a strong protest should the mechanical system be abandoned in favour of doing it by hand just because of a few complaints by some of the newly arrived Southern men, whereas S&D men had been managing it successfully for the past 50 years. So things remained as they were and complaints from the Bournemouth men gradually died away until eventually most of them could operate the catchers as well as any S&D man. Actually it must be admitted that firemen on the S&D line had to expose themselves to some danger whilst inserting and retrieving tablets from the catcher with the train at speed. But during the 50 or so years that this method of tablet exchanging was in use on the line, only two injuries of any seriousness can be recalled. The more serious of the two accidents happened as late in the day as the mid 1950's. But it did not involve an S&D man. In fact the unfortunate person involved was Fireman White, a Southern man from Bournemouth Central shed. It occurred at Stalbridge whilst he was engaged in working the 6.48 pm up, in the impenetrable blackness that typified this sparsely populated part of North Dorset. Losing his bearing slightly he left the operation of placing the out-going tablet too late, and he was still partly outside the engine manipulating the tablet when he was struck by the Stalbridge signalbox catcher. The impact caused serious injury to one of his arms resulting in his being taken to hospital. He was subsequently off work for many weeks.

One of the more obscure problems associated with the operation of the mechanical tablet apparatus, was (for the fireman) losing one's cap; one had to stand right outside the engine in the full blast of the slipstream and bend down to foot level to insert the pouch into the apparatus or collect it in, and the wind frequently whipped one's hat off without warning. One S&D fireman reckoned that every cow that grazed in the fields adjoining the line from Blandford to Templecombe had a footplate man's hat — and a spare one for Sundays. Personally after experimenting with various forms of headgear ranging through issue caps, corduroy caps and berets, I eventually settled on wearing a beret, for besides not having a tendency to blow off, they felt light on the head. However I reverted to the regulation cap when carrying out driving duties.

But if losing one's cap was one thing, losing a tablet catcher was another. Catchers were supposed to be rendered operational on the engine when passing the distant signal preceding the single line section ahead. This was no problem with the type that could be swung or slid into position by mechanical means as fitted to many ex S&D engines. But the system whereby catchers had to be "put out" by hand as applied to later engines, presented a considerable hazard to firemen inexperienced in their use. To do this it was necessary to hang out from the footplate by one hand — in the teeth of a tremendous slipstream if travelling at speed — and holding in the other the heavy catcher, by gripping it in the middle of "the arm". This required considerable strength in the wrist. Once outside it was necessary to keep the catcher level whilst trying to engage the square end of the arm into the slides of the tender bracket — which at night could not be seen. If that sounds difficult, believe me it was. The worry that this operation caused drivers, when paired with say, a young passed cleaner, occasionally prompted them to instruct their mate to place the catcher out at the last stopping place before reaching the tablet section. This was sometimes a considerable way in advance of it.

One winter's evening in the 1950's, Driver Dick Evry of Bath shed was working the 8.25 pm Templecombe — Derby 'Perishable' on the first stage of its run, with a BR standard class '4' 4-6-0. On the way the train stopped at Evercreech Junction and Dick told his fireman to place the catcher out ready to take the tablet at Midford some 22 miles further on. Thereafter matters proceeded normally — or so they thought — and on this dark night the 'Perishable' stormed up to the heights of Masbury Summit. Then came the usual fast descent down the northern slopes to Radstock, followed by brisk running on the undulating and sinuous stretch towards Midford. But something happened back up in those mysterious hills of which the crew, as yet, were unaware. When Dick shone his torch at the approach to Midford in order to watch the tablet exchange, he was staggered to see that the engine catcher had disappeared. This resulted in an emergency brake application with the train grinding to a halt just north of Midford Station. The fireman ran back and collected the tablet and the train continued on to Bath.

After arrival on shed, Dick reported the incident and next day was interviewed by Mr. Morris the Bath Shedmaster, who asked if he had any idea what caused the mysterious disappearance or where it had occurred. "Haven't a clue" said Dick. "All right, I will have someone walk the line between Midford box and the up distant signal to see if there's any sign of it", replied the Shedmaster, thinking that the catcher was put out between these points as the rule book demanded. "I think your man will have to walk further than that 'gaffer'", said Dick. "I put the catcher out at Evercreech". Instantly realising that the rule book had been disregarded the Shedmaster had a few crisp words to say to Dick on the subject because that ruling had been framed with good purpose. For example, when a catcher was positioned for "pick up" there was always the danger — slight though it might be — of it striking someone standing near a platform edge when passing through. (Here it should be said that it was standing orders in the S&D appendix to the working timetable that station staff must prevent passengers from being near the tablet exchange apparatus when fixed near the platform, and also keep them from standing too near the platform edge when trains were arriving or passing through). But be that as it may, Dick in turn outlined his problems and responsibilities as a driver when supplied with a 'green fireman' — as on this occasion — explaining the dangers of inexperienced men positioning catchers in the dark, a difficulty which under these conditions was eventually conceded by the shedmaster.

A search of the line was made and the catcher was found eventually at Chilcompton, and its disappearance was established as being caused by the breach of another rule. A light engine running in front of the 'Perishable' (probably a banking engine returning to Radstock from Masbury Summit) had stopped for water at Chilcompton on the up line. After its tank had been filled, the heavy leather studded water bag was thrown out of the engine water tank, but the safety chain that should have been used to secure it to the column was left undone. The engine disappeared into the night and the trap was set.

Down the bank whistled the 'Perishable' and the water column bag, waving about close to the line like an elephant's trunk, made contact with the engine's catcher, whipping it out of its bracket and flinging it down the embankment towards some watercress beds. It was indeed fortunate that nobody was in the path of its trajectory.

An unusual sequence of events occurred one Saturday in 1957 when a 'West Country' Pacific and the Whitaker lineside tablet catching apparatus came into conflict. The local 3rd division football team, Bournemouth and Boscombe Athletic, was doing unusually well in the F.A. cup that year and on the Saturday in question were playing the mighty 1st division side Wolverhampton Wanderers. In consequence six special trains were laid on to convey supporters to the match at Wolverhampton of which two were routed via the S&D line.

Branksome crews worked the S&D specials on a 'short rest' basis from Bournemouth Central to and from Bath, with motive power supplied by Bournemouth Central shed and almost inevitably these were Bulleid light Pacifics. Driver Jack Thorne and fireman John Curtis were on the second special via the S&D and Jack had hardly covered half a dozen miles before finding out that the steam reverser on his mount (the number of which cannot now be recalled) was virtually uncontrollable and would not stay fixed in the desired position but continually lengthened the cut off without any alteration by himself. This was a mere precursor of what was to come.

Whilst travelling at around 60 mph on the Blandford – Templecombe single line stretch, a section of the Pacific's air smoothed casing worked loose near to the left hand outside cylinder, and at one end of the tablet exchange places, the flapping thin sheet metal struck the lineside standard hurling it aside which naturally caused the locomotive apparatus to 'miss'. Instantly Jack 'dropped the handle' bringing the train grinding to a halt some ¼ mile past the exchanging place whereafter his mate ran back to effect the tablet exchange by hand. Jack meanwhile went forward to attend to the piece of offending casing. Upon inspection he found that some of the small bolts necessary for securing the sheeting were missing, and those in position could not be removed to expedite a temporary repair by relocating the available bolts without the proper tools and necessary time, both of which he did not have. The trusty coal pick was therefore brought into play and the casing was unceremoniously battered into a position which Jack hoped would wedge it firmly in place.

When his breathless fireman had returned with the correct tablet they set off once more and all seemed well – except for that fiendish steam reverser, which continued to give constant trouble.

This train was made up to eight coaches totalling some 260 tons tare. This was under the limit of 270 tons permitted to these engines between Evercreech Junction and Masbury therefore the engine was booked to make the climb unassisted. But there was no such luck, the steam reverser playing a considerable part in the contretemps that followed. It would not stay put in any intermediate position and to add to Jack Thorne's troubles, following a rousing start away from Evercreech Junction with the Bulleid Pacific on the lower slopes of the Mendips emitting its characteristic rasping sound from the chimney top which someone once likened to rhythmic sandpapering, the engine started slipping and on the 1 in 50 gradient the speed got lower and lower. Eventually Jack dropped the engine into full forward gear and by continually pumping the regulator and keeping the steam chest pressure as low as possible, he somehow inched his slippery footed steed up to Shepton Mallet. With all that had gone before, the train was by now very late, and with some three and a half miles still to go of mainly 1 in 50 climbing Jack decided not to risk it further, so an out of course stop was made here for assistance on the remainder of the climb. This was rendered by a '7F' 2-8-0, which fortuitously happened to be standing in the station at the head of a stone train. This engine was rapidly removed from its train and coupled on ahead of the Pacific which then submitted to being ingloriously piloted over Masbury Summit by the goods engine.

At Binegar a further special stop was made to detach the 'helper' but with favourable grades from here on to Bath – apart from the stiff climb out of Midford to the North end of Combe Down Tunnel – there was an attempt to recoup some of the considerable lateness by now incurred. Thus it was later on that the train sped down the 1 in 50 into Bath on the Midford – Bath single line section, having clawed back a few minutes on schedule, and Jack Thorne began braking hard as the Pacific negotiated the sweeping bend leading onto the Midland line from Mangotsfield at Bath Junction. John Curtis had the tablet positioned in the catcher ready for collection by the lineside apparatus at Bath Junction when to their dismay, both men looking ahead saw the airsmoothed casing swing out in the slip stream again. The fast descent from Masbury had obviously vibrated it loose. As speed dropped it swung out suddenly, rather like a sail, just in time to strike the signalman's waiting tablet catcher and knock it aside again. Once more the train ground to a halt and fireman John Curtis wearily trudged back to hand over the errant tablet to the signalman after which the final half mile into Green Park station was completed without incident! Here mercifully, the Southern engine came off the train and a 'Black Five' took over for the journey to the Midlands.

Arriving on shed Jack Thorne found awaiting him a veritable covey of railway officials, including Mr. Morris the Bath Shedmaster, and from the look on their faces, Jack's murder had been strongly mooted. However after hearing the sorry tale and following a thorough mechanical inspection of the engine it was eventually agreed that blame for the fiasco lay elsewhere. Not only was the reverser and the locomotive's airsmoothed casing found defective but the sand in the sand boxes and pipes was damp and none of the sanders were working. Mr. Morris promptly failed the engine and the return trip to Bournemouth that night was worked by a Bath class '5'.

To round off I must just mention the unofficial usefulness of the tablet catching apparatus. The engine crew when in charge of an express passenger train were in some ways isolated from the outside events of the world. But on the single line section when retrieving a tablet just collected from the signalman's apparatus it was nothing unusual for the fireman to spot a protruding slip of notepaper tucked just inside the pouch, which, when perused, would impart many types of information of interest to the engineman ranging from the news that a high ranking official was at such and such a point, "so watch your speed", to (say) the latest score in the current cup final or test match.

Chapter Seven

KALEIDOSCOPE OF TRIALS AND TRIBULATIONS

I
During S&D and LMS Days Mainly

One of the attractions of footplate work in days of steam was its variety and freedom from close supervision. In addition by the very nature of the job there was an almost complete lack of boredom endemic in so many other professions and which has now, to some extent, permeated to the daily round of the modern footplateman. Usually many different types of loco-motives were encountered by crews over the years, to be worked in their various states of maintenance over a variety of routes, at all times of the day and night and in every possible condition of weather. But if variety be the spice of life out on the road then there was a great deal of spice in the loco depots amongst enginemen themselves. There were fat ones, thin ones, tall ones, and short ones. Personality wise, there were happy ones, miserable ones, the optimistic and the pessimist, some you could hate, and some you could like, but collectively this combination of men, machines, and the elements, in all their different moods, human and otherwise, made footplate life in steam days one of the most exciting and interesting of careers as I hope in some small way subsequently to show.

When locomotive drivers are discussed amongst railway enthusiasts it is not infrequently in connection with a particularly fine piece of locomotive performance for which that worthy was responsible, or some other similar sportsmanlike event as described in the 'Locomotive Practice and Perform-ance' columns of the 'Railway Magazine' and its contemporaries. But like all professions, footplatemen consisted of all sorts and included its share of the more doubtful characters.

In the early twenties a certain driver at Bath — 'Ginger' as he was known — carried on for years a vendetta with the local railway police inspector. This driver was basically of easy going and cheerful disposition who carried out his exploits for the sheer thrill of adventure, and certainly his exploits were the talk of the line. More than once when he was returning to Bath "spare", travelling in the coaches of a passenger train, other crews had observed him at the beginning of his journey entering the train wearing a pair of old black boots and later detraining at Bath wearing a brand new pair of brown boots. The local railway police inspector was very aware of what was going on, but unable to obtain proof. However he left this driver in no doubt of his intentions towards him for whenever he had occasion to pass, the police inspector would hiss, "I'll have you yet". Illiciting the reply from 'Ginger', "You'll have to get up early in the morning". Nevertheless, the inspector did once corner him, and on information received, detained 'Ginger' on Bath shed and questioned him in connection with a tea service which had gone missing in transit. This news spread down the railway telephone lines like wildfire. However 'Ginger" was not without friends. The missing tea service was indeed at 'Ginger's' home and whilst he was being carted off for further questioning, a colleague, aware of all the facts, shot off to his own home, packed up his wife's best tea service and nipped it round to 'Ginger's' house substituting it for the stolen one. This was accomplished none too early, for the police arrived soon after and unknowingly picked up the substitute to exhibit at the subsequent court hearing. When 'Ginger' appeared in court the railway police inspector was looking as pleased as a dog with two tails. The crunch for him came when during the hearing a representative belonging to the firm who had manufactured the missing tea service was asked to identify the one on exhibition. Taking a cup and saucer he examined both in detail before at length making the statement that completely spoilt the police inspector's day. "This tea set was not manufactured by my firm and it is not the one .we dispatched", he intoned.

As 'Ginger' left the court a free man he gave his adversary a wink of his wicked eye, and it must be chronicled the poor police inspector never did have the satisfaction of catching him.

Another driver at Bath who stands out as quite a character was not in fact an original S&D man. He had transferred to Bath after the LMS had absorbed the line in 1930. This driver was a man to whom every fireman enjoyed firing. Tall, handsome, full of the joys of life, he enjoyed every minute of his existence and could talk the birds out of the trees — for example herewith a story told to me by one of his former firemen, Lou Ricketts.

During the last war this driver — who I will refer to as 'R' — and Lou were relieved from a down freight at Shepton Mallet at around 7.00 am one bitter winter's morning with snow and ice lying on the hills around. It was cold and miserable as they sat in the dimly lit and dismal porters room munching their sandwiches in a sort of defeatist silence, when out of the blue the driver said to Lou, "How would you like a nice cup of hot coffee laced with rum to cheer you up?". "Don't talk daft, there's no coffee and rum around here", returned Lou somewhat contemptuously. Standing up and opening the door the driver beckoned, "You come with me and keep your mouth shut", whereupon he stepped out into the darkness followed by his fireman shivering in the icy blast blowing over the Mendips.

They walked to a small hotel a short way from the station and finding a light on and a door unlocked, entered. Inside was a young girl on her knees washing the floor. Looking up she not unnaturally appeared startled at seeing two grimy faces staring down at her. "Good morning", said Driver 'R' in a most charming voice. "Could I speak to the manager please?". "He's asleep in bed, and I dare not disturb him" said the girl. "Oh that will be all right", replied 'R' soothingly. "Tell him two important gentlemen would like to see him". Though not quite convinced the girl nevertheless got to her feet and went upstairs. 'R' turned a grinning face at his mate — who was feeling decidedly uneasy now — and placed a finger over his lips.

The maid returned followed soon after by the sleepy tousled looking manager attired in pyjamas and dressing gown, and looking none too pleased at being summoned from a nice warm bed. "What do you want?" he rasped, eyeing the grubby pair. This is it, thought Lou, we'll be out on our necks any second now. But the driver really turned on the charm and his verbal dexterity, and told the hotel manager at the same time such a plausible tale of privation by his mate and himself. This he said had been occasioned by their being on duty for 16 hours continuously whilst working an ammunition train down from Birmingham to Bristol which in turn, due to a heavy air raid on Bristol had been diverted over the Mendips to gain Bristol by way of Evercreech Junction and Highbridge. Now, having been relieved at last and waiting for the first up passenger train of the day to take them to Bath they craved a cup of coffee. Lou still uneasy watched the manager's fingers drumming on a table and was getting ready to make a rapid exit. But the tale was accepted completely, and quite soon afterwards a tray appeared on which stood a silver coffee set, two cups and saucers, a cream jug and sugar bowl. Nearly filling with coffee the two cups the manager enquired, "I take it you would like a little spirit in it?" The driver's thanks were more like a blessing as two measures of rum swirled into the coffee.

As they sipped the steaming delicious liquid 'R' gave mine host a fabricated running commentary on his night's trip. The manager was by now most interested in it all, and proffered each man a second cup which the driver accepted on behalf of both of them. Lou supped his second cup at the same time idly wondering what the inside of Shepton jail was going to be like, for he was convinced that that was to be their ultimate destination and instinctively he edged closer to the door. I might mention here that neither had a penny piece on them.

Finishing his coffee this intrepid driver proceeded to embarrass mine host with his most grateful thanks. Then dipping his hand deep into his empty trouser pocket he enquired confidently, "Now, sir, how much do we owe you?". Watching his mate groping in his empty pocket nearly caused Lou to panic. But the manager positively beaming now raised a restraining hand, "Please gentlemen, don't worry, that is quite all right, I can see that you have both had an extremely trying night whilst I've been warm and snug in bed, please accept the coffee with my compliments". Lou Ricketts never forgot that trip or the generosity of that Shepton Mallet hotel manager, and least of all the cool nerve and silvery tongue of his driver.

However, with that I will return to matters bearing more directly on footplate work and remember instead that it is the collective vigilance and skill of all railwaymen that has made railways the safest form of transport devised by man.

One of the many qualities required of footplatemen (and of many other grades of railwaymen) was, and is, vigilance and quick thinking, However in an industry that operated 24 hours a day 365 days a year, inevitably there were occasions when someone was caught with his guard down or a vital rule was broken, the consequences of which could be quite fearful. Consider for example a mishap which occurred on Bath shed in the late twenties in which Johnny Walker was involved.

Johnny was cleaning an engine standing in three shed road when the shed turner arrived telling Johnny he was going to move his engine, S&D 2-8-0 No. 82, to No. two road. Passed cleaners who happened to be working on engines which required to be moved were liable to be pressed into service. On this occasion the turner told Johnny he was going to draw with his engine, both the 2-8-0 and a 'Scotty' standing in front of it up the steep gradient out of the shed to the summit of Albert Road Bridge, whereafter No. 82 would be uncoupled and Johnny was to drop her down by gravity, inside the shed to the bottom of No. two road. With a tooting of whistles the engines were drawn up out of the shed to Albert Road Bridge where the three engines halted. Here Johnny applied 82's tender handbrake and allowed the engines in front to sink back on to him slackening the coupling and thus allowing the turner's mate to uncouple 82! This done Johnny released the tender handbrake, noting at the same time that 60 p.s.i. was showing on the boiler pressure gauge — sufficient to provide at least some braking with the steam brake though much caution would be required. The big 2-8-0 began to roll back down the gradient towards the shed. Before passing the coal stage Johnny acted to check the speed by applying the steam brake — but horror of horrors, upon grasping it, the brake handle slid limply into the 'on' position, but without the accompaniment of the clang of brake rigging and blocks slamming onto the engine's wheels. The steam brake supply isolating plug had been screwed in. Johnny was, to put it mildly, shocked, but nevertheless displaying presence of mind, whipped the reversing gear from backwards to forward gear, opened the regulator full and then feverishly screwed on the tender handbrake — though not necessarily in that order.

The alternate blast of steam hissing from the cylinder drain cocks, until Johnny found time to close them, caused Tom Rudd, the running foreman to turn from the engine diagram board which he was in the process of updating inside the shed. Taking in the situation at a glance he hollered out, "Jump lad, Jump for it!". But Johnny still hoping to save the situation was looking around frantically for a 7/8" spanner to undo the isolating plug, but no luck. So with 82's whistle blowing its warning and Johnny giving out cries at the top of his voice and in between times straining on his already tight tender brake No. 82 — albeit now at a much reduced speed — headed relentlessly for the wooden stop blocks at the bottom of the shed, then with a splintering crash the stout wooden blocks were felled and flattened to the ground by 111 tons of locomotive. By some good and overdue fortune the big 2-8-0 shivered and ground to a halt seconds later, the tender buffers just inches from the back of the shed structure itself.

Johnny Walker climbed down off the footplate shaken, but otherwise unharmed, and silently surveyed the wreckage as shed staff hearing the crash came running to the scene. But Johnny was never a person not to see a silver lining to almost any situation. He suddenly brightened and took off from the scene in some hurry towards the loco office. Tapping a door he entered one of the offices and approached a desk behind which sat Mr. Davis the chief clerk. "What can I do for you son?" he enquired. "Can I have a staff purchase chit please, I want to purchase some broken stop blocks". "Sorry son", replied Mr. Davis, "we haven't any that are damaged". "Oh yes you have", grinned Johnny, "I've just knocked down the stop block in No. two shed road". He got his chit and the block. About two minutes later one of the shed fitters — George Adams — entered the office with the same request. "Too late" said Mr. Davis. "They have been booked already by the chap that knocked them down".

The first rebuilt Bulleid light Pacific to appear on the S&D line was No. 34039 *Boscastle* in June 1959 on the up 'Pines Express' returning to Bournemouth on the corresponding down train and it was one of these engines that soon after their introduction on to the S&D, and about 30 years after the foregoing contretemps with the 2-8-0, became involved in a very similar incident.

The Pacific got out of control whilst dropping down the same gradient into the shed. It happened on a summer Saturday when the engine was being shifted by a Radstock driver who was on loan to Bath shed for the day to assist with the preparation and disposal of the many engines which used the shed on such days. The driver was unused to these engines which in turn was itself low in steam pressure — like old 82 years earlier. The situation developed with the Pacific getting out of the driver's control whilst dropping down into the shed, and culminated when the 137 ton locomotive — picking up the shed ash wagon en route — rammed into a '7F' 2-8-0 berthed on the stop blocks at the bottom of No. three shed road. The collision reduced the meat in the sandwich — the unfortunate ash wagon — to instant matchwood and the impact drove the 2-8-0 tender first through the buffer stops, bulldozing it on through the outer brick wall of the enginemen's cabin, accompanied by a cloud of dust, splintered wood, flying bricks and mortar. The '7F' finally came to a stand with its tender half way in the cabin, filling the gaping hole in the wall and with the 'West Country' hard up behind.

The cabin contained quite a number of men at the time of this collision, but from their position within they could see nothing. However, hearing a cacophony of fearful noise, rending crashes and screeching metal heading in their direction, a mass exodus of seething humanity attempted to escape through a window at the far end of the cabin. One shortish shed worker was first at the window but not the first to get out. Someone behind jumped on his back and vaulted outside to safety. The 'stumpy' rose and tried again, only to be used as a take off pad by someone else. It took three or more attempts before the poor chap made it. As with the incident of yesteryear fortunately nobody was at all hurt — only the pride of the short one. When the enginemen's mess room was subsequently rebuilt, a window was strategically placed in the new wall so that the lads could "see 'em coming!".

At least the foregoing collisions were out of the gaze of the general public and one can only but commiserate with the driver of an early morning Bristol — Bath Queen Square local passenger train sometime during the 1920's, who, upon entering the Bath Terminus, misjudged things completely and, not taking into account the state of the rail on a dewy morning, put his engine — believed to be a Johnson 0-4-4T — clean over the buffers and through the flower arrangement beyond. Upon hearing about the crash a keen local newspaper reporter dashed, in company with a photographer, to the scene to write up his scoop. Attempting to collect his facts he asked the unfortunate driver if he would pose alongside his engine where it reposed amongst the debris. To say the driver was not cooperative is putting it mildly. "This isn't a bloody peep show you know", the harassed driver bawled as he chased the photographer away from the scene. Seconds before the train crashed through the blocks, several drowsy workmen, not long out of bed, sat on a seat directly behind the buffers apparently mesmerised by the sight of the rapidly approaching train — they must have thought they were still in bed dreaming. Then — crash! and they jumped in all directions like frogs on a river bank.

The blastpipe 'choppers' I have mentioned in chapter three. But another piece of 'do it yourself' equipment in prevalent use during the 1920's on freight locomotives was the steam brake clip. To explain its use is inevitably a little technical but is of interest. The 'clip' was manufactured from a stout type of split pin and the object of using this gadget was to run with the vacuum steam ejector shut off, thus economising in coal and water. The 'clip' was fashioned in such a way that it could be fitted over the driver's combined vacuum and steam brake control valve as fitted to Midland and LMS locomotives, and held in the fulcrum rod (which operated the steam supply to the steam brake cylinder) thus keeping the steam brake piston control valve closed. There was a small steam brake clip already fitted on this equipment to hold the fulcrum rod in position when the vacuum ejector was shut off, and meant for use when the engine was standing with the tender handbrake applied. But with the train in motion it was just possible for this small clip to become dislodged, which with the vacuum shut off, would cause the fulcrum rod to fly out propelled by boiler steam pressure, and a full application of the steam brake took place, a happening which with a long train of loose coupled wagons could have dire results — particularly for the guard. When in motion with the illicit 'clip' in position, vacuum turned off and requiring to use the brake, the driver merely opened up his small ejector to create 21" of vacuum, the vacuum piston on the top of the fulcrum rod was then held in by atmospheric pressure on its outer side, and with the two to one pull of the fulcrum rod the smaller steam brake piston positioned below on the rod was thus held closed preventing steam from passing down to the brake cylinder. The driver then removed his illegal steam brake 'clip' and braked his train in the normal way.

It is doubtful if Inspector Wells or anyone else in authority knew of their existence (indeed so furtive were drivers in their use that many a fireman would probably not have been aware of whether or not his mates used one) and many S&D drivers have wondered if 'the clip' might have had any influence on the runaway 2-8-0 No. 89 on 20th November 1929 when the 3.25 pm Evercreech Junction — Bath freight made up to 37 wagons plus a brake van and hauled by No. 89 running tender first got out of control in Combe Down Tunnel after the engine crew had been overcome by fumes in its foul interior. The train hurtled down the 1 in 50 into Bath goods yard at high speed where it piled up in disastrous fashion causing severe damage and killing three persons including the driver, Henry Jennings of Bath shed. His fireman Maurice Pearce was seriously injured. Some enginemen speculated privately that Henry had a 'clip' on the brake. It is known that the engine was steaming badly on this occasion and was labouring very slowly up through the just over one-mile-long bore of Combe Down Tunnel (thought to be the longest unventilated tunnel in the country). Even though travelling tender first, and the chimney behind the direction of travel, No. 89 was moving so slowly that fumes and the attendant searing heat started pouring into the cab the intensity of which caused fireman Maurice Pearce to pull his coat up over his head for protection. He eventually lost consciousness and it is to be assumed that sometime shortly afterwards Henry Jennings did also.

Now engine crews working into Bath would at this point be running down their fires so as to facilitate engine disposal duties on the shed. Due to the prolonged climb at 1 in 100 up through the tunnel and 1 in 55 at its approach, it is fairly certain that with a poorly steaming engine being worked hard with a low fire and receiving no attention for a considerable time from its unconscious crew, steam pressure would have dropped, resulting in a fall in vacuum until eventually with no one in a fit state to take preventative action the inherent design of this brake equipment would allow the steam brake piston to open, gradually to begin with, but progressively as boiler pressure fell. Once the vacuum had fallen to about 12" or a little less, the steam brake would be firmly applied, thus bringing the train to a stand, particularly with this load and on this gradient. But if the 'clip' was in position with the vacuum turned off the fulcrum rod would have been clamped tight, and a drop in steam pressure would not then have applied the steam brake.

One man who might have known whether or not the 'clip' was in fact in position on the brake apparatus was the first man into the wrecked cab of 89 immediately after the disaster. This was driver Billy Bowles, a kind gentle Christian man who was on his way home from work when he heard the violent collision. No 'clip' was found on the engine when it was examined officially and no irregularity came to light as a result of the official enquiry. But for some time after S&D drivers talked about the possibility in guarded tones and wondered, but no one asked Billy directly, and he told no one. One way or another he took his knowledge to the grave. From that time onward the steam brake 'clip' passed from use.

Donald was inside the nearby loco shed that fateful evening and upon hearing the fearful crash dashed with several other men to ascertain the cause. Many of the lights in the goods yard were extinguished but such lights as existed revealed a grim scene. It might be appropriate to mention at this juncture that the ambulance movement amongst workers of all grades has always been strongly promoted by railway management mindful of the daily hazards inherent in railway work. During their time both Bath and Branksome sheds had champion teams emerge from various first aid competitions and Donald was for years a leading light in this field. Thus on this occasion he was quickly on the scene to render what assistance he could. When Donald arrived the driver and fireman had been extricated and taken inside the shunters cabin. The immediate impression of those present was that both were dead. Seeing Donald, the yard foreman asked him to identify each man and, on entering the cabin, he found them laid out on wooden forms. Both figures were covered in thick coal dust which all but blanked out their features, and even Donald, who knew both men well, found it difficult at first readily to distinguish them. It was the small moustache that Henry Jennings sported that enabled his identity to be established. It was just after this that it was confirmed that Henry Jennings was indeed dead, but his more fortunate fireman was in fact still alive though badly injured.

Two other features of this tragedy which are established fact are that Driver Jennings had been off work ill with bronchitis a short time before the accident. Also, his fireman had very recently been transferred from Radstock to Bath and had little previous knowledge of the differing conditions to be encountered in the two treacherous tunnels between Midford and Bath. The combined aftermath of Henry Jennings' recent respiratory illness allied to the fumes in the tunnel, together with the inexperience of his fireman to these severe conditions, might have played their part in the mystery of what really went wrong on the footplate of No. 89 on the evening of 20th November 1929.

Incidentally at the rear of the train was Guard Wagner, and his guard's van brake blocks became nearly white hot from his efforts to retard the runaway train in some way during its terrifying headlong descent toward certain catastrophe. With all hope abandoned the guard finally jumped from his flying van near Bath Junction and suffered two broken knee caps as a result. By an odd freak when rescuers went to his van after the crash it was still upright with his oil lamp standing at the base of the hand brake burning brightly.

Driver Henry Jennings met his death as a direct result of Combe Down Tunnel as we have just seen, but even before this the Gods of the Tunnel seemed to have singled out this unfortunate driver as some sort of sacrifice. He was once driver on the assisting engine coupled to the down 'Diner'. His engine was a 'Scottie' 0-6-0 No. 47 and upon closing the regulator inside Combe Down Tunnel a serious "blow back" occurred on the footplate. A sheet of white hot flame shot out of the firebox dramatically splitting the smoky impenetrable blackness. An attempt by driver Jennings to combat this by re-opening his regulator was foiled by the searing heat and he received serious burns to his hand and arm. His fireman Bill Bidiscombe had already been forced outside the cab and stood in the darkness on the swaying and vibrating framing halfway to the smokebox. Henry Jennings was soon forced to do likewise. When the train shot out into daylight near Midford the crew on the train engine realised their colleagues' desperate plight, slowed the train and brought it to a stand in nearby Midford station. Here Henry received first aid, but insisted upon carrying on and seeing the job through, despite his pain and the fact that all the fittings on the footplate were still burning hot, with the inside cab paint blistering and peeling. The fact of getting the 'Diner' through to Bournemouth came first. Having seen it safely to Masbury station — where on this occasion the assisting engine was booked to be detached — Henry Jennings was satisfied, and officially reported his injuries. He was subsequently off duty for some weeks. Footplate life in steam days was not for those lacking resolution and nerve. This is yet another story in the annals of those two wicked single line tunnels between Bath and Midford whose presence commanded the utmost care, forethought and respect of all footplate crews who had to negotiate them.

II
The Continuing Theme under British Railways

In 1949 Bath shed first received an allocation of Ivatt class '4' 2-6-0s of somewhat revolutionary outline by British standards then, and still in their original double blastpipe and chimney guise. These rapidly gained an unenviable reputation for erratic steaming and fortunately the stay of these 2-6-0s was relatively brief. S&D footplatemen nicknamed them 'Doodlebugs' which in itself tends to indicate the regard in which they were held.

During one summer Saturday of intense traffic a brace of these engines were double heading a heavy 12 coach express bound for Bournemouth. The train engine No. 43036 was being driven by Donald Beale, and Johnny Walker, now a passed fireman, was in charge of the pilot No. 43017.

Getting away from Bath the engines got to grips with the 1 in 50 up to the north portal of Combe Down Tunnel, and soon a most laborious climb ensued. The boiler pressure on Donald's engine was only maintained by virtue of leaving the injector off as long as possible. But when it was applied pressure fell with a rush so that when the train emerged from the smoky depths of Combe Down Tunnel, into the cool fragrant air, and magnificent scenery of the Midford Valley, neither Donald nor his fireman had much of an eye for the beauty around them. After passing Midford station they struggled on – none too surely – towards Wellow, and it crossed Donald's mind that if his own engine was not doing too well then the pilot engine was not exactly setting the world on fire either. Approaching Wellow boiler pressure on 43036 was right down in the doldrums and the water level was nearly out of sight in the bottom of the gauge glass. With the Radstock – Masbury climb looming in front of them Donald decided to stop at Wellow for a 'blow up' and, with the aid of the engine whistle and sign language, signalled ahead this intention to Johnny Walker. Having come to a stand in Wellow station Donald dismounted and walked ahead to 43017 to explain. "Sorry I had to stop Johnny, but we are right down the pan on that old 'Camel'", he exclaimed apologetically jerking his thumb at the innocent looking smokebox of 43036. Johnny smiled benevolently, "Don't worry old pal, if you hadn't stopped I would have had to", he returned, adding impishly, "but you signalled your intention first so you can write out the report". Donald glanced over Johnny's shoulder and found conditions on the footplate of 43017 mirrored very much those on his own engine – about 80lb of steam on the clock and the water just bobbing in the bottom of the gauge glass being surveyed by a sweating and dirty fireman obviously fed up to the back teeth with the situation.

The stop here was prolonged whilst the boiler of both locomotives was refilled and steam pressure restored to blowing off point. It was useless to attempt to climb to Masbury "half right" with engines of proven poor steaming ability. On this occasion although the 'Doodlebugs' managed the climb over the Mendips without a further 'blow up', Masbury Summit appeared in the front cab windows none too soon; both engines crawling over the top in much the same state as they had earlier arrived at Wellow for their enforced stop.

This was an all too typical story of the 'Doodlebugs' hence their eventual removal from the S&D, only in effect to return again in 1955 in single chimney guise, improved in steaming ability and thinly disguised as BR standard class '4' 2-6-0s – the 76000 breed.

Compared to the 'Doodlebugs' the SR 'West Country's' would be termed exceptionally free steaming. But human frailty could render them 'breathless' – even under the most favourable circumstances of mechanical well being – illustrated by an unfortunate error of judgement which occurred on one of the early trips over the line of a light Pacific during the summer of 1951. The engine was prepared on Branksome shed by a crew who had never been on this type of locomotive before and, more to the point, the young fireman had never had any dealings with a wide firebox engine which required a completely different firing technique than that used on engines with long fireboxes. A friendly Nine Elms crew – who were of course familiar with these engines – happened to be on shed early that Saturday morning and the fireman was asked, "What's the best way to fire one of these?" "Nuffing to it mate!", replied the cockney, "just keep the back corners well filled, in fact", he continued, "get as much coal as you can in the back of the box, she'll steam all right". It was this state-ment that was to prove the undoing of the S&D summer Saturday schedule that morning. Thus armed with this knowledge, straight from the horse's mouth as it were, the Branksome fireman took his Nine Elms colleague literally and went to work with a will and, it must be admitted, without too much thought about what he was doing. In fireman's parlance he well and truly "soled and heeled" her. Something like a third of the coal in the tender was transferred into the Pacific's firebox onto a rather low fire until it was literally blocking the firehole door. So in this condition the engine was handed over to the unfortunate crew who were rostered to work it to Bath on an up express. The preparation fireman had of course thought that he was doing his colleague a favour, but even a glutton like a Bulleid light Pacific was liable to indigestion when fed on such an enormous diet of Welsh coal. Thus the horrified main line crew went off shed, more in sorrow than in anger, and more in hope than in the conviction that they were going to get very far. Nevertheless engine and crew made a fight of it and somehow or other managed to make Templecombe No. 2. Junction, albeit much behind schedule – where they expired very much 'down and out', and with a veritable procession of expresses queued up behind. Templecombe shed had been previously alerted of the circumstances and here the Pacific was removed from the train and a waiting '4F' substituted.

Driver Vic Williams, a kindly understanding sort, was acting shedmaster at Templecombe that day, and appreciating the mistake that had originated back at Branksome – made in all good faith – he arranged that the subse-quent report submitted by both himself and the Pacific's driver would attribute the engine's failure to a badly fitting smokebox door causing air ingress to the smokebox resulting in bad steaming. It was thus reported and completely accepted by authority so saving the preparation crew from receiving a considerable rocket. The only remaining problem materialised when that tremendous heap of coal in the 4-6-2's firebox came really to life – which it did not so very long after its arrival on shed. The vast majority of Bulleid light Pacifics at that time – and including the locomo-

177

tive in question – were not fitted with ashpan dampers. This inevitably made the fireman's job of tailoring steam production to demand rather difficult. In this case once the fire had coalesced into a homogeneous red hot mass there was no easy way to stop it raging uncontrollably and ironically, though now producing steam in vast quantities, the engine could not be sent out on an alternative job since officially it had been failed to enable a repair to be made to the smokebox door. Therefore the deafening sound of intermittent blowing off from the safety valves was much in evidence in the environs of Templecombe during much of that day and on into the early evening before the pent up energy in the fire started to subside. It was a good thing that this particular depot was situated in the midst of open country and well clear of anything that would be described as a built up area otherwise searching enquiries from an irate local public might well have ensued.

In similar vein to the foregoing – another escapade of which even now it might be policy not to mention names, numbers or even when it occurred. It concerned an engine crew and a grossly manipulated steamraiser – all Branksome men. The crew were in the mess room at about 5.45 am playing cards although in fact they were booked to prepare a '2P' 4-4-0 prior to working an early morning passenger train to Templecombe. The driver had completed the oiling and examination of his engine and his fireman had partly completed his appointed tasks, but the fire still required making up, so the fireman decided on a piece of cruel psychology to kid the steamraiser to carry out this chore for him and avoid interrupting his game. It was first suggested to this worthy that he wasn't very good at his job, which caused quite a commotion. "What!" he roared. "I could do your job anytime". "Prove it", said the fireman artfully, "go and make my fire up. I'll bet you can't get enough in the firebox to see me through to Templecombe". "Oh no, we'll see about that", said the gullible victim of this exercise in kidology and stormed out of the cabin to the engine. But if our card playing heroes had seen the way he was shovelling slow burning Welsh coal, much of it slack, into the firebox with the aid of a large square mouth shovel onto a very low fire, they would not have felt so happy for unknown to them the joke was about to rebound onto the pair. As soon as they boarded the engine half an hour later, they knew their goose was all but cooked. The firebox was full to the brick arch with coal but there was hardly a flame to be seen. It looked futile even to leave the shed, let alone work a train. But the driver was very much aware that he could give no valid excuse for not going without dropping himself into very hot water so they departed, hoping to work something out, and backed on to their train in Bournemouth West station. Blower, pricker, dart, all had little effect on livening up the black sticky mass which could least be described as a fire. They even tried shovelling coal out of the firebox back into the tender – which must be fairly unique – but to little good effect. They did depart on time with their three coach load, but this was the last time that this particular train was on time that day. By the time Broadstone was reached, the train was already behind schedule and the engine had but 80lb per square inch on the steam pressure gauge with the water in the bottom nut of the gauge glass. By now the engine was unable to maintain the required 21" of vacuum in the train pipe, so the driver decided to continue — to use a colloquialism — without it. The large and small vacuum ejectors were shut off on the engine, the strings pulled on the train thus releasing the brakes, and the train was run on freight train lines in as much as only the engine steam brake (such as it was with 80lb of steam) tender hand-brake and guards brake in the coaches were now available for braking the train. In this rather risky fashion they departed from Broadstone, but nemesis was now close at hand, and after a few more painful miles our intrepid crew were forced to "throw in the sponge". Another engine was ordered by telephone from Bailey Gate signal box and the crew sat down to await its arrival.

It was this period of sojourn that gave the driver an opportunity to consider how best he could extricate himself from this tricky position. There were bound to be enquiries made into the cause of the delay and he was musing on the best line of approach with regard to the report he would have to write at the end of his duty. But Branksome men were nothing if not resourceful in any situation and this one was no exception. He noted that the brick arch was in a rather poor condition. So getting the 'heavy dart' down off the tender with considerable effort he managed to knock the brick arch down in the firebox. With the bricks now spreadeagled across the 'fire' — which was beginning to show signs of life — he was now able to introduce an element of truth into the report by relating how with the brick arch collapsing during the journey to Bailey Gate, combined with poor quality coal, the engine had failed to steam etc. etc. causing loss of time. In fact he made such an excellent job of this report that the area locomotive inspector ultimately commended the crew on the efforts they had made to time the train in the face of very difficult circumstances. He could say that again!

In case some people consider this tale casts a poor light upon this crew, I would like to say that they were usually as conscientious as any at Branksome shed and had done their share of 'keeping the job going' beyond the call of duty when necessary. But on this one occasion, their bit of seemingly harmless fun at the steamraiser's expense, had rebounded most unfortunately, and I like to think that by turning a personal adversity to his advantage and to the apparent satisfaction of management, this driver showed considerable initiative which, I know for a fact, had often been used in other more worthy circumstances to facilitate a repair, or nurse an ailing engine along the road with considerable benefit to the smooth running of the job, and the travelling public's convenience.

A legitimate failure occurring during 1953 brought an unusual Southern visitor to the S&D line, this was a Maunsell 'Q' class 0-6-0 No. 30548, which had to deputise for a 'West Country' Pacific on the 9.25 pm goods from Poole Yard to Bath. I was present when the light Pacific was failed on Branksome shed after working the down 'Pines' due to the regulator gland blowing furiously on the footplate and directing a scalding jet of steam under pressure towards the cab roof just above the fireman's seat, where it condensed and dripped filthy water continuously. No amount of judicious pulling up of the gland nuts had any effect on stopping the blow so Bournemouth Central sent over the 'Q' class to cover the next part of the Pacific's diagram. The 0-6-0 did not cover itself with glory as the substitute on this then heavy duty, and had to pause for breath on no less than six occasions on the way to Bath that night, the first stop being as early in the journey as Broadstone following the two mile climb at 1 in 75. However, lack of familiarity on the part of the enginemen with their mount might well have been the cause as '4F' 0-6-0s (essentially similar in size and concept) had managed this job on several occasions.

On 26th November 1955 an unusual failure befell Standard class '5' No. 73052 which blotted its copybook whilst hauling the southbound 'Pines Express' over the Mendips. The engine was in the charge of Driver Eric Elford and Passed Fireman Steve Penney. Steve mentioned at one stage to Eric (one of the most economical of drivers) that the engine appeared to be burning an excessive amount of coal — as well he might for unknown to him at the time, the rear half of the engine's rocking grate was slowly collapsing and gradually depositing the firebars and with it the fire into the ashpan. Approaching Binegar the entire rear section of the grate and its fire suddenly disappeared down into the ashpan which action effectively welded up the ashpan doors. Eric halted the 'Pines' at Binegar. As was customary on this train from 1949, 73052 was being piloted as far as Evercreech Junction by a '2P' 4-4-0 — 40563 on this occasion — and after conferring with her crew it was decided to remove the class '5' from the 11 coach train which formation included a heavy 12 wheeled dining car and 40563 took over, now in the charge of Driver Elford and Passed Fireman Penney to carry on unaided. The train was still over a mile on the wrong side of Masbury Summit, and to restart its 360 ton train the '2P' required some rear end assistance from a 'Jinty' 0-6-0 tank which was fortunately in the sidings at Binegar. Initially Eric was game to continue through to Bournemouth without further help, but upon subsequent reflection, thought better of it. The train was already late, and its weight was way above the permitted maximum for a '2P', particularly up the 1 in 80 Corfe Mullen Bank and the even steeper 1 in 60/50 gradient of Parkstone Bank and a signal check or stop at the beginning of either climb would have meant almost certain stalling so a stop was made at Templecombe to attach an S&D 'Armstrong' 0-6-0 No. 44559 as pilot onwards to Bournemouth.

Earlier in that month of November 1955 there had been a locomotive failure that caused a fair amount of chaos. This occurred on 10th November when a Standard '4' 2-6-0 No. 76013 — in the charge of Bournemouth

Central men — failed at Broadstone with injector trouble on the 6.40 pm Bournemouth West — Bath and the only engine readily available to carry on with the train was a Southern 'T9' 4-4-0 No. 30728. The engine carried on working the 2-6-0's diagram during the next day and in the evening headed the 6.25 pm Bristol — Bournemouth West train over the S&D. But somewhere on the journey, in the darkness of an S&D night, the 'T9' lost its feet in such a severe bout of slipping that a coupling rod became bent and began to knock the splasher. Thereafter the engine had to continue the journey at reduced speed and Bournemouth West was reached 40 minutes late. The unfortunate 'T9' was eventually towed away to Bournemouth Central shed shortly after midnight by the Pacific off the 7.30 pm from Waterloo to Bournemouth West.

Breakaways were always a distinct possibility on the loose-coupled freight trains so long a primitive feature of moving goods by rail in this country. An occurrence of this kind happened on the Highbridge branch on January 15th 1958.

The train involved was the 6.30 pm freight from Highbridge to Templecombe consisting of 32 wagons plus a guards van. The train was drawn by an S&D 'Armstrong' 0-6-0 in the charge of Driver Ron Spiller of Templecombe shed and Fireman Peter Guy then also of Templecombe but who later transferred to Branksome.

It was just before 9.00 pm and a dirty night of rain and heavy mist as 0-6-0 No. 44557, panting hard and having a bit of a struggle came up the 1 in 105/86 bank from West Pennard towards Pylle. After several bouts of slipping the '4F' managed to get somewhere near Pylle station when a wagon coupling parted leaving only one vehicle still attached to the engine tender. The remainder of the train proceeded to run back down the bank at ever increasing speed despite the valiant efforts at the rear of goods guard Ted Scovell who stuck to his post in the brake van in an effort to retard the train — not that there was much hope of this on these gradients. Mrs Higgins the crossing keeper at Cockmill Crossing first spotted the runaway and immediately telephoned the West Pennard signalman informing him of the situation heading rapidly in his direction, thus confronting him with a hideous dilemma. The signalman had two options open to him. Either let the train run on back down the line towards Glastonbury in the hope that on more level grades extending thereafter the train would lose its impetus and come to a stand, or alternatively divert the speeding train into a siding at the Glastonbury end of West Pennard station. There was little time to cogitate " the pro's and con's" and the signalman chose the latter course. The heaving and swaying wagons lurched wildly as they negotiated the points into the siding and then became derailed and overturned in hideous confusion. The guards van and several of the wagons turned a complete 180 degrees. When helpers arrived at the overturned van guard Scovell could not be found. It transpired that after crawling from the wreckage Ted, suffering from severe shock, had wandered off from the scene, down the track and was eventually found near Pennard Lane Crossing. Poor Ted had a lucky escape but he never really recovered from the shock of that accident.

Mr. Pike the then Evercreech Junction station master was quickly informed of the accident and hurried to the scene to take charge of the situation. He immediately sent for the steam crane at Bournemouth Central to clear the site, but for some reason this was not available and the Salisbury crane was provided instead. This arrived at about 3.00 am the next morning and cleared the tangle of debris from the line in time for the 2.20 pm Highbridge — Templecombe passenger. The rest of the clearing up was done on the following Sunday. The wrecked train's cargo consisted mainly of coal, and some covered vans of tinned milk en route to Avonmouth for an export order. Despite the severity of the derailment the eventual loss of goods was minimal, consisting of about a ton of coal and several boxes of tinned milk. The latter were quickly replaced and the whole consignment was despatched to Avonmouth in time to catch the scheduled ship and fulfil the export order.

West Pennard was in the news again on March 7th 1961, when a W.R. Pannier tank No. 3795 failed there whilst working the 7.05 am Highbridge to Evercreech Junction. The Western engine was itself a "stand in" on the diagram having been substituted the previous afternoon on Templecombe shed for Stanier class '3' 2-6-2T No. 40126 (which had a split side tank) to work the 4.00 pm Templecombe — Evercreech Junction and the 5.00 pm Evercreech Junction — Highbridge. Next morning and on the second leg of the diagram No. 3795 lost one of its left hand big-end bolts and shortly afterwards the other sheared off whilst travelling between Glastonbury and West Pennard. This precipitated the chain of events leading to the failure of the Pannier tank. Bringing his train to a stand the driver found (or did not find as the case may be) upon examining his engine the left hand connecting rod somewhat bent and resembling a letter 'S'. The reversing shaft had been sheared off and the big-end strap was missing. This was later discovered on the dynamo bracket of the third coach back from the engine. Finally part of the locomotive's ashpan had been smashed. With some failures of this kind it was possible for the engine crew to 'take down' the damaged side of the motion and work the engine home on the other. The damage done to 3795 on this occasion — plus the lack of suitable tools on the engine — made this impossible and the driver called out the "break down gang". Templecombe fitter Peter Pike and his mate Frank Ray collected some gear together and in company with 'Jock' Gordon the Templecombe shedmaster, hastily dispatched themselves to West Pennard to restore some order.

They got to West Pennard at about 10.00 am just as the cripple was being pushed with extreme caution into the siding behind the down platform by the following goods train. Peter Pike and his mate now got to work stripping down and securing one side of the locomotive's motion and making it fit to tow back to Templecombe shed. This proved a cramped and fairly difficult task on this particular class of engine and with no pit in which to work. But just before midday after a bit of a struggle, the left hand connecting rod had been taken down and everything was made secure.

Naturally by now the lads were feeling a bit "peckish", hot and thirsty; a nearby pub shimmered like an oasis in the desert but money was short. However Peter, Ray and Mr. Gordon thrust their filthy greasy hands into their pockets and pooled what money they had. It was sufficient to buy a pint bottle of beer each, a single french loaf and some cheese. So returning with their wares to the station they took over a platform bench seat for an improvised picnic whereat their recent purchases went down uncommonly well – grease and all, whilst awaiting an engine to pull them home to Templecombe. At about 2.00 pm Templecombe Driver Ben Dyer arrived with a '7F' No. 53807 to perform the task, Peter riding back most of the way on the side framing of 3795 to watch out for further trouble, but the journey was completely without incident.

This story I hope illustrates a little of the work performed by the running shed fitter in steam days. They got little of the limelight, unlike their footplate colleagues, but all the same performed no mean task. Their work was mostly done on shed, frequently under horrible conditions of cold, damp and in poor light, a routine only interspersed by the occasional call to off shed breakdowns or derailment at any hour of the day and night when just about anything might be met with, requiring much skill and improvisation.

That story involving Peter Pike reminds me that he once lived at Evercreech Junction station where his late father was station master for many years. Both were (indeed Peter still is) thorough going railway enthusiasts as well as being professional railwaymen. This is typified by a "little job" in which both involved themselves on Sunday 14th July 1957.

Mr. Pike had seen the 9.45 am Bournemouth West – Bristol away from the station and then proceeded with his son to walk up the line in order to collect the time books from the shunters' cabins in the up and down goods yards and that belonging to the North signalbox, for him to do the paybills. It had been raining earlier and the rail was not too good. As they walked up the line alongside the up side marshalling yard the engine of the 9.45 am could be heard slipping in the distance as it set about the climb up to Shepton Mallet with its eight coach train of about 260 tons. The train engine was Southern Pacific No. 34110 *66 Squadron* in the charge of a Bath crew who had just taken over the 4-6-2 at "the junction" from the Branksome crew who had brought the train up from Bournemouth. Knowing the reputation of these engines for slipping, Peter remarked to his father "They won't get far". Walking on to the North signal box they could then see the train in the distance and watched as the Pacific grappled painfully with the 1 in 50 gradient. It was moving very, very slowly, and sure enough it finally expired on Prestleigh Viaduct. Deciding that they might be of some assistance to the train crew, Messrs Pike senior and junior (despite the fact that Peter was officially off duty) hurried back down to the station. Mr. Pike dived off to get a taxi from a nearby garage whilst Peter, suspecting that the Pacific had defective sanding gear, collected some wire, corks, spanners and a hammer, and then, as a final thought, picked up four small bags of sand purloined out of the guards compartment of an old two coach Southern set of coaches kept at Evercreech and used for strengthening "the branch" trains on summer Saturdays.

The taxi was soon speeding them towards Prestleigh and upon arrival they clambered up the damp and grassy embankment to the viaduct where they found Driver Reg Beasley rather fed-up with life at that moment. The trouble was what Peter had suspected — the sanders were not working and without these the engine was completely devoid of adhesion. Reg was alone, having sent his fireman walking on to Shepton Mallet with a 'wrong line order' requesting assistance. The guard was protecting the train three quarters of a mile in the rear with detonators and red flag.

Deciding to find out what was what Peter thought he would check the sandboxes, but compared to conventional locomotives this was difficult on these air-smoothed Pacifics, a ladder being normally required to effect the task. Nevertheless by dint of standing on Reg Beasley's shoulders Peter was able to check the sandboxes interiors and found the righthand ones were empty as was one on the left side of the engine. The remaining box had some sand in it but the sand trap was blocked. Emptying a little of the sand which he had thoughtfully brought into each of the empty boxes and clearing all the sand traps, Peter eventually got the sanders working. Whilst this activity was taking place at Prestleigh — watched incidentally by many of the stranded passengers hanging out of the carriage windows — the Pacific's fireman had arrived at Shepton Mallet with his official request for an assistant engine and at length arrived back at Prestleigh — travelling wrong line — on board a BR standard class '4' 2-6-0 No. 76026 in the charge of Driver Harry Shearn of Bath. The engine had been taken off the head of an engineers train at Radstock. The 2-6-0 was coupled to the Pacific and an attempt made to continue the interrupted journey. So deadly was the combination of gradient and curvature at this point that even with two engines several attempts were required before they could get the train on the move which was now well over an hour late. The Pacific, despite having the sanding gear now working, slipped repeatedly, and most of the initial effort to start was thrown on to the class '4' which itself was hampered by reason of the fact it was travelling tender first and was only equipped with one set of back gear sanders. But once on the move both engines buckled down and got the train away from Prestleigh and over Masbury Summit, some five miles off, while Station Master Pike and his son returned home to Evercreech Junction satisfied in the knowledge that whichever way one looked at their contribution to getting the train through they had done the best they could. It is nice to record here that Driver Beasley mentioned in his subsequent report the help he received from the Pike family that day, and this illicited an official letter of thanks and appreciation to them from the District Motive Power Superintendent at Eastleigh.

This incident meant a black mark for someone at Bournemouth Central Shed in sending out the Pacific in this condition, but unfortunately it was very representative of engines turned out by that depot then.

A Bulleid Pacific slipping to a standstill was not unique in the Mendips for sometimes even when their sanders were (apparently) working these engines would slither to a standstill such was their lack of adhesion at times. But for some years these engines were rostered to work this Sunday (summer service only) train until at length it was decided wisely to turn the job over to a class '5' locomotive; in 1960 I fancy it was. But the problem was that this duty was diagrammed for a Bournemouth Central engine which had nothing more suitable than a 'West Country' on its books. So a Bath locomotive diagram had to be altered in order to leave a class '5' at the Bournemouth end of the line on Saturday nights for working the up and down Bristol service the next day. The class '5' finally completed its amended diagram by returning to Bath with the Monday morning up Sheffield relief to the 'Pines Express'. This alteration in turn resulted in a Southern Pacific laying idle on Bath shed following its arrival on Saturday before mid-day until it returned to Bournemouth on the down Sheffield relief to the 'Pines Express' on the following Monday afternoon. Not an economic procedure on the face of it. But as regards their use on the S&D these SR Pacifics — though occasionally performing something of note — contributed more to the business of keeping the traffic moving smoothly by staying off this route if other types of suitable engines, such as the class '5's, were available. Whereas the class '5's may have appeared less glamorous to some railway enthusiasts, they were considerably more reliable and acceptable to the professional footplatemen whose responsibility it was for actually doing the job.

Marshalling yards were locations that saw some trials and tribulations with a fair frequency of minor derailments and collisions. But Driver Eric Elford and I were involved in a rather curious incident one day whilst performing the Bournemouth West carriage shunting duty. Carriage shunting here was very busy during the day. Indeed virtually a non stop occupation and Eric was having a 'blow' on the fireman's side and I was doing the actual driving as 'M7' No. 30127 dropped on to a seven coach rake standing in No. five road in the carriage sidings, prior to propelling them down to the station to form the 12.20 pm to Waterloo. In true Bournemouth West tradition the shunter dived under to couple us on and was out again in next to no time and was vigorously giving us the hand signal to set back down to the station. I immediately opened the large and small ejector, set about creating a vacuum, and when the needle got over the 19″ mark opened the regulator whereafter 30127 gradually got them rolling. Once nicely on the move — probably about 15 mph — I shut off. By then the coaches were on to the 1 in 90 gradient leading down into the station and speed started to increase rapidly. Then suddenly I realised with astonishment that the coaches were travelling slightly faster than the engine and in fact leaving us behind — I could hardly believe my own eyes — and before I knew what was happening the outstretched vacuum pipes between the engine's bunker and the first coach parted with a hiss of in-rushing air to fill the train pipe vacuum. The brakes on the coaches squealed as they pulled the train rapidly to a standstill. But our 'M7' which was now trailing several yards behind the coaches had no chance whatsoever of stopping in that distance. "Hang on Pete" yelled Eric, and — wham! — we ran full tilt into our train. The 'M7's trailing buffer beam folded up under the impact and one of the buffers dropped off. The air was thick for a while with coal dust and several oil bottles were overturned spilling their gooey contents all over the footplate. Damage in the train too was quite severe, especially in the restaurant car where tables and chairs and crockery lay in profusion and both the set of coaches and the engine had to be withdrawn from service for repair. The cause of all this was quite simple. In his desire to keep things moving smoothly and rapidly the shunter had when coupling on our engine, only connected the vacuum pipes, but had quite inexplicably forgotten to place the coupling over the hook. Surely a case of the old axiom — more haste, less speed.

One instance on which Donald and I look back with a certain amount of amusement (although not at the time of its happening) occurred on the 7.33 am passenger train from Broadstone to Bath. It was a few days prior to the Christmas of 1959. When we made the scheduled stop at Bailey Gate station, Donald and I noticed that the porter/shunter there, was standing on the end of the up platform with a well filled sack, "Mornin', Donald" he called. "Mornin', Charlie", Donald returned. "Um, do you think you could put this sack in your firebox please?" enquired Charlie. "It's full of chicken feathers and innards, I've been plucking and drawing chickens for Christmas, and thought the best way of getting rid of this lot would be in your firebox". That seemed reasonable, and in any case Donald and I had both ordered our chickens from him at bargain price, so our co-operation was assured really. But if only we had given some thought to what we were agreeing to do we would not have been so keen on the idea.

With some difficulty I managed to squeeze the sack through the firehole door of our standard '4' 4-6-0 75072 and we departed. We had not progressed far before our mistake became apparent. The engine was steaming well on her mixed diet of coal, chickens innards and feathers, but oh! the smell! A most unpleasant odour of burning meat pervaded everywhere in the confined space of our cab, and the forward movement of the engine was driving the smell straight into us and even leaning over the cab side we could not escape its pungent attention. I have only once before felt so sick whilst on the footplate that it caused me to reach, but that was due to physical exhaustion towards the end of an all out session of firing, on a class '9' being flogged over the Mendips on the up 'Pines'. But this ghastly smell had very much the same effect. Eventually I climbed up on the coal in the tender, but there was no escape, and it was two pale and drawn enginemen, who gratefully stepped off the footplate for a breather when the train halted at Blandford station — by which time anyway the intensity of the smell was gradually subsiding.

After the Southern take over of S&D motive power matters in 1950, Johnny Walker was transferred to Bournemouth Central depot as a driver, and naturally featured less in S&D affairs. But his name still cropped up at times in all sorts of ways such as an occasion during the summer service of 1961, when Donald and I were on the down 'Pines Express'. But to start the story at the beginning — on the day in question the Express ran into Bath from the north some 20 minutes late behind a Stanier 'Jubilee' 4-6-0 No. 45649 *Hawkins*, coincidentally driven by a Bath driver of the same name, 'Jumbo' Hawkins as he was known to his S&D colleagues. As the engine ran in past us his fireman gave the thumbs down and implied that the blame for the train's lateness could be placed at the door of the 'Jubilee'. Nevertheless the load was certainly heavy comprising 13 coaches — which it sometimes did on the down train on Fridays around this period — of BR standard rolling stock, and with a crowded passenger complement probably weighed around 500 tons full. Heading the train onwards to Bournemouth was our favourite class '5' No. 73052, with '2P' No. 40634 as pilot to Evercreech Junction.

At this time the rostered motive power for the 'Pines Express' was a '9F' 2-10-0. But for one reason or another none of the four 2-10-0s shedded at Bath was available to haul it that day. So by a curious inversion of things the heaviest train of the week was entrusted to a 4-6-0, as happened more than once. But this situation presented no problem. Any of the BR class '5's then shedded at Bath was fully capable of handling the job.

As we drew away from Bath Donald remarked, "Right time Bournemouth my son". This went without saying really as it was a point of honour to reach Bournemouth punctually if at all possible. Despite receiving a tremendous hammering for mile after mile 73052 steamed with consistent freedom and turned over the crest of the bank at Masbury Summit with full boiler pressure and just under a half glass of water — engineered by me to prevent blowing off during the fast coasting descent to Evercreech Junction.

Here the '2P' came off and the class '5' had the 500 tons on her own to Bournemouth. There was no let up in the effort, and 73052 continued to put up a sparkling performance. Perhaps the star turn of the whole journey was the brilliant acceleration away from the Blandford re-start with speed up to 60 mph just after Spetisbury followed by a maximum speed of all but 80 mph attained at the bottom of the short 1 in 100 leading down to Bailey Gate station. Thus the hard ten minute schedule from Blandford to Corfe Mullen Junction was kept. After a brief easing here to negotiate the junction and take to the "cut off" line to Broadstone the hard effort was renewed, with a glorious assault on Corfe Mullen Bank, the two miles of 1 in 80 being breasted at fully 30 mph and the 'Pines Express' was back on schedule as we ran into Broadstone where an air of satisfaction pervaded the footplate — justifiably I feel. It's easy to say that one recovered 20 minutes of a late start but results like that did not just happen.

Nevertheless the day appeared to be won at Poole. Only Parkstone bank remained as the final obstacle before Bournemouth West. With the proven form of 73052 what could stop us now? What indeed? But after the *tour de force* came nemesis.

From the awkward sharply curved start at Poole, there was just a mile of level track to get a run at Parkstone Bank consisting of one and a half miles of 1 in 60 interspersed with a short strip of 1 in 50 and of 1 in 300 through the station platform. Now if one thrilled to the sight and sound of a steam locomotive being worked really hard, then to watch a class '5' or '9F' hauling the 'Pines' up Parkstone Bank, performed unassisted as it was day in, day out, despite loads of well over 400 tons, was one of the most exciting weekday spectacles to be seen and heard anywhere on British Railways. The summit of the bank was rarely passed at a speed less than 30 mph or most probably nearer 40 mph if '9F' hauled. On the trip being described, once clear of the level crossing gates at Poole, Donald opened the regulator fully, the cut off was set on 50% and our class '5' was really 'digging in'. The train was accelerated up to around 40 mph with a machine gun like exhaust as 73052, now dropped down to 55% with the needle of the steam pressure gauge pinned on "the mark", launched onto the 1 in 60. Above the din I suddenly heard a smothered exclamation from Donald's corner. Parkstone up intermediate colour light distant signal was on, this was a cruel check indeed. The engine was eased immediately. Up went the safety valves and speed dropped rapidly as a cautious approach was made to the up intermediate home signal at the end of the Parkstone station up platform. Being brought to a stand with a trailing load of 500 tons in the middle of this climb was not the happiest of circumstances, and we approached the signal like a cat approaching an unsuspecting mouse, but it proved to no avail and we were brought to a dead stand.

After waiting a couple of minutes or so I got down from the footplate and went to the track side telephone to remind the signalman at Poole High Street crossing box (Poole A) of our presence in his section to the background of roaring safety valves from 73052. "O.K. mate, wait until it clears", came the 'bobby's reply over the phone, "and by the way", he added, "I've been asked to pass on a message from the driver of the train that's delaying you. He sends his kindest regards to Driver Beale and expresses regret for the delay caused by circumstances beyond his control. Furthermore, he trusts your good driver will not experience any difficulties in starting away from Parkstone". Before the signalman had finished I knew who was mixed up with this. "That's got to be Johnny Walker", I replied. "Quite right", said the chuckling voice over the telephone. "He's stuck in Branksome station with the 4.7 pm Brockenhurst – Bournemouth West local passenger train". It appeared that the climb up to Branksome had left Johnny's Drummond 'M7' 0-4-4 tank engine – with its three coach load – all but bereft of steam, and it was a good five minutes before sufficient was generated for it to lift its load out of Branksome and proceed on to Bournemouth West.

Donald and I were naturally disappointed at being stopped here particularly after all the very hard work that had gone before and when a punctual arrival in Bournemouth seemed certain; we were eventually over ten minutes late into the West Station. But at least Johnny's "tongue in cheek" message caused a chuckle from Donald when I passed it on.

That is the end of the anecdote as such, but I cannot leave the 'Pines' stranded in Parkstone station, it remains for me to chronicle that when the signal did clear 73052 made no fuss about starting this heavy train and accelerated away up the curving 1 in 60 in thrilling style. The tremendous exhaust of the engine echoed back at us off the sides of the deep cutting and it seemed as though we might blow sky high the overbridges in the vicinity as we barked our way under them. What remarkable engines those BR class '5's were for their size. When capably handled there seemed to be nothing they could not do, and they always seemed to be able to pull something out of the bag, they thrived on hard work and the harder you worked them the better they steamed. Yet they did it without becoming wildly extravagant on fuel.

When Johnny Walker transferred himself from Branksome to Bournemouth Central depot to gain promotion from passed fireman to that of registered driver, it broke up something of a love affair between Johnny and a Stanier 'Black 5' No. 45056. He thought the world of that engine. When at Branksome if rostered on the 'Pines Express', whether driving or firing, Johnny would the day previous telephone the Bath shed shift running foreman, probably Arthur Elliott, saying, "I'm on the 'Pines' tomorrow Arthur, so put 5056* on the down Mail (the first part of this particular diagram) in the morning would you please?" This frequently provoked from the recipient some unprintable comments, the gist of which was, "What the hell do you think we are up here, employed to administer to your every whim? anyway I've already made out tomorrow's engine diagrams and your not getting 5056". "Thank you very much Arthur, I'm

---

* The prefix number acquired by most engines under BR ownership was often omitted by professional railwaymen.

189

most grateful to you", the grinning Johnny would reply, before replacing the telephone receiver, knowing full well that despite all that had been said his favourite 'Black Five' would if at all possible, be rostered on the 2.40 am down Mail from Bath; and Johnny when signing on at Branksome the following morning to work the up and down 'Pines Express' would find her prepared for him on the pit ready for another day hauling this veritable Queen of S&D passenger trains.

Broadly speaking ex S&D and ex Southern men kept to their respective spheres of activity, therefore when Johnny transferred himself to Bournemouth Central he lost contact with 5056. It seemed almost as if this severance was too much for 5056 to bear, and around about the time of Johnny's departure she too departed from the S&D for pastures new.

I have included this final anecdote in order to show that by no means all the fun and games were confined to members of the locomotive department.

Late one evening during the 1950's Bert Moody the Templecombe Upper Station Inspector watched an up West of England line train run into Templecombe station. Included within its formation was a cattle van containing a highly valuable prize bull in transit to Australia. It was necessary for the beast to be watered here and Bert entered the van's dark interior clutching a bucket of water in one hand and his trusty hand lamp in the other. Placing the bucket near the tethered bull, it occurred to Bert that the partition in the van was lying on the floor and that the animal seemed to be able to move around rather freely when suddenly fear gripped his stomach as he realised that the bull was not tethered at all, but had somehow freed itself.

Bert flattened himself against the inside of the van as the bull lunged in his direction and to Bert's horror disappeared out of the open van door, onto the station platform. Thereafter such waiting passengers as there were disappeared like magic, and the refreshment room did good business. After roaming the platform for a bit the bull took it into his head to set off at a fair trot down the West of England main line towards Milborne Port with Bert Moody, who had warned the Templecombe station signalbox to stop all trains in the vicinity and alert the surrounding boxes, in hot pursuit. But suddenly the positions were reversed; the bull was now seen to be chasing Bert who was heading back to Templecombe at considerable speed. One wag watching from a safe distance reckoned Bert had covered this length faster than the up 'Atlantic Coast Express'.

But by now Bert was tiring, and it was blessed relief when the bull veered away from the main line, and ran between the lines of goods wagons in the upper goods yard before heading down an embankment towards some cows which had attracted his attention in an adjacent field. Here Bert was joined by another railwayman who, claiming to be an expert on bulls, started to approach, cooing, "Come on Billy, good boy Billy". "You leave that bull alone", exploded Bert, anxious that the now much quieter bull should remain in that placid state whilst he worked out the next move. "I know all about bulls" returned the other fellow boastfully and despite further protest from Bert continued to approach the now very watchful animal. Suddenly without warning the bull lowered his head and tossed the offending human into an adjacent brook. After watching this retribution Bert said, "I could have kissed that bull".

Eventually matters were resolved. Aided by the allure of the aforementioned cows the prize animal was captured, and Bert all but near exhausted from his physical exertion, got home in the very early hours of the morning. But next morning when "the powers that be" who govern from on high — but only from 9 'til 5 — heard about the previous night's escape at Templecombe, telephone bells were soon ringing to seek explanation and enquire after the bull's welfare. Thus Bert was summoned somewhat earlier from his bed than he would have liked, to explain the facts. It remains to chronicle that all concerned survived the enquiries and the bull subsequently continued his interesting journey to Australia.

Chapter Eight

SPECIAL WORKINGS AND EXCURSIONS

Special trains and the bank holiday and summer services were keenly anticipated by passed firemen and passed cleaners as one or another such
trains provided driving or firing turns for those respective groups, and in
the 1920's, could mean the difference between employment or joining the
thousands of others in this country then without jobs. In any case, it was
for the cleaners, much more exciting being out on the road than on shed.

A large number of excursion trains and other specials ran over the S&D
line during its lifetime, from a wide variety of places and for various
reasons, and although it would be difficult, or even impossible to list these
now, perhaps a few specific recollections of this traffic since the 1920's
might be of interest for the record and catch something of the flavour of
these specials.

Between the wars, excursion trains from Bath and Bristol to Bournemouth at weekends, and on bank holidays, were common enough during
the summer months, as were trains from places even further afield, for example, Cheltenham, Worcester, and Birmingham, and as such were not
really remarkable. But of greater interest were the excursion trains from
these locations to either Swanage or Weymouth which were routed via the
S&D. From Broadstone they would take the 3½ miles of single line which
was part of the original Southampton and Dorchester Railway (the 'old
road') to Hamworthy Junction, there joining up with the SR Weymouth —
Waterloo main line for the completion of their journey. Both crews normally worked these trains through to their destinations usually handling
'4F' 0-6-0s, although briefly after 1938 until the beginning of the war
Stanier Black '5's could be seen on these workings. Sometimes Branksome
men would relieve Bath crews at Broadstone and work the excursions
forward to their destination.

Annually around April time the pigeon racing season would start with
the arrival at Bath of the first 'specials' from the North of England, and it
was quite a sight when the homegoing birds were released from their
baskets. Thousands of them would circle the station rising higher in ever
widening circles, until eventually little bunches would break away and
head back northwards and home. A week or two later the first 'pigeon
specials' booked for destinations further south would be observed traversing the S&D heading for Templecombe or the Bournemouth area. Besides

This siding alongside Branksome shed was where 'West Country' Pacifics loaned for the weekend used to assemble on Friday evenings during the summer services of the 1950's waiting to work some of the holiday trains which would flood over the S&D line next day. By comparison with those golden days of steam, on 14th May, 1964 the siding contained five ex SR 'M7' 0-4-4Ts Nos. 30036, 30048, 30029, 30067, and 30108 withdrawn from Bournemouth Central shed and stored here awaiting their final call.

Photo: A. Trickett.

BR standard class '5' No. 73051 has just passed through Parkstone station and thunders up the final 1 in 60 length of Parkstone bank with a packed Bath – Bournemouth excursion, during the summer of 1964.

Photo: Ivo Peters.

A most sad event took place on 5th Septen ... ... iving member
of the S&D '7F' 2-8-0s No. 53807, worked ... ... eech Junction and back. Following its arrival back a ... ... 'd, the fire then
dropped, and the last of these outstanding locc... ...

... when ... from Ba... 53807 ...wn from service. ...es was Photo: Ivo Peters.

Late arrivals on the line were the BR 2-6-4 tank engines. No. 80037 was passing
Wyke Champflower with the 4.15 pm up local from Templecombe on 15th May
1965.

Photo: Ivo Peters.

An 'LCGB' farewell special running between Binegar and Moorewood on 5th March, 1966. Donald Beale, together with fireman Tom Upshall, was in charge of the leading engine, 'West Country' Pacific 34006 *Bude*. The train engine was 'Battle of Britain' class No. 34057 *Biggin Hill*.

Photo: Ivo Peters.

Four specials ran over the ex S&DJR during the weekend of 5th/6th March, 1966 as a prelude to its closure. Stanier '8F' 2-8-0 No. 48706 has just passed Templecombe Lower Platform and is approaching No. 2. Junction from the direction of Bournemouth. The special was organised by the Great Western Society and traversed the line on Saturday 5th March, 1966.

Photo: M. K. Lewis.

From 1914 until 1928, the through Bournemouth – Manchester dining car express (named the 'Pines Express' in 1927) was hauled by 4-4-0s built for the S&D to the standard Midland class '2' design. No. 68 heads the up 'Diner' at Broadstone circa 1920. The bowler hatted figure of S&DJ Locomotive Inspector Wells is visible on the footplate.

In 1928 the LMS resumed building what were essentially Midland class '2's, and in the same year three of these were completed for the S&D and generally assumed haulage of the 'Pines Express' up until 1938. No. 698 in immaculate condition at speed just north of Wellow with the up train in 1936.

Photo: L. T. George collection.

During the period from 1922 – 1938 should the load of the 'Diner' or 'Pines Express' exceed the usual six coach formation then a class '4' 'Armstrong' 0-6-0 might well deputise for the usual 4-4-0 or a double headed formation with any combination of class '2' and class '4' locomotives being employed depending on train weight – as was the case when '4F' 0-6-0 No. 4046 was photographed piloting '2P' 4-4-0 No. 629 on the down 'Pines' near Radstock in 1936.

Photo: L. T. George collection.

1938 saw the introduction of Stanier 'Black Fives' onto the line which quickly super-seded the class '2's on the 'Pines Express'. Destined to be a long serving member on the S&D No. 5440 breasts the 1 in 97 climb away from Broadstone on the 'cut off' line to Corfe Mullen Junction with the northbound train during September 1938.

Photo: G. W. Puntis.

The reinstatement of the through Bournemouth — Manchester service following the second world war saw the 'Black Fives' generally in charge again. But on summer Saturdays up until 1949, Horwich 'Crabs' could sometimes be seen heading the train. 2-6-0 No. 42922 had charge of the down 'Pines' near Stalbridge one Saturday in 1949.

Photo: L. T. George collection.

Following the Southern takeover of S&D locomotive matters 'West Country' Pacifics took up the reins on the 'Pines' from 1951 until 1954. Here the down train is approaching Cole with Donald and myself in charge of No. 34040 *Crewkerne,* photographed on Saturday, 18th July, 1959 by which date, in fact, these engines were not the trains daily rostered motive power but only for Saturdays during the summer service.

Photo: R. C. Riley.

During 1954 successors to the SR Pacifics were being sought for S&D main line work which ultimately proved to be BR class '5' 4-6-0s. Thereafter these locomotives remained in effect the staple motive power for the 'Pines Express' right up until its re-routing in September 1962. With over 400 tons behind the tender No. 73047 rouses the echoes in the cutting at the approach to Broadstone station as it nears the end of the two mile climb at 1 in 75 with the up 'Pines Express'.

Photo: Ivo Peters.

The locomotives finally associated with the 'Pines Express' were the BR '9F' 2-10-0s which were rostered to haul it during the summer service of 1960/61/62. No. 92220 *Evening Star* hauled the last up and down 'Pines Express' over the S&D line and was here photographed passing Cole on the last up train on 8th September, 1962 in the charge of myself and Fireman Aubrey Punter. *Photo: Ivo Peters.*

... later on the same trip we were photographed triumphantly breasting Masbury Summit – marked by the overbridge – No. 92220 having hauled the 426 ton train unaided up the 7¾ mile climb from Evercreech Junction, much of it inclined at 1 in 50. Of all the locomotives associated with the 'Pines Express' over the years the BR '9F' 2-10-0s and the BR class '5' 4-6-0s were the classic performers.

Photo: Ivo Peters.

these special pigeon trains, individual baskets of pigeons would arrive by passenger train destined for Blandford or Wimborne. Some of the pigeon specials would travel through to Weymouth hauled by S&D engines (usually '4F's again) and manned by S&D crews throughout. In common with the passenger excursions to Weymouth (or Swanage) earlier mentioned, this entailed stopping at Broadstone and picking up a Southern driver to act as pilotman to and from Weymouth.

After berthing the vans at Weymouth — usually on a Friday night — S&D men ran light engine back to the Southern depot at Dorchester, where they would clean the fire and coal their engine ready for the return trip with the empties on the following evening. The Southern Railway Company had a lodging house at Dorchester which was used by the S&D crews on these occasions and very clean and comfortable it was too. The initial start out of Weymouth on the return journey the following day was made up the formidable Bincombe bank, but this held no terror for men born in the rough and tumble of the S&D line. The climb out of Weymouth up to the east end of Bincombe Tunnel just over four miles away, though severe, was not as difficult as the southbound start out of Bath, and if the climb depleted the boiler somewhat then this could soon be righted as this initial hard work was followed by very easy gradients for the next 22½ miles as far as Hamworthy Junction where trains bound for the S&D left the Weymouth — Waterloo main line and the stiffish climb mainly at 1 in 100 up to Broadstone commenced. The whole run required considerably easier locomotive work compared to the 18 struggling miles from Bath to Masbury Summit. The returning pigeon empties by virtue of their weight invariably qualified for assistance out of Weymouth but S&D men would have none of it. The look of consternation on the face of the pilotman after having informed the S&D driver that he had arranged for a banking engine was often comical, because the driver usually told the pilotman, "We don't want a banker, mate, she'll do 'em all right on her own". But the Southern pilotman would look less than confident when the S&D guard came up to inform his driver of the load. "Ten on, mate, for 250 tons, don't want a banker, do you?". The '4Fs' for all their faults were quite powerful engines, with excellent adhesion, and given the steam could handle the task comfortably. Thus an 'Armstrong' with her 'throat cut' would trot them up the 1 in 51 past Upwey, and through the dreaded 814 yards long Bincombe tunnel on an incline of 1 in 53 which Southern and Great Western engines and men seemed much to dislike, but which inside, compared to the inferno of the S&D's own narrow single line bores of Devonshire and Combe Down Tunnels, seemed as cool as a mountain stream and its roof as high as a church steeple. Then on over the top and around the bend to Dorchester where a toot of farewell was given to Southern friends in the lodging house, and the Bath men were heading back for S&D rails again.

During the season pigeon specials regularly ran via the S&D line to

Christchurch – just east of Bournemouth – right up until the early 1960's. These particular trains were invariably heavy and hauled almost exclusively by '7F' 2-8-0s manned by Branksome crews who were the only S&D men who knew the road throughout from Bath to Christchurch. These trains were run into the siding just east of Christchurch station which at one time formed part of the old Christchurch to Ringwood line. I personally fired to '7F's hauling these trains on several occasions during the mid 1950's, sometimes with as many as 16 vans behind us. But even with this load these engines would comfortably storm the two miles of 1 in 80 up Corfe Mullen Bank and the even worse 1¼ miles of 1 in 60 up Parkstone Bank. In this connection there was an occasion when a very lengthy Christchurch bound pigeon special was being worked throughout manned (rather unusually) by a Bath engine crew, and in consequence had stopped to pick up a Southern pilotman at Broadstone. After leaving Poole, the train was wending its way round the curving causeway which separates the placid waters of Poole Park lake on one side and the more turbulent waters of Poole Harbour on the other, when the Southern man happened to look back along the train for the first time and observed its full magnitude. "Crikey! that's done it", he exclaimed to the Bath driver, "you should have requested a banker at Poole, you'll never get up through Parkstone with this lot on". "We don't require any assistance thank you", declared the Bath driver firmly. Ahead lay the difficult 1 in 60 climb of Parkstone Bank and the S&D man determined to put up a good show really opened up the big 2-8-0 whereafter it breasted the summit without faltering at a fine rate of knots with the exhaust shooting high into the air to the accompaniment of a tremendous 'Derby roar' from the chimney. Later on, the amazed Southern pilotman was gracious enough to congratulate the S&D crew on their effort adding, "You've got a wonderful engine here, driver, we haven't a single type on the Southern that could do what this engine has just done".

The big snag for drivers on these trains during the 1920/30's was their composition, for they were usually made up of a ramshackle collection of parcels stock and vacuum fitted box wagons, all in various conditions of maintenance. On the saw-tooth gradient profile of the S&D where it was possible to have one's train on several different gradients at once, it often happened that on application of the vacuum brake a tug would be felt transmitted through the tender drawbar, and a glance at the vacuum gauge would reveal the needle pointing to zero, this confirming the driver's worst fear that somewhere along the train's length a coupling had parted, and the train was now running in two portions – although severance of the vacuum pipes would quickly bring them to a stand. Because of this danger it became standard practice – if drivers consider that they had a particularly motley set of vehicles behind them – to work them like a goods train over certain sections of line: that is without using the continuous vacuum brake (although of course it was still coupled up and the vacuum maintained for use if required) recourse being made to the engine's steam brake and tender hand brake only. This meant cautious running and a slow approach to stopping places at times, but it was better than having bits of trains stranded all over the place. One snag with this method of braking was caused by that Midland brake control valve again which was designed to apply simultaneously the steam brake on the engine and the automatic vacuum brake on the train, but provided no real provision for operating the steam brake independently. To overcome this therefore, drivers held a wad of cotton waste over the top of the steam brake fulcrum rod, fitted on the front of the combined steam and vacuum brake application valve, and by using the cotton waste to pull on the fulcrum rod, steam could be admitted to the engine steam brake cylinder and thus apply the engine and tender brakes only and so avoid any snatches in the train itself.

Between the wars "the branch" often saw excursion trains during the summer months, mainly from Weston-super-Mare, Taunton, Burnham and Wells, to Bournemouth or vice versa, sometimes worked throughout by GWR 'Bulldog' 4-4-0s or after 1930 'Collett' 0-6-0s, thus anticipating the regular use of the latter type on the line by some 30 years. But after the war these summer excursions off the Highbridge line were more occasional. I personally recall several such trains running through to Bournemouth from Taunton and Weston-super-Mare during the 1950's and early 1960's when Highbridge men worked them throughout to and from Bournemouth, which was unusual, because their regular duties by this time confined them entirely to the Highbridge, Templecombe Upper section of the S&D, working pick-up freights and ambling local passenger trains.

During the week before the "great day" was due, the driver involved would spend his time riding between Templecombe and Bournemouth West having a 'road refresher'. The excursion trains themselves were more often than not hauled by a Templecombe '4F' 0-6-0 loaned for the occasion (usually 44557 or 44417) and made up to 10 coaches and with point to point timings on the main line little less easy than those of the 'Pines'. Altogether a vastly different proposition for its Highbridge crew than their normal duties.

On one weekend trip, a Highbridge crew, who shall be nameless caused something of a traffic jam in the Bournemouth area. But before proceeding further with the story perhaps I ought to mention that rail traffic particularly over the section between Poole, Bournemouth West and Bournemouth Central on summer weekends during the 1950's and early 1960's was very intense with passenger trains, empty stock trains, and light engines, passing any given place inside that area every few minutes throughout the day. But the operation of the three flat junctions comprising the Branksome triangle was perhaps the key to successful traffic operation in the Bournemouth/Poole area. All trains whether they were Southern trains approaching it from the East, or Southern and S&D trains approaching from the West, had to use two of the three junctions during their passage of this area, and light engines being turned on it prior to going to Branksome shed, situated inside the triangle, had to use all three junctions. These complex operations made planning of the timetable for the area and its observance very difficult, and regular drivers in the area having a keen appreciation of these difficulties were always alert to moving off promptly from signal stops or checks, and generally moving briskly through the area in order to clear the sections and keep traffic on the move. Again a situation as far removed from the placid and occasional happenings of the Highbridge branch as can be imagined. So with this situation in mind it was no small surprise to some when one day a Highbridge driver, unused to, or unaware, of what was expected from him, whilst turning his engine on the Branksome triangle and booked to go on to Branksome shed, drew gently to a stand on the main line outside Bournemouth West Junction signal box with all signals clear, and shouted up to the signalman for a 'Pilotman' saying he wished to go to Bournemouth Central shed for coal. With trains occupying just about every section of track for miles around the harassed signalman nearly had apoplexy and with raised arms screamed at the driver. "Now you tell me. Do you think I've got a stock of spare pilotmen up here or something? Get bl . . . . going, and get it sorted out somewhere else!" – or words to that effect. Thus chastised and not at all enamouted of all this unseemly rush and tear, the driver ambled off again to complete his turning procedure before going on to Branksome shed where coaling facilities were not available. Engines when working to Bournemouth were supposed to be coaled sufficiently to perform a round trip from their home depots. Here the Highbridge man again requested to go to Bournemouth for coal, occasioning a Branksome driver who was present to go out and have a look at the quantity of coal in the '4F's tender. Giving it a brief look he exclaimed, somewhat surprised at what he saw. "B . . . . . me, you've got enough coal there to go to Honolulu let alone Highbridge"."Ah, I know" confessed the Highbridge man, "but I burn a lot you see". Actually the Highbridge driver's concern about coal was probably due to his unfamiliarity with the road plus the heavier than normal load causing a certain crisis of confidence on his part, albeit perhaps understandable under the circumstances. Anyway the Branksome driver read the psychology of the situation well enough and therefore volunteered himself to take the engine over to Bournemouth Central shed for a couple of tubs of coal, and consequent peace of mind for the Highbridge man. Nevertheless the same crew were certainly entering into the spirit of main line running when that evening I watched from my back garden the return excursion flying down Parkstone Bank at a good mile a minute. The '4F', blowing off hard, was rocking and rolling all over the place during its headlong coasting descent giving the impression of almost falling over itself. But on board, the Highbridge fireman looked happy enough; capless, with shirtsleeves rolled up above his elbows and peering ahead into the slipstream through half closed eyes, obviously enjoying the unaccustomed speed at which he was travelling. Speed on "the branch" was limited to a maximum of 45 mph.

After the second world war, excursion trains from the Bournemouth direction to destinations on "the branch" were rare. But I recall two Sunday "pilgrim" specials in the mid 1950's running on separate occasions to Glastonbury. Both trains were worked by Branksome crews — with a pilotman between Evercreech Junction and Glastonbury, this section not being part of Branksome men's route knowledge. Both trains were hauled by Eastleigh based BR standard class '4' 2-6-0s a type not normally seen on "the branch". 76028 was one of the engines concerned. Before 1930 when the LMS assumed responsibility for supplying S&D motive power, SR engines were sometimes used to work excursions from Bournemouth to Bath, Burnham-on-Sea and Weston-super-Mare — 'T9' or 'L11", 4-4-0s being the usual types employed.

Between the wars excursion trains to Clifton Down were run in connection with visits to Bristol Zoo, but after the war these were only run for special booked parties. Bert Brewer and I worked two such specials to and from Bath on consecutive midweek days around 1957, as I recall. The party consisted of schoolchildren from various schools in the Poole, Bournemouth and New Forest areas, who had combined to make up the occupants of an 8 coach train hauled by 'West Country' Pacific No. 34108 *Wincanton* (then still in unrebuilt form) on loan from Bournemouth Central shed. Because of the lengthy nature of this turn of duty in terms of hours away from home, it was designated as a 'short rest' turn, which translated meant that we booked off duty at Bath for some hours during the day signing on again at around teatime to prepare the engine and work the return special to Bournemouth. A 'short rest' duty was thus similar to a lodging or 'double home' turn except that one did not in this case actually lodge at an appointed place.

I remember the first day's trip well enough because of the heated argument that Bert had with one of the coalmen on the coaling stage at Bath. Due to our being rostered to use 34108 on the following day's 'special', it had to be sufficiently coaled to do a return trip from Bath to Bournemouth and back with the engine spending the night intermediately, berthed on Branksome shed. So bearing in mind the voracious coal burning appetite of the 'West Countries', I adopted the usual procedure necessarily used on these engines when working such a roster, I made up a huge fire under 'the door' whilst standing under the coal stage and followed this by stacking lumps of coal on the tender footplate while Bert supervised the coaling up on the tender to the extreme limits of its capacity, nominally five tons. However the coalman thought we were carrying things too far and at one stage refused to tip any more coal into the tender giving it as his opinion that we had plenty for our needs. This led to a fine old set to. However with the aid of Mr. Morris the Bath shedmaster pouring oil on troubled waters, order was eventually restored and yet more coal was poured onto the tender whilst Bert patiently explained to the still truculent coalman that this type of engine was rather extravagant on coal and that crews often had a job to eke out supplies on a round trip to Bournemouth and back, and that by the time we arrived back at Bath on the following day virtually all of the coal that he had tipped on the tender would be burnt. The coalman, still simmering well, was not at all convinced of this — until next day that is, when we again slid 34108 under the Bath coal stage. I doubt if there was a hundredweight left in the bottom of the tender and the coalman, with whom we had now re-established cordial relations, cheerfully agreed that we had indeed been right in our estimation of the Pacific's coal burning capacity. Glancing scornfully down at the engine he commented "They greenbacks (as Southern Pacifics were referred to at Bath) are certainly heavy on their rations". Considering 34108's train in each direction had consisted of only eight coaches, he could certainly say that again.

The S&D line had quite a steady trade in school specials. Sometimes a special train was put on for pupils of Bryanston School, near Blandford, at the beginning and end of each term; at the very least extra coaches were attached to certain local passenger trains to transport the pupils and their luggage. For this purpose also the up 'Pines Express' usually had an extra coach attached, sometimes making it up to a 13 coach load. In the late 1950's and early 1960's when this train was composed almost entirely of BR standard coaches, this meant a gross load of around 500 tons — a formidable task on this road for a class '5' to get to Evercreech Junction unassisted and usually with nothing more than a '2P' as pilot from there over the Mendips to Bath. The 4-6-0s fireman did not get a lot of rest either. Actually one of my own last driving turns over the S&D line towards the end of 1962 was with one such early morning "school special" hauled by an S&D 'Armstrong' 0-6-0, No. 44558, and is of some interest because the pupils from Claysmore School joined the train at Charlton Marshall Halt. This tiny station with its two short platforms — which wanted some finding in the pitch dark — was actually closed in 1956, and it was specially opened for us to pick up this contingent of pupils from the nearby School. Up until 1950 Chilcompton station in the Mendips also had regular beginning and end of term special trains to and from Waterloo via Templecombe Upper, for the benefit of pupils at Downside School.

I would like to mention here two summer "Saturdays only" express trains which ran throughout the 1950's and into the early 1960's which remained 'Midlandised', as it were, and revived pre world war II memories by reason of the motive power rostered to haul them. As the 1950's progressed Stanier and Standard class '5's, standard '4' 4-6-0s, Southern Bulleid 4-6-2s and latterly BR '9F' 2-10-0s, were between them hauling most of the line's holiday traffic between Bournemouth and Bath whereas, when compared to former years, ex S&D or Midland engines gradually became rare birds on these holiday expresses other than in the capacity of assistant engines over the Mendips. But the two trains which took turns in steadfastly remaining loyal to ex Midland designs almost to the end of through traffic were the 11.40 am Bournemouth West — Derby and from the summer service of 1958, resulting from some changes in the locomotive diagram, the 11.12 am Bournemouth West — Sheffield received the doubtful privilege of being drawn by an ex Midland 0-6-0. Respectively both these trains took their turn at being drawn by a Templecombe '4F' at times loaded up to 10 or even 12 coaches which the 0-6-0 was called upon to haul unassisted from Bournemouth West to Evercreech Junction. This was well above the maximum laid down load for an engine of this type and in pre war days such a train would probably have been double headed throughout to Bath. But such was the volume of traffic on summer Saturdays in the 1950's, and the consequent strain on motive power resources, that one engine had to suffice on this train. The Sheffield train was rostered for Branksome men and originally diagrammed for a 'West Country' Pacific, but after the 1958 diagram alteration the '4F' previously rostered to the 11.40 up was switched to the 11.12 departure in place of the Pacific. Some change! Thereafter referred to as "a rough turn" Donald and I performed this duty with a '4F' 0-6-0 on a number of occasions, the recollections of so doing are indelibly stained on our memories. The 11.12 am was booked non stop from Poole to Evercreech Junction and with the general sluggishness in running which was the hallmark of these engines, combined with the rising tendency of the road in the northbound direction, caused the regulator to be open almost continuously throughout from Poole to "the Junction" — representing an hour and fourteen minutes running time. Here five merciful minutes were allowed in which to attach a pilot engine — usually a '2P' 4-4-0 and take water before setting about a laborious climb up the South face of the Mendips followed by a pell-mell descent down the other side in an effort to recoup some of the inevitable lost time. Actually in the working timetable the 11.12 am was, during its run up, booked to stop at Shillingstone to cross a down train in the loop. But in practice so much time had been lost by the time this station hove into view that the down train could be seen safely stowed in the loop with all signals for us on the Sheffield train showing "right away". What with the water level bobbing in the bottom nut, the injector continually blowing out with a roar from under the footplate and requiring resetting; the pressure gauge defying you to keep it on 'the mark', dirt and dust blowing around the footplate — which was usually appalling on these engines when on the run — Oh! how we grimy, perspiring firemen longed to see a distant signal against us at, say, Shillingstone, Sturminster or perhaps Stalbridge, just to give us a chance to pull the boiler round; but always, it seemed, the signals were off beckoning on the '4F' with a sort of stately amusement. Incidentally, the return working for this crew on the amended summer Saturday diagram was with the down 'Pines Express', often with a Bulleid Pacific in high summer on which train these engines swallowed coal in considerable quantities and could be guaranteed to make us firemen sweat profusely from start to finish, and so make our day complete! But there was some satisfaction in this case in that our efforts did produce sufficient steam for the job in hand. As Kipling might have said, "If you can survive that and still smile at the end of the day, then you'll make a fireman, son".

Thus the '4F's had their final regular fling on a through express train working throughout from Bournemouth to Bath on the 11.12 am up during the summer of 1958. Due to their dismal running the motive power authorities recognised that something better was needed on this duty and the following year the stalwart S&D '7F' 2-8-0s were the rostered motive power. Though not superior to the '4F's in matters of free running, and barely so in comfort on the footplate when on the run, they did have superior boiler capacity and would at least steam freely enough (just) to prevent Branksome drivers and firemen from having nightmares during the night before they were booked to work the 11.12 am up.

Thereafter the '7F's remained largely unchallenged on this duty until the end of the summer season of 1961 by which time extra BR class '4' 4-6-0s had been drafted to the line, and it was one of these (indeed a pair of them from Evercreech Junction to Bath) which regularly hauled the 11.12 am Sheffield during the last summer of through working over the S&D line to the Midlands and the North in 1962 and by comparison with what had gone on for years before the job was, during this swan song of S&D summer services, simplicity itself.

Most years during the summer months of the late 1950's and the early 60's saw at least one Sunday return excursion from Christchurch departing at 9.35 am for Paignton, via Templecombe Upper — again worked as far as Templecombe by Branksome men on a 'short rest' basis. On this account the duty was not universally popular, because there was not much to occupy the men during their eight hour lay over at the sleepy village of Templecombe.

However Driver Eric Elford and I worked one of these 'short rest' excursions one Sunday in the mid 1950's and turned it into a most pleasurable day. At that time Eric had only fairly recently been transferred from Templecombe to Branksome shed, and although he was lodging in Parkstone, as yet, his home, together with his wife and family, was still situated at Henstridge near Templecombe. Prior to our Sunday trip Eric informed me that his wife had invited me to lunch and tea during the layover period if I would care to accompany him to Henstridge, and of course I was only too pleased to accept this very kind hospitality. I remember this as an essentially happy day despite the fact that on the up journey our engine — standard class '4' 2-6-0 No. 76011 — did not steam too well as was forewarned by the Eastleigh fireman when I relieved him after his arrival at Bournemouth Central Station. He had worked the train in from Brockenhurst where it had originally started as empty stock. "She ain't doing too gay, mate", he announced, with only 160lb per square inch showing on the boiler steam pressure gauge to back up his statement. "Keep her bright", he grinned as he climbed down on to the platform. However, although things were not much better when we departed from Bournemouth Central, before leaving Poole Station — following the coasting descent of Parkstone Bank — I had improved the situation considerably, and we did not encounter too much trouble timing our 10 coach train onwards to Templecombe No. 2. Junction, although to be sure No. 76011 never steamed as she might, and was a well worn common user engine demonstrated by the numerous steam leaks that emanated from her — particularly from the injector clack valves that were letting by furiously so that the engine rather resembled a mobile laundry — and by her rattling and banging progress up through the Dorset countryside. At Templecombe Bulleid Pacific No. 34037 *Clovelly* was waiting to take over the train.

On a personal level this trip had been planned to a nicety and that day our bicycles travelled on the train in the guards van to and from Templecombe so that after turning, coaling and bedding 76011 down for the duration, we could use them to transport ourselves on a truly rural ride to and from Henstridge — and a very nice ride it was too.

The return trip to Bournemouth Central was a virtual duplication of the up run as far as the engine working was concerned, though 76011 apparently steamed better. But the going was generally easier in this direction. Aesthetically this homeward run was completely different and provided a clue to the compensation experienced by some enginemen for having to work at all hours around the clock. We left Templecombe in the cool dusk of a midsummer evening with daylight fading fast across the meadows and streams as evening gradually gave way to the darkness of night. Passing through oil and gas lit stations and halts on the way, we eventually emerged out of the Dorset fastness at Broadstone into the electric light sodium strip of the Poole/Bournemouth conurbation before finally pulling up at Bournemouth Central on time, at around midnight, and handing 76011 over to a set of Bournemouth Central men. It just remained for us to ride our bicycles back to Branksome, book off, then cycle home for some food, a good wash, and bed, probably by around 1.15 am — having left home at around 8.30 am the previous morning.

The S&D line saw a number of football excursions over the years and perhaps the most interesting of these was the one that occasioned what appears to be the first trip of a Bulleid Pacific over the line when No. 21C149 worked a football excursion destined for Bristol from Christchurch to Bath and back with a 420 ton load. The engine was piloted by ex Midland '2P' No. 40505 between Evercreech Junction and Bath, and it occurred during the latter part of 1948 — for the record, the interesting point being that this was some two and a half years before these Pacifics were officially tested over the line prior to taking up regular S&D line work in 1951.

It is obviously not practical or reasonable to draw conclusions from just one return run, and every day experience is the best teacher, as was brought forcibly to my attention over the years. Several end-of-platform assumptions made about certain classes of locomotives, perhaps making them a favourite of mine, were rudely dispelled in later years when I came actually to work on them. Nevertheless, even on this initial outing of a Bulleid Pacific over the S&D there were signs that perhaps it was not the most suitable type for this line. There was a fair amount of slipping en route and on the return journey that night the locomotive rounded off its trip by nearly stalling on the 1 in 60 climb up Parkstone bank with a load similar to that with which a class '5' daily romped up this bank, and with never a second thought whilst hauling the southbound 'Pines'. Parkstone Bank whilst steep, was short in its extent, and was considered as nothing by S&D enginemen compared to what lay north of Evercreech where tractive effort combined with the adhesion factor of a locomotive really counted: here there was little opportunity of storming the major climbs with the aid of impetus gained from a flying start.

By 1954 and with something like three years of daily operating conditions under their belts on the S&D main line, it was apparent that the Bulleid light Pacifics were only a partial success in the role cast for them. Besides their liability to fits of slipping and poor braking on unfitted freight trains, mechanical failures were fairly frequent. Bath shed's remaining 'West Countrys' or class '5's were often not immediately available to stand in for a sudden failure, which situation often necessitated a '4F' and '2P' combination throughout from Bournemouth to Bath and back, deputising for a failed Pacific on the 'Pines Express'. In the past Bath shed would have borrowed a visiting 'Black 5' to do the honours — there were usually several about the shed on lay over between out and home working — but then the London Midland Region put their foot down and reminded the Southern that they were now responsible for supplying the motive power for this line and to discontinue the practice of purloining LM engines. So with the 'West Countrys' continuing to disappoint it became obvious that the Southern Region now had something of a problem in finding suitable engines from amongst its fleet to power the line's heaviest trains.

It was eventually decided therefore to try out in March 1954 a Maunsell two cylinder 'U' class 2-6-0 No. 31621, and also a three cylinder 'U1' class 2-6-0 No. 31906 for assessment as possible replacements for the Pacifics. Each spent a week on the line hauling test trains between Bournemouth and Bath on the 11.40 am Bournemouth — Bristol semi-fast and returning to Bournemouth on the similar 4.25 pm Bath to Bournemouth service. Strictly speaking neither train was a special nor an excursion. However they were special in as much as their normal weekday formation (excepting certain days during the summer season) consisted of four coaches only. For the trials both up and down trains were strengthened considerably, both engines being tried for three days with 8 coaches unassisted throughout and a further three days hauling 12 with a pilot over the Mendips.

A Southern locomotive inspector accompanying these locomotives during the 1954 trials inexplicably declared himself confident that either engine could equal the work of the LMS class '5' 4-6-0s despite the fact that the Southern engines were rated as class 4P/3F only. One can only assume that this worthy was not familiar with the difficulties of this line or with the work of the 'Black '5's which was on an altogether higher level of performance than the Southern 'Moguls' — as one would expect. However that hopeful statement was made prior to the start of the trials and, following their conclusion, the inspector frankly admitted he had been over optimistic and that these engines were not after all really man enough to work the line's summer holiday trains and a job such as the 'Pines Express' was beyond their capabilities. He mentioned that his earlier forecast was based on his experience of the 'U' class, in particular, on the Salisbury — Portsmouth service via the Netley line. This he had previously considered a hard road. The gradients of the S&D came as something of an eye-opener.

Of the two, the two cylinder 'U' class No. 31621 emerged as the better performer but both types had to be worked virtually flat out at various points with the 12 coach test train, sometimes to counteract a falling off in steam pressure. Not only on the climb over the Mendips but also the ascent of Corfe Mullen and Parkstone banks proved a rather gruelling business requiring full regulator allied to not far short of full forward gear resulting in a rapidly falling water level in the boiler particularly on the three cylinder 'U1' class No. 31906. Not only this, but time was not absolutely maintained. Under the circumstances both engines did quite well with performances that were acceptable for their size rather than memorable. Faint praise, maybe, but considering the performance of certain other engines, both SR and LMS, used for S&D line work at various times over the years, a quite respectable battle honour. But there was no getting away from it, neither the 'U' nor the 'U1' classes were quite powerful enough, so it looked as though the 'West Countrys' would have to stay. At least their boiler power was up to the job. After the trials neither the 'U' nor the 'U1' engines worked regularly on the line again.

The motive power situation was saved for the Southern by the continued building of the various BR Standard locomotives with which types that region eventually discharged much of its motive power responsibility with regard to the S&D line. It is undeniable that basically the BR locomotives lineaments owed more to the ex LMSR than to any other railway hence the strong LMS locomotive atmosphere continuing to pervade the line right up to its demise. The absorption into the Southern region stock book of most of the ex LMS locomotives operating on the S&D after nationalisation also aided this atmosphere, which was heightened by the London Midland Region later relaxing its opposition to Bath shed borrowing its engines, resulting in 'Black 5's continuing to be used on the line when necessary up until the end of through traffic. Naturally this need was infrequent thereafter. As for the 'West Country' locomotives, they were finally superseded at Bath in 1954 by BR class '5's, following which the Pacific's use on the line was mainly confined to extra passenger workings at weekends during the summer season and at other bank holiday periods throughout the year, when one normally powered the Monday and Friday only, Sheffield relief to the 'Pines Express'. On these occasions the Pacifics were loaned from Bournemouth Central shed.

Although throughout its official lifetime the S&DJR remained largely untainted by diesel fumes, for the record it should be mentioned that the odd Diesel Multiple Unit did traverse the line on excursions. The first occurrence of this sort was a special organised by the Gloucestershire Railway Society on May 10th 1958 formed of a WR cross country unit. On Whit-Sunday of the same year another D.M.U, formed this time of Derby alloy units, was used for an excursion from Birmingham to Bournemouth and back. Offhand I do not recall which of them it was, but I remember passing one of these excursions near Masbury station when I was firing on an up express. The first thing that struck me was that although by now on most lines D.M.Us were nothing unusual this one looked most out of place. The S&D was first and foremost a steam railway.

No diesel locomotives worked over the line until after its closure following which several types appeared heading demolition trains. On at least one occasion a works outing special chartered by a brewery at Blandford was seen traversing the Blandford — Broadstone section during the outward and homeward leg of its journey hauled by a Southern Region based diesel electric. Here I should add that at the 1966 official closure the Blandford — Broadstone section of line was retained primarily for freight traffic, though this service too was withdrawn in 1969.

Railway enthusiasts specials were fairly common on the S&D during the last six or so years of its existence, but more particularly in the final months prior to its closure when a good number of farewell specials were organised. At first these were hauled if possible by one of the dwindling class of '7F' 2-8-0s, the last of which, No. 53807, was withdrawn in September 1964. Later a diverse selection of locomotives was used to power these trains ranging from Ivatt 2-6-2 tanks through to '8F' 2-8-0s '9F' 2-10-0s and Pacifics of both the 'West Country' and 'Merchant Navy' classes. (The latter type working between Bournemouth and Templecombe only). But perhaps the most interesting post war locomotive visitor to the line occurred years before on Sunday 25th April 1954, when an enthusiast special worked through from Waterloo to Bath via Bournemouth, hauled by an SR 'Schools' class 4-4-0. The 'Schools' was originally scheduled to be paired with a 'T9' 4-4-0 from Bournemouth Central onwards to Bath, but due to last minute problems in fitting an automatic tablet catcher to this locomotive, Branksome instead sent over a rather grimy ex LMS '2P', No. 40601, as substitute which was coupled inside the 'Schools' at Bournemouth Central. This engine was No. 30932 *Blundells*, then of Bricklayers Arms shed, and fitted with a unique (for this class) high sided tender. Branksome crews were closely involved with this special with Alec Bollwell and Steve Penney crewing 40601, and Bert Brewer piloting Southern men on *Blundells*. For the return journey from Bath to Waterloo the special was routed via Templecombe Upper (where reversal took place) and the SR West of England main line through Salisbury joining up with the Waterloo – Bournemouth main line – which the train had taken on the down run – at Worting Junction near Basingstoke. As the 'Schools' could not be turned on the turntable at Templecombe, it ran light engine ahead of the return special from Bath to Evercreech Junction, where it was turned on the table thereafter continuing tender first on to Templecombe to await its train which followed on, hauled by two '2P' 4-4-0s, No. 40601, still with its Branksome crew, and 40698 in the charge of Bath men, who treated their passengers to a lively descent from Masbury Summit to Evercreech Junction.

These sort of outings were enjoyed immensely not only by the enthusiasts, but also by the participating enginemen who frequently derived great enjoyment and entered wholeheartedly into the spirit of the occasion.

Of several tales that Alec Bollwell told me following the Waterloo – Bath excursion, one small incident that sticks in my memory concerns a group of young enthusiasts having their photographs taken with the crew of 40601. Despite attempts by the photographer to coax some spontaneous laughter from the youngsters, initially they started posing for the camera in that contrived way that so many people do in that situation. Thus it fell to Alec to divert attention from the camera and raise some smiles. Now Alec always carried with him on the footplate a bottle of tea which he drank without the addition of any milk, and pretty vile stuff it looked too as it lay menacingly on the tray above the firehole door. Suddenly picking up his bottle on impulse, Alec made as though to take a swig. Lifting the bottle to his lips, some of the tea spilt down the front of Alec – apparently accidentally! The surrounding retinue immediately burst out laughing at Alec's discomfiture and the camera's presence was quite forgotten – and the photographer (hopefully) got the picture he wanted.

Because of his long association with the line Donald Beale was asked prior to this 'last weekend' if he would like to take part in working a special that the Locomotive Club of Great Britain had booked to tour the S&D system on Saturday the 5th March. For the portion of this working with which Donald was involved the train was hauled by two unrebuilt Bulleid light Pacifics No. 34006 *Bude* and No 34057 *Biggin Hill.*

During the early days of the S&DJR its operation was to say the least, less than well organised, a state culminating in the well chronicled, fearful single line head on collision which occurred shortly before midnight on August 7th 1876 near Foxcote signal box between Radstock and Wellow, when twelve passengers were killed. But as a result of this tragedy drastic reforms concerning the operation of the line took place transforming it into one of the most efficient and smartly worked cross country lines in England. However, Donald's trip of 1966 had a faintly familiar ring about it reminding one of those early days of lackadaisical operation when lack of communication between all parties concerned led in part to the Foxcote disaster — though it must be immediately emphasised that as far as the working of this special was concerned, not for one moment was there any danger to the train or its occupants.

At Evercreech Junction — prior to departure for Bath, a Western Region locomotive Inspector joined Donald on the footplate of 34006 which was coupled ahead of sister engine 34057, and informed him that he was to make an unscheduled 'photographic stop' at Chilcompton. However, those organising the working had not thought fit to inform the signalmen at Binegar and Midsomer Norton (Moorewood and Chilcompton signalboxes were closed) of the changed circumstances. So when the special, having safely passed Binegar signalbox, duly stopped at Chilcompton, it was not long before the Midsomer Norton signalman, alarmed at the train's non appearance at his end of the section, began making frantic telephone calls to his colleague at Binegar trying to trace the whereabouts of the LCGB special. The Midsomer Norton signalman's dilemma was not resolved until at length — and after the photographers had satisfied their requirements — the train came into view descending the bank towards the box with all on board completely unaware of 'the flap' that had taken place during their sojourn at Chilcompton. Thus the line approached its end with just the merest hint of the same disorganisation that characterised its very early days.

RE-ROUTING OF THE 'PINES EXPRESS' AND PASTURES NEW

One link that was not immediately severed as a result of the re-routing of the 'Pines Express' in September 1962 was Branksome enginemen's association with this train for initially it was rostered to our shed for several weeks over the new route, working it to and from Oxford.

The first trip that Donald and I had together on this re-routed train, was one that neither of us will ever forget, and if in describing the events it appears as though I am rather getting away from the S&D, then I hope some mitigation can be found in the fact that it did occur on the 'Pines Express' when still in the hands of S&D men. The run took place on a Monday morning in early October 1962 at the start of which Donald and I presented ourselves for duty at Branksome shed. Donald was attired in neatly pressed pale blue overalls, spotless white shirt, together with his shiny-topped uniform hat, and boots in a high state of polish for his first trip into what was then "foreign territory". He looked the perfect ambassador for the S&D. Driver Harry Woods of Bournemouth Central shed acting as pilotman was to accompany us through to Oxford, and so it was in his company that we set off from Bournemouth. The 'Pines' comprised its usual 12 coach load weighing some 425 tons tare, our engine was unrebuilt 'West Country' Pacific No. 34105 *Swanage* of Bournemouth Central shed which now, due to the re-routing, had taken over from Bath shed the long held responsibility for providing regularly the motive power for this duty (Bournemouth No. 399 duty). Although 34105 was not the worst engine of its class shedded at Bournemouth Central, it was far from being the best in 1962. On the opening stretch to Southampton, boiler pressure see-sawed up and down between the limits of 250/180lb. However the engine coped in an undistinguished way on the first stage of the run to Southampton Central where we drew carefully to a halt at the water column to take water. It was here that things started going wrong on that fateful day. Before proceeding with the story however, perhaps I may be allowed a digression here to say that when compared to the S&D main line, the gradients between Bournemouth and Oxford were of little consequence and the 'Pines' schedule on this route not difficult. At no stage during the run to and from Oxford was there any necessity to indulge in the virtually all out type of locomotive handling such as was the case at certain points between Bournemouth and Bath. So notwithstanding the load on this occasion it should not have bothered a locomotive of class '7P' capacity. But the standard of locomotive maintenance at Bournemouth Central shed at this time was frankly not of the best, and a good many engines were in rather poor condition. Several light Pacifics including Nos. 34085, 34105, and worst of all 34043 were such indifferent performers (due to their marked reluctance to steam freely and compounded on 34105 by its valve setting being awry) as to be unofficially banned at that time from express passenger work east of Bournemouth, unless there was just nothing else to send. Much of their time was spent languishing at the rear of the shed or perhaps employed as substitute for broken down 'M7' Push and Pull tanks on the 'Old Road' from Bournemouth West to Brockenhurst. Working the weekday morning and afternoon Brockenhurst to Christchurch school trains on the main line was another of their regular jobs. Nevertheless during the year of through traffic from Bournemouth to the North via the S&D 34043 and 34105 in particular (admittedly amongst other more puissant machines which occasionally strayed onto the line) had been regularly supplied at summer weekends to the S&D for the heaviest of trains. They were a couple of real 'old irons' and much sweat was expended on their footplate, wangling them over the road, and thus did not enhance the popularity of the class amongst S&D footplate crews. Similarly during the time that Branksome crews were rostered to work the 'Pines Express' to and from Oxford after its re-routing, Bournemouth Central depot continued its policy of shipping off if possible the lame ducks to Branksome crews causing some recriminations.

Getting back to the main theme but bearing the foregoing in mind Donald and myself and I suspect Harry Woods were not surprised at 34105's somewhat mediocre steaming coming through the New Forest, and as we drew up at Southampton Central, Donald indicated that I should stay on the footplate saying that he and Harry Woods would see to matters at the water column, leaving me free to get the fire organised for the next part of the journey. This included the lengthy collar work mostly at 1 in 252, from Eastleigh up to Roundwood which was the real crux of the up run for heavy trains and liable to expose any engine to doubtful steaming. I was thus engaged in putting the finishing touches to the fire (strictly speaking it was bad form to fire whilst in a station, but sometimes needs must) when suddenly I heard a 'rumpus' from the vicinity of the tender (one could not see back into the bunker from the enclosed footplate of a 'West Country' with its high fronted tender) followed by torrents of water and black slurry spewing out on to the shovelling plate and footplate. Almost immediately there was a violent banging from the other side of the tender and shouts of anguish from Donald. Seeing water spraying everywhere I immediately guessed what had happened. The water column pressure at Southampton Central was fierce, and the water column pipe had doubled itself up inside the tender and forced itself up and out through the filling hole, catching Donald — who was standing on top of the tender

208

studying the track layout and signals at Southampton Central — completely unawares. Following his first wetting he immediately jumped in the only direction that he could with safety, over the coal, toward the cab, which sent him slithering down the coal sloping towards the shovelling plate. Given reasonable luck this would have kept him out of trouble, but the rubber water column pipe, now free from the restriction of the tender and able to direct its solid jet of water in any direction, chose to home in on Donald with all the assuredness of a guided missile. When it is considered that this column delivered water at the rate of something like 1,000 gallons a minute, Donald's watery plight may be better imagined!

Harry Woods, was in the porter's room adjacent to the water column making a can of tea and upon hearing noises of distress, came dashing out, and quickly turned the water off whereupon I opened the tender access door letting Donald scramble off the coal onto the footplate — and my word, was he wet! Water was pouring from his clothing and running out of the lace holes of his boots. Poor Donald — as we departed from Southampton Central that day he could have been seen removing his clothes right down to his vest and pants and his humour understandably was not of the best. The cabs of the Bulleid light Pacifics got very hot at times, indeed in the summer, temperatures of well over 120°F have been recorded on their footplates. But though most uncomfortable and fatiguing on this account when hard firing was called for, they were like mobile drying rooms and ideal for watery disasters such as this. So some of Donald's wet and dripping clothes were hung on the various steam control valves which protruded into the cab from the steam manifold, whilst the rest were draped over the whistle cord which extended across the cab roof. Meanwhile Donald himself huddled up to the boiler front not entirely for warmth — because as indicated earlier there was no lack of that on a 'West Country' but to keep out of the gaze of others and so save his blushes and maintain his self respect.

Whilst all this was going on pilotman Harry Woods had got the 'Pines' briskly away from Southampton and was soon hurrying it up through Eastleigh at some 60 mph. 34105 was always regarded by us at Branksome as being as 'weak as a robin', therefore, to achieve 60 mph here, the engine was being worked hard — indeed considerably harder than the schedule demanded with a long cut off and the regulator "in the roof". Since the usual mode of driving employed by Bournemouth Central enginemen was of a distinctly more gentle nature I rather felt this display of verve was being done to impress the "foreigners" from the S&D. But it was taking its effect on the boiler. 34105 didn't like it at all and started adding to the confusion by "turning her nose up" at being hustled along at such an unseemly rate, and boiler pressure gradually began falling back. I commenced firing with some vigour amidst the "washing" but it was an awkward, hot and frustrating job with a ceiling of wet shirt tails and dripping trouser legs hanging all around and flapping me in the face — particularly when once or twice I had to get the pricker down and stir up the fire in an effort to encourage the old girl to percolate. With myself sweating profusely, and with water dripping all over me from Donald's washing, I was definitely water cooled on this occasion.

The scheduled stop at Winchester was made well ahead of time, thus giving *Swanage* several minutes of extra time in which to recover her breath. But once under way pressure soon dropped back in the doldrums again. That laboured climb through the chalk cuttings and tunnels leading to Litchfield was neither exhilarating nor comfortable with our losing steam pressure all the way. The summit of the climb was breasted at just over 40 mph with some 160lb per square inch on the clock and about an inch of water showing in the gauge glass. But nevertheless the train was still more or less on time and thenceforward as far as power output from the engine was concerned, the outward part of the job was over. What was more the 'washing' was drying nicely now, and Donald was able to run into Basingstoke Station decently attired in his trousers, shirt and waistcoat — although the overalls still required a little more airing.

The road from Basingstoke onwards to Oxford is almost entirely favourable and 34105 was easily on top of the job now, and a rather more buoyant air gradually began to pervade the footplate. As we swung on to the Oxford line at Didcot East Junction, Donald put on his cap and overalls and was able to run into Oxford station claiming that on this washday Monday at least, he had "washed", "dried" — although not yet "ironed". A glance in his direction was sufficient enough to convince one of that, as it was very apparent that his clothing had lost something of the crispness with which they had started the day.

It might reasonably be assumed that this was the end of the saga — but there is more. Running into Basingstoke on the down 'Pines' later in the day, Harry Woods decided to take water. The steaming of the Pacific was still as tricky as ever and the climb from Reading West up to Basingstoke had somewhat exhausted 34105 and had me sweating hard from my efforts to make the engine boil. As we drew up at the column Donald shouted, "I'll put the pipe in, kid", and he once more motioned me to stay on the footplate and see to the fire, whilst Harry and himself attending to filling the tender tank, but mindful of the morning and noticing my questioning expression, Donald added with a grin, "They say that lightning never strikes twice in the same place". Perhaps I should have reminded him that we were not in the same place as the morning incident.

I was working on the fire when I heard a yell and a whoosh which sounded suspiciously like a noise I had heard before that day and my immediate reaction was, "Oh no! not again". I rushed to look over the side of the cab and was greeted by the sight of water gushing down the side of the tender and down over the station platform. Incredibly this water column pipe too had worked its way up out of the tender filling hole. The result was that Donald's much washed clothing was yet again hung up to dry that day.

Well trouble always comes in threes or so they say so it did, but Donald — and I — were to be gleeful spectators this time. Whilst accelerating away up the 1 in 249 from Basingstoke towards Worting Junction we noticed in the up side goods yard the driver of a Maunsell 'S15' 4-6-0 turning off a water column control valve having just filled his engine's tender tank. But his fireman up on the tender — obviously keen to be on the move — threw the water column pipe overboard a shade before his mate below had turned the water off, and he had no chance of stepping clear. The flexible section of these water column pipes usually retained a residue of water after being turned off and this one was no exception, its icy contents cascading down all over the unfortunate and somewhat shocked figure of the driver, thoroughly drenching him. Human nature being what it is, this, I fear, considerably amused Donald and me. Donald blew our engine whistle and waved vigorously to the bedraggled figure. This was meant as a gesture of comradeship to a fellow victim, but I fear the driver suspected that he was being made fun of — if only he had known.

After his arrival back home that evening, Donald's wife stared unbelieving at her unhappy dishevelled husband, commenting crisply, "If that's the state you are going to come home in now you work on the Southern, then the sooner you get back on the S&D the better".

However there was to be little more chance of this for events occurred towards the end of 1962 which at the start of 1963 culminated with Branksome shed's closure, thus anticipating the fate of the remaining S&D motive power depots by some three years. When these depots did eventually close in 1966 a number of the older men took an early retirement, including several ex members of the erstwhile Bath cleaning gang whose exploits are chronicled in chapter one. The remainder were distributed amongst sheds in the Western Region mainly where many still remain. But when Branksome closed in 1963 the enginemen, shed staff, and the shed's diagrammed duties were transferred to the opposition's establishment on the other side of the town at Bournemouth Central — although engines still used the Branksome shed yard in between trips during the daytime. So the tremendous gradients of the S&D main line were exchanged for the greatly contrasting easily graded and beautifully aligned lengths of the Weymouth — Waterloo main line and the cross country link to Oxford. Thereafter most Branksome crews lost regular contact with their old line although the link in which I and my Branksome colleague Bill Harford (both of us passed firemen) were placed by virtue of our seniority did have two ex Branksome diagrams in it covering regular turns of duty to Templecombe and back, but speaking for myself I can't truthfully say I enjoyed working over the line by then. It was obvious that the line was suffering a long, lingering, but inevitable death, and the morale of the staff remaining on the line was understandably low. Many men throughout its length, from various grades resigned their jobs for alternative employment rather than trust their future to fate and the politicians. Those who hung on waited and worried. In general, filthy unkempt locomotives ambled around more or less aimlessly on four coach locals (the various S&D farewell specials being notable exceptions to this rule), weeds began to grow amongst the ballast on certain sections of track — a manifestation almost unknown in previous years. The unfair sobriquet by which the S&DJR was often referred to throughout its history 'slow dirty and jolly rotten' almost became an accurate description of the line during its last three and a half years. As far as I and most other S&D men are concerned the S&D line as we knew it ended when the last 'Pines Express' ran over it in September 1962. The transfer of Branksome men and duties to Bournemouth Central finally broke up the partnership between drivers and firemen at that depot including my own with Donald Beale that we both had enjoyed at Branksome for several years previously. I think it was slightly unfortunate from the point of view of those lay enthusiasts who were interested in train timing and locomotive performance generally, that the two Branksome drivers — Donald Beale and Bert Brewer — whose seniority at the time of the transfer would have placed them in the top link at Bournemouth Central never actually took their rightful position. The reason being their age and close proximity to retirement. Both management and the two drivers concerned were aware that it would require many months of 'road learning' before they could confidently sign for the various routes covered by the top link, and viewed realistically this was not really a practical or profitable proposition. So instead these two Branksome drivers, both of whom had performed some outstanding feats of locomotive performance over the S&D main line, eked out their final days on the footplate engaged on mainly local freight and passenger workings. Had fate decreed different, I can't help but think that Donald and Bert might well have set the Bournemouth — Waterloo main line ablaze — probably literally if there were any arrears in schedule to make up — by their performance on the fasts, and the train timers scurrying for their watches and notebooks.

This transfer brought about other manifestations. It meant for us working at a depot with generally different traditions to those formerly applying and in some instances totally opposed methods of how work on the footplate should be performed, which situation did cause the odd confrontation. I was most fortunate in that my own new driver, Roy Lovell, proved to be a very pleasant man, quiet, thoughtful and a good engineman. He was a dyed in the wool "Southern Man" whereas, though Southern based, my own leanings as far as locomotive matters were concerned lay with the LMS therefore we occasionally exchanged good natured badinage on the relative merits or otherwise of LMS and SR engines. Strangely Roy did not originate from within SR territory in its purest sense but came from Temple Cloud, in Somerset, a small village situated not so very far from the S&D main line. Once again therefore I was paired with a Somerset man and for the next year or so we had many interesting trips together on a wide variety of jobs ranging through pick up goods trains to Wareham and Swanage with Maunsell 'Q' class 0-6-0s, local passenger trains to Salisbury, Weymouth or Eastleigh with 'U' class or BR class '4' 2-6-0s to the other extreme of working the "Bournemouth Belle' Pullman between Waterloo and Bournemouth with a rebuilt 'Merchant Navy' Pacific.

I found it rather sad when during the Summer service of 1963 I was rostered to work Saturday only extras from Bournemouth destined for towns and cities in the North of England trains which during previous years would have commenced their long journey by traversing the S&D. Now the majority of these trains were routed by way of Basingstoke, Reading and Oxford and hauled mainly by Southern Pacifics. However by way of a change Roy Lovell and I were booked one Saturday to work a northbound extra routed via West Moors, Salisbury and Westbury, which was as far as we went with it. The train was made up to eight coaches hauled by a BR class '4' 2-6-0. I was interested to note that it was a Stanier 'Black 5' that took over the train at Westbury.

This change of environment brought Branksome enginemen into close contact with several types of locomotives which, though seen daily, had not been actually worked on by most enginemen, excepting a number of passed cleaners of my own seniority and including myself, who for a period in the mid 1950's were frequently loaned to Bournemouth Central shed to cover a temporary shortage of firemen there. We few thus had some previous footplate experience of many ex SR classes some of which had been rendered extinct by the time of our 1963 transfer. Many of these locomotives were superseded in the main by BR standard and LMS Ivatt types — and not before time. I quite appreciate the fact that the continued existence on the Southern up to and in some instances into the 1960's of many types of old pre and post grouping classes was the cause of considerable satisfaction and interest to many railway enthusiasts, but speaking from a professional stand point it was obvious that most should have been swept away years before. Their continuance in service made the daily task of Southern enginemen more burdensome than it might have been. According to the adage, 'the grass is always greener on the other side'. Well this wasn't always so, and after sampling a fair selection of Southern types, most of my Branksome mates referred to LMS engines in terms of almost extravagant endearment — excepting possibly the dreaded '4F's. Of all the older Southern engines on which I have worked I think I enjoyed the 'King Arthur' 4-6-0s the best: good reliable work horses and how those engines could steam. But my out and out favourite Southern type was without doubt the rebuilt 'Merchant Navy' Pacifics. The difference between these and the smaller 'West Countrys' as regards their performance on the road and the general comfort as experienced on the footplate was as marked as chalk is to cheese. I developed a healthy respect for the 'Merchants' and enjoyed all my trips on their footplates. Included amongst the locomotives regularly handled by some ex Branksome men from 1963, were not only former Southern Railway locomotives but also the GW 'Hall' class 4-6-0s working from Oxford to Bournemouth on the through train from York. Towards the end of steam this duty became rostered for a Stanier 'Black 5' working through from Banbury to Poole. Unfortunately most of the engines concerned were rather run down, rough riding, and able to show little of their true form.

But the greatest pleasure for me as I know it was for several of my ex Branksome colleagues, was to get on the footplate of a class of engine which was always one of our favourites at Branksome — the BR standard class '5's — and prove they could do virtually anything that a 'West Country' Pacific could do hauling the crack trains on the Waterloo — Weymouth main line. On the S&D line the class '5's had already proved they could better the Pacifics, being better starters and stronger at low speed in the banks on heavy trains. I was most interested therefore to see how the two classes of engines would compare on the very fast Bournemouth — Waterloo main line, where there was an almost complete absence of any steep gradients, and which terrain was very much to the liking of the speedy Pacifics.

On those occasions over the years when Southern and S&D men spent their cabin time mildly insulting the capabilities of each others locomotives, Southern crews often referred to our LMS 'Black 5's as 'bloody old goods engines'. This usually earned the retort "Well those old goods engines as you call them could work with ease any train you've got on the Southern". Such baiting rarely failed to bring forth much invective and ribald comment from the Southern men. However the outstanding work over a number of years of the standard class '5's (which were derived from the 'Black 5's and can justifiably be regarded as an extension of that class), when towards the end of 1955 ten apiece were allocated to Nine Elms and Stewarts Lane sheds on the Southern Region, surely proved the judgement of the S&D camp of years before as being a fairly accurate assessment. At first the standard '5's shedded on the Western section of the Southern at Nine Elms got little opportunity to perform on the top jobs against the over-supply of Bulleid Pacifics, and were largely employed with great success on semi-fast trains such as those between Waterloo and Bournemouth. But due to the notorious unreliability of the Southern Pacifics, particularly in their unrebuilt form, the class '5's did occasionally get the opportunity to deputise, and most ably too, for the Pacifics on Bournemouth — Waterloo two hour trains including the 'Bournemouth Belle' Pullman and at times on 'The Royal Wessex' running between Weymouth — Waterloo. I can add further weight to this statement of class '5' prowess by mentioning that Mr. S. C. Townroe one time District Motive Power Superintendent at Eastleigh records on page 93 in his book 'The Arthurs, Nelsons and Schools of the Southern' that some enginemen preferred a BR '5' to a 'Merchant Navy' on the 'Bournemouth Belle'.

I recall a memorable trip between Bournemouth and Oxford and back on class '5' No. 73042 — then a Weymouth engine I think — which had been hastily substituted on Bournemouth Central shed for a failed Bulleid Pacific in October 1962. The train — need I add — was the 'Pines Express', and it seemed far more fitting and much more like old times to have what was in effect an LMS engine at the head end once more. The Bulleid engines always appeared incongruous on this train to any S&D man. The most outstanding feat of 73042 that day was the climb from the Winchester stop up the 1 in 252 to Roundwood. With a trailing load of 430 tons tare, probably 470 tons gross, the engine accelerated up the incline until speed reached 50 mph at Micheldever and, still slightly accelerating, a shade over that speed by the time the summit at Roundwood was reached, in a time of just under 15 minutes from the Winchester re-start. At this point the engine was on 35% cut off, with full regulator and boiler pressure comfortably maintained "on the mark" throughout with water at the top of the gauge glass sustained by relatively easy firing. I never saw a 'West Country' Pacific improve on that with such a load unless the boiler was substantially mortgaged which could of course have been done with 73042 to achieve a faster time. The rest of the trip required no special effort from 73042 in order to keep time. Indeed both the Oxford road and that to Waterloo required little in the way of exceptional power output relative to the size of locomotives used and normally loaded, it was in the recovery of lost time that locomotives were sometimes extended and allowed to show their powers.

It is nice to record how at this late stage an original S&D driver although no longer working regularly on his native line was partly instrumental at least in a consultative sense in helping to decide the final shape of its locomotive history. Bournemouth Central depot was in 1963 responsible for providing the power for a number of S&D diagrams and officially these were rostered for BR standard class '4' locomotives. But towards the end of 1963 with the ranks of steam locomotives at Bournemouth suitable for use over the S&D line becoming depleted due to scrappings, it became increasingly difficult for Bournemouth shed daily to turn out an engine of this class for certain diagrams and frequently a 'West Country' was substituted. But these were sorely required on the Southern main line to bolster the dwindling ranks of express passenger locomotives. With the continual mass transfers from depot to depot of steam engines displaced by dieselisation and electrification which was a feature of the closing years of steam on BR, Bournemouth acquired several BR standard '4' (80000 number series) 2-6-4 tank engines and whilst chatting in Bournemouth Central Loco yard one day to Donald Beale, Mr. Pringle the shedmaster happened to mention his problem of finding suitable engines for his S&D diagrams whereupon Donald suggested using these big tank engines. "Think they could do it throughout to Bath, Donald?" enquired Mr. Pringle. "Yes. Ideal on stopping and semi fast trains," Donald replied, "bags of power, fast, comfortable and with sufficient coal (3½ tons) capacity to work through over the 71½ miles from Bournemouth to Bath on three, four, or five coach trains"

— which were the norm by then. Donald was very much aware that these engines were no more than a "tank" version of the 75000 standard class '4' 4-6-0s which had worked on the S&D line most successfully since 1956, and the only factor that really needed to be considered with regard to their use on these diagrams was the sufficiency of their fuel carrying capacity. On November 4th 1963 therefore Mr. Pringle was moved to sending out for the first time on the 1.10 pm Bournemouth to Bath a Standard 2-6-4 tank. Its performance proved satisfactory and from then onwards engines of this class did a fair amount of main line work — such as it then was — between Bournemouth and Bath for the final two or so years of the S&D line's existence. Some were allocated for a time to both Templecombe and Bath sheds.

However care was needed with these engines during their preparation on shed to ensure that the bunker was completely filled with coal as there was not much to spare when working through from Bournemouth to Bath or vice versa. With tender engines it was customary for them to work through from Bath to Bournemouth West (visiting Branksome shed intermediately even after its official closure where the coal was shovelled forward on the tender) and back to Bath on the contents of a tender of coal. Obviously this was doubtful of attainment with the 2-6-4 tanks and it was sometimes necessary for them to run over the busy 2½ mile section of track from Branksome to Bournemouth Central shed for coal on certain turns which was rather inconvenient. However this situation was facilitated when from 2nd August 1965, Bournemouth West station became temporarily unavailable to Somerset and Dorset trains due to engineering work, in the event S&D trains never again returned to Bournemouth West and it was subsequently closed on 4th October 1965. In consequence S&D trains were diverted to Bournemouth Central which made it easier for the big tanks to call in at the adjacent motive power depot for coal. With a water carrying capacity of 2,000 gallons, water was something else that had to be watched, with the 2-6-4 tanks. But there was an ample supply of water columns between Bournemouth and Bath from which to replenish them and this was not a major problem, more of a nuisance.

Despite the undoubted thrill that I had of doing 100 mph through Winchester Junction on 35016 *Elders Fyffes* hauling the 12 coach (488 tons tare) down 'Bournemouth Belle' Pullman one Sunday in August 1963, one occasion that delighted me very considerably during my period of work on the Southern was in the awful winter of 1963 when an S&D 'Armstrong' 0-6-0, No. 44560, turned up at Eastleigh one freezing January night on the 11.46 pm Eastleigh — Poole goods on which I was rostered. I was intrigued to know how on earth it came to be on the job. It transpired that a Bournemouth Central BR class '4' 2-6-0 had failed at Bath a day or two earlier and the '4F' had deputised on the 7.05 pm Bath — Bournemouth passenger train and subsequently carried on working through the 2-6-0's normal diagram duties instead of being removed at Bournemouth in favour of a Southern based engine as usually occurred under these circumstances, hence it turning up at the head of the 11.46 pm goods. This would have been some "cop" for any insomniac train spotters east of Bournemouth Central who might have been near the lineside that night. I have never been an ardent admirer of the Fowler '4F's, but for old times sake I did enjoy the run to Poole that night. We had 60 wagons hung on behind the tender, and the husky exhaust of 44560 echoing out into the damp night air as, completely out of her usual setting, she dragged her unwilling load up the 2½ mile gradient at 1 in 176-103 across the snow covered heathland beyond Brockenhurst, which reflected a brilliant moon and took on something of the appearance of a lunar landscape, brought back nostalgic memories of similar sounds heard many times before echoing out across the rolling Mendip Hills. But how times had changed for the S&D line and its men since those hills first echoed to the sound of No. 44560, or I should say No. 60, as she then was in far off 1922.

Detailed arrangements in connection with private special train Southern Railway to Blandford and return empty train Blandford to Southern Railway via Broadstone, Tuesday, May 14th, 1940.

Private Special Train Southern Railway to Blandford and return empty train Blandford to Southern Railway (via Broadstone) Tuesday May 14th.

		a. m.
Broadstone	arr.	2. 13
"	dep.	2. 21
Corfe Mullen Jcn.	pass	2§26
Blandford	arr.	2. 38
Blandford	dep.	11. 30
Corfe Mullen Jcn.	pass	11§43
Broadstone	arr.	11. 50

Notice No. 43 S.O.O. dated May 11th, 1940, which has been issued by the Southern Railway and has been circulated to stations concerned on the S.&.D. Joint Line is to be observed in regard to the working over the S.&.D. Joint Line.

On a Single Line, should it be necessary for a train travelling in the opposite direction to cross the special train such train must arrive at the crossing place, and be clear of the line on which the special train will run 10 minutes before the special train is due to pass the signal box in rear and the "Is line clear" signal for the special train must not be acknowledged until the train in the opposite direction has arrived in the Loop Line clear of the single line. The Signalman must verbally inform the Driver of the circumstances and instruct him not to allow the engine to move. The Station Master will be responsible for seeing that the train is clear of the Loop Line over which the special train will pass and that the hand brake in each van of the train is hard on and properly secured.

During the time shunting movements are being made at Blandford and also whilst the special train is standing at the down platform line at Blandford no train to be allowed to leave Shillingstone in the direction of Blandford.

Monday, May 13th

Class 5 Mixed Traffic Engine No. 5274 will be worked light from Saltley to Templecombe as under:—

		p.m.			p.m.
Saltley Loco	dep.	12.10	Standish Jc.	pass	2.35
Landor St. Jc.	pass	12.14	Berkeley Road	pass	2.52
Camp Hill	pass	12.19	Yate	pass	3.20
Kings Norton	pass	12.27	Mangotsfield Nth.Jc.	pass	3.30
Blackwell	pass	12.38	Bath	arr.	3.50
Bromsgrove	pass	12.44)S	do.	dep.	4.50
Stoke Works Jcn.	pass	1. 0)L	Midford	pass	5. 0
Dunhampsted	pass	1. 8	Radstock	pass	5.16
Abbotts Wood Jc.	pass	1.19	Shepton Mallet	pass	5.30
Ashchurch	pass	1.40	Evercreech Jcn.	pass	5.48
Cheltenham	pass	1.53	Templecombe No. 2	pass	6. 5
Gloucester	arr.	2W5	Templecombe Loco.	arr.	6.10
do.	dep.	2✳15			

Mr. Sealy will arrange for engine to be worked forward from Templecombe to Branksome for working the special train.

The engine to be chimney leading from Saltley and will be turned at Bath and Branksome.

Class 5 Mixed Traffic engine No. 5289 will be worked from Bristol to Blandford for the station movements at Blandford and for working the return empty train forward to Broadstone.

This engine to be at Blandford by 1.45 am and will stand on the down line until the arrival of the special train.

Class 7 engine to be provided at Templecombe to act as "stand-by engine".

The men selected for working the special train from Broadstone are:—

> Driver J. E. Flynn of Branksome.
> Fireman D. E. Beale of Branksome.

to be relieved by:—

> Driver A. J. Good of Templecombe.
> Fireman H. Jeans of Templecombe.

The engine for making the station movements at Blandford will be manned by:—

> Driver W. J. Cox of Templecombe.
> Fireman D. M. Norris of Templecombe.

to be relieved by:—

> Driver A. Bollwell of Branksome.
> Fireman H. Grant of Branksome.

The Guards selected are:—

> Guard W. J. Prior, Bournemouth
> To be relieved by W. Hodges, Bournemouth.

Mr. Sealy will be in charge of the whole of the movements at Blandford and no movement must be made without his authority.

The special train will come to a stand on the Up Line at Blandford clear of the crossover road at the south end of the station and with the cab of the engine opposite a point at which a man will be stationed exhibiting a hand signal.

Mr. Sealy will authorise the movement of Class 5 mixed traffic engine No. 5289 from the Down Line to the rear of the special train standing on the Up Line and for engine to be attached in rear.

The train will then be drawn from the Up line to the Down line and come to a stand on the Down line clear of the trailing points at the South end of the station leading to the goods yard and with the cab of the engine opposite a point at which a man will be stationed exhibiting a hand signal. This movement will be made with an engine attached front and rear of the special train. The engine at the South end of the special train to then be detached and proceed light to Branksome.

The train will afterwards be drawn from the down line into the middle road of the goods yard and come to a stand with the cab of the engine opposite a point at which a man will be stationed exhibiting a hand signal.

After the special train has come to a stand the vacuum must be entirely destroyed. The engine drawing the special train into the Goods Yard at Blandford to remain attached to the train throughout the night and until the engine for making subsequent movements of the special train has been attached.

Class 5 Mixed Traffic Engine No. 5289 to leave Branksome Shed light for Blandford to arrive by not later than 9.0 am.

At 9.30 am this engine to be attached to the rear of the special train standing in the Goods Yard, and the special train to then be drawn from the Goods Yard on to the Down line, and come to a stand clear of the cross-over road at the South end of the station leading to the Up line, and with the cab of the engine opposite a point at which a man will be stationed exhibiting a hand signal. The train to afterwards be drawn from the down to the up line and come to a stand at 9.45 am at the up platform with the cab of the engine opposite a point at which a man will be stationed exhibiting a hand signal. These movements will be made with an engine attached front and rear of the special train.

The special train to then be drawn back from the Up platform line through the crossover road on to the down line, and come to a stand clear of the trailing points leading to the Goods Yard and with the cab of the engine opposite a point at which a man will be stationed exhibiting a hand signal. This movement will be made with an engine attached front and rear of the special train. The engine at the South end of the special train to then be detached, and the train to afterwards be drawn from the down line into the Goods Yard and come to a stand with the cab of the engine opposite a point at which a man will be stationed exhibiting a hand signal.

At 10.45 am the special train will again be drawn from the Goods Yard on to the down line and come to a stand clear of the crossover road at the South end of the station leading to the Up line and with the cab of the engine opposite a point at which a man will be stationed exhibiting a hand signal. This movement will be made with an engine attached front and rear of the special train. The train to afterwards be drawn from the down to the up line and come to a stand at 11.0 am at the up platform with the cab of the engine opposite a point at which a man will be stationed exhibiting a hand signal. These movements will be made with an engine attached front and rear of the special train. After arrival at the up platform line and the station duties are completed the leading engine to be detached and the train will stand in the Up platform line until ready to leave at 11.30 am for Broadstone.

Class 5 Mixed Traffic Engine No. 5274 to leave Blandford for Templecombe after the special train has been set to the Up Platform line at Blandford.

In connection with movements of an engine attached front and rear of the train the leading driver in the direction of travel will be in entire control of the brake and the driver of the rear engine must have his ejector shut off. *(Special attention to this)*.

Special Train

Composition of special train (G.W.Stock) leaving Broadstone will be as under:—

Engine		
First Brake	8020	
Restaurant Car	9005	
Sleeping Saloon	9090	
Sleeping Saloon	9091	
Sleeping Saloon	9093	
Restaurant Car	9004	
Compo Brake	7061	7 vehicles approx.
		255 tons.

Total length of special train (excluding engine)   420′ 0″

The District Engineer will arrange for pegs to be placed at the points where the men will be stationed exhibiting the necessary hand signals.

When the special train is ready to leave, the guard must not sound his whistle.

All points which become facing and are not fitted with facing point locks and bars (or track circuit controlling the facing point lock lever) to be clipped for the movements at Blandford.

The District Controller to make the necessary arrangements and to be personally in attendance at Blandford to supervise the movements.

The Police Inspector, Bristol, is arranging to provide the necessary uniformed Police whilst the special train is at Blandford. The County Constabulary have already been communicated with.

Mr. Rider, Bristol, will arrange that no member of the public be allowed in the Goods Yard at Blandford between 6.0 pm Monday, May 13th and 11.45 am on Tuesday, May 14th.

Mr. Sealy will arrange for a red lamp to be provided and fixed at the point beyond which the engine drawing the special train must on no account pass.

Steps etc.

Steps will be provided for use at Blandford.

The District Engineer will arrange for the lavatory pans to be placed in position under the special train after arrival. After departure of the special train the pans to be emptied, cleaned and afterwards placed in the van together with the steps ready to be returned to Wolverton.

Staff (to be provided by District Engineer).
Flagmen.

To be stationed at the points where the pegs have been placed and where the centre of the cab of the engine drawing the special train will come to a stand.

Men for clipping points.

The men required to clip points at Blandford to report to Mr. Sealy at 2.0 am on Tuesday, May 14th, and after the train has been set in position the men will assist in placing steps, etc. in position. Similar men to be also provided from 9.0 am.

Standby arrangements for engines and breakdown train.

The Class 7 engine at Templecombe will act as "stand-by" engine.

Mr. Sealy to arrange for 8 copies of each of the following morning papers to be handed to Inspector Shaw on the special train by not later than 7.30 am on Tuesday, May 14th:—

> Times
> Telegraph
> Mail
> Express
> Herald
> Chronicle

The P.O. telephone at Blandford Station will be manned continuously during the time the special train is at Blandford.

HAROLD RUDGARD

Divisional Superintendent of Operation

Oil Engine 4826 (22C), 9.45 Express Bournemouth – Bath, 10.10.47

Driver Beale, Fireman Pollard, Branksome. Agreed loading 270 tons. Actual loading 248 tons.

Mileage	Galls.of Oil used	Estimated weight of one Gall. of oil	Lbs.of oil consumed	Lbs.of oil consumed per mile	Galls.of oil consumed per mile	Galls.of Water consumed	Galls.of Water consumed per mile	Lbs.of Water consumed per lb. of oil.
71½	250	9·758	2,439·5	34·1	3·49	2,500	35.0	10·247

The performance of the Engine and Crew was exceptionally good, no difficulty was experienced to maintain a full head of steam on any part of the journey.

Loading Table for S.Rly Engines working over S. & D. Rly.
Loaded coaches.

Class of Passenger Engines (S.R.)

	K.10	S.11	T.9	T.1	U1,N1, U, N.	West Country
	Tons	Tons	Tons	Tons	Tons	Tons
Bath to Masbury	200	180	170	145	240	270
Masbury to Corfe Mullen (including Templecombe Upper)	300	270	255	215	365	405
Corfe Mullen to Bournemouth West	270	240	220	195	320	380
Bournemouth West to Corfe Mullen	270	240	220	195	320	380
Corfe Mullen to Evercreech Junction (including Templecombe Upper)	300	270	255	215	365	405
Evercreech Junction to Binegar	200	180	170	145	240	270
Binegar to Bath	270	240	220	195	320	380
Templecombe Upper to Templecombe Junct. (This weight not to include the engine at rear of train)	450	425	400	335	450	450

Loading Tables for Engines working over the S&D Railway.
Loaded coaches.

Ex L.M. & B.R. Std Freight Engines

Class of Engines	3 Ex Midland 0-6-0	4 Ex Midland 0-6-0	5 Horwich† 2-6-0	7 Ex S&D 2-8-0	8 Ex L.M.S. 2-8-0	9 B.R. 2-10-0
	Tons	Tons	Tons	Tons	Tons	Tons
Bath to Masbury	190	240	240	310	310	410
Masbury to Corfe Mullen N	290	365	365	450	450	410
Corfe Mullen to Bournemouth West	260	320	320	415	415	410
Bournemouth West to Corfe Mullen	260	320	320	415	415	410
Corfe Mullen to Evercreech Junction N	290	365	365	450	450	410
Evercreech Junction to Binegar	190	240	240	310	310	410
Binegar to Bath	260	320	320	415	415	410

Ex L.M. & B.R. Std Passenger & Mixed Traffic Engines.

Class of Engines	1 Ex Midland 0-4-4T	2 Ex Midland 4-4-0	2 Ex L.M.S. 4-4-0	3 2-6-2T	4 Compound 4-4-0	4 B.R. 2-6-4T 2-6-0 4-6-0	5 L.M.&B.R. 4-6-0s	6 B.R. 'Clan'* 4-6-2
	Tons	Tons	Tons	Tons	Tons	Tons	Tons	Tons
Bath to Masbury	130	190	200	220	225	240	270	290
Masbury to Corfe Mullen N	200	290	310	335	340	365	405	425 (a)
Corfe Mullen to Bournemouth West	175	260	275	300	310	300	380	–
Bournemouth West to Corfe Mullen	175	260	275	300	310	300	380	–
Corfe Mullen to Evercreech Junction N	200	290	310	335	340	365	405	425 (b)
Evercreech Junction to Binegar	130	190	200	220	225	240	270	290
Binegar to Bath	175	260	275	300	310	320	380	400

NOTES:

N	– Including Templecombe Upper.
(a)	– Masbury to Templecombe Upper only.
(b)	– Templecombe Upper to Evercreech Junction only.
*	– This class never actually worked on the line.
†	– Strictly speaking, the Horwich 2-6-0 ought to come under the heading "Passenger and Mixed Traffic Engines", but in the Loading Tables contained in the various appendices to the S&D working timetables it was listed as a "Freight Engine".

The above figures, although largely representative of the locomotives concerned during their working life on the S&D, were liable to amendment. For this reason certain figures quoted in the text of this, and my previous book, are not identical to those quoted here.